POLITICS AS USUAL

POLITICS AS USUAL

Thomas Dewey, Franklin Roosevelt, and

the Wartime Presidential Campaign of 1944

Michael A. Davis

NIU PRESS *DeKalb, IL*

© 2014 by Northern Illinois University Press
Published by the Northern Illinois University Press, DeKalb, Illinois 60115
Manufactured in the United States using acid-free paper.
All Rights Reserved
Design by Yuni Dorr

Library of Congress Cataloging-in-Publication Data

Davis, Michael A.
Politics as usual : Thomas Dewey, Franklin Roosevelt, and the wartime presidential campaign of 1944 / Michael A. Davis.
pages cm.
Includes bibliographical references and index.
ISBN 978-0-87580-711-9 (pbk : alk. paper) — ISBN 978-1-60909-169-9 (e-book)
1. Presidents—United States—Election—1944. 2. Roosevelt, Franklin D. (Franklin Delano), 1882-1945. 3. Dewey, Thomas E. (Thomas Edmund), 1902-1971. 4. United States—
Politics and government—1933-1945. I. Title.
E812.D38 2014
324.973'0917—dc23
2014025214

TO HOLLY—

*my "needle girl in a haystack world"**

*"Needle and Haystack Life," on the album *Hello Hurricane*, by Switchfoot. Atlantic Records, 2009.

CONTENTS

ACKNOWLEDGMENTS

In his 1971 memoir, *Vantage Point*, Lyndon Johnson observed that a political campaign is "a blur, a whirlwind, an excitement—frustrating, exhilarating, exhausting, and necessary." The same, perhaps, could be said of writing about a political campaign. While this project was the result of over ten years of effort, it has in many ways seemed like a blur. It also certainly has had its moments of exhilaration and exhaustion—all made better by the many people who have helped me along the way. I am especially grateful to my colleagues in the History Department at Liberty University, including David Snead, Sam Smith, Carey Roberts, Roger Schultz, Doug Mann, Tim Saxon, Chris Jones, Chris Smith, Rob Ritchie, Donna Donald, and Homer Blass for their friendship, encouragement, and support. Unfortunately, Dr. Blass, a beloved professor and devoted bibliophile, did not live to see this manuscript completed. I hope it is a book that he would have been proud to place in his very large personal library. I am appreciative too of our department secretary, Kris Burdeaux, who—besides always making the office a pleasant and efficient place—was of tremendous logistical assistance. I also owe sincere thanks to the staff at Northern Illinois University Press, including Linda Manning, Susan Bean, Kenton Clymer, and Mark Heinike for approving of this project and guiding me through the publication process with patience and great care.

I want to thank Marist professor Stan Mersand, one of the leading authorities on Thomas Dewey and the director of the Thomas E. Dewey Center in Pawling, New York, for being generous with his time and providing invaluable insight and assistance. I also want to thank Mary Huth, Lori Birrell, and Melinda Wallington at the University of Rochester library, Tom Rieder at the Ohio Historical Society in Columbus, Elizabeth Safly at the Harry S. Truman Presidential Library in Independence, Missouri, and Matt Schaffer and Craig Wright at the Herbert Hoover Presidential Library in West Branch, Iowa. At the University of Arkansas, my alma mater, I want to thank Randall Woods, Patrick Williams, and Todd Shields—all members of my dissertation committee—for their scholarly advice and for encouraging me toward publication.

I am deeply indebted to my family, including my parents, Jimmy and Diane Davis, and my brother, Kevin. Mom and Dad worked hard and sacrificed much for me and my brother to have the opportunities we have today. I love them both very much. I am also thankful for my grandparents, Floyd and Bertha Davis and O'neal and Oleta Moody—all passed now—who left behind a legacy of hard work, generosity, faith, and service. I am blessed because of them. I am grateful too for my own children, Sadie, Shiloh, and Savannah. They are a source of great joy and pride. They are also a source of many questions, including "How many more pages, Daddy?" and "Are you done yet?"

Ultimately, this book would not have been possible without the love and support of my wife, Holly. Without complaint, she accompanied me on all my research trips, lifted my spirits when I was down or overwhelmed, and made our home a place of refuge. In 2006, not long after this project began (and when our three girls were very young), Holly suffered a massive brain hemorrhage, the result of a brain A.V.M. that she was born with and that we did not know she had. She was in a coma for two weeks, and over the course of 2007 had to relearn to eat and walk, and undergo multiple procedures in an attempt to cure the A.V.M. Thankfully, she experienced a complete recovery and continues to be a shining light in our home. She is the love of my life, my best friend, my staunchest advocate, and my motivation. This book is dedicated to her.

POLITICS AS USUAL

INTRODUCTION

The presidential election of 1944, which unfolded against the backdrop of the Second World War, was the first since 1864—and one of only a few in all of American history—to take place while the nation was at war. After a brief primary season, the Republican Party, in late June, settled upon New York governor Thomas Edmund Dewey—the former district attorney, and popular special prosecutor of Legs Diamond and Lucky Luciano—as its nominee for president of the United States. Dewey, age 42, was the first presidential candidate to be born in the twentieth century. His running mate was the conservative governor of Ohio, John W. Bricker. The Democratic nominee for president, of course, was the three-term incumbent, 62-year-old Franklin Delano Roosevelt. Although there was little doubt about Roosevelt seeking a fourth term, much speculation existed concerning his choice for a running mate. Vice President Henry Wallace was widely unpopular among party elites, especially those from the South, who objected to his liberal views on race, and who feared that Roosevelt—rumored to be deteriorating in health—might not survive a fourth term. In the end, Democratic professionals replaced Wallace with Senator Harry S. Truman of Missouri.

Sensitive to the wartime setting of the election, both Roosevelt and Dewey, early in their campaigns, adopted dignified and low-key electoral strategies. For example, at the very subdued Republican National Convention in Chicago in late June—only a few weeks after D-Day—Dewey quietly observed that "we now pass through dark and troubled times. Scarcely a home escapes the touch of dread anxiety and grief; yet in this hour the American spirit rises, faith returns—faith in our God, faith in our fellow man, faith in the land our fathers died to win, faith in the future, limitless and bright, of this, our country. In the name of that faith," he concluded, "we shall carry our cause in the coming months to the American people."[1] Similarly, Roosevelt, speaking that July from an undisclosed location by radio hookup to a more raucous Democratic National Convention, announced that he would not campaign "in the usual sense." "In these days of tragic sorrow," he explained, "I do not consider it fitting. And besides, in these days of global warfare, I shall not be able to find the time."[2]

Within a few weeks, however, the campaign degenerated—as *Newsweek* noted in early October—from "Solemn to Silly."[3] The 1944 presidential campaign, then, was a typical campaign in that the candidates and the parties held nothing back in their criticisms of one another. In fact, the campaign was especially harsh and negative. FDR called it "the strangest campaign" of his lifetime, while the *New Republic* insisted that it was "A Bad Campaign" full of such misrepresentation and falsehood as to "cause for the deepest alarm. . . ."[4] *U.S. News,* meanwhile, described it as a "free-swinging" partisan affair, complete with political "body punches and head-rocking."[5]

"Political campaigns, like war," Dewey once observed, "depend on much more than money, mathematics, and pure reason. They are characterized by faith and often by high feeling, by the music of ritual and tradition, by the public clash of personalities."[6] This was especially true in 1944. Indeed, this was the campaign of Roosevelt's famous Fala speech, and Dewey's electric (if lesser known) Oklahoma City response. It was during this campaign that Democrats accused Republicans of scraping and sinking "more of our fleet than was destroyed by the Japanese at Pearl Harbor."[7] It was during this campaign too that Republicans warned that Roosevelt was "little by little distorting our democracy into a dictatorial Bumbledom," and that he "is the only American President who ever lied us into a war because he did not have the political courage to lead us into it."[8] This was the campaign of Harry Truman's first "whistle stop" tour, and the Republican slogan of "Clear Everything With Sidney."

On Election Day, the Roosevelt-Truman ticket received a comfortable 53 percent of the popular vote, and a sweeping 432 votes in the Electoral College. Still, this was the narrowest of FDR's four victories and the closest election since Woodrow Wilson's 1916 upset over Charles Evans Hughes. Only about 3.6 million votes (out of 47 million cast) separated the two candidates, and in 13 states numbering 175 electoral votes, FDR's margin of victory was 150,000 votes or less. A shift of 800,000 votes in the right states would have given Dewey an Electoral College win and the presidency. Despite first appearances, then, the election was actually close.

Not surprisingly, the 1944 campaign has interested few scholars. After all, as most historians and political scientists insist, Roosevelt, performing his role as commander-in-chief during World War II, was all but assured of victory. The campaign was simply the crescendo of his partisan career, the last act of his political drama—or as one scholar put it, his extraordinary "Final Victory."[9] Furthermore, 1944 did not conform to what Harvard political scientist V.O. Key described in the 1950s as a "critical election."[10] Critical elections, he insisted, "occur periodically in American history, generating high levels of voter interest, upsetting the previous balance of power among competing parties, and producing durable changes in the compositions of the voter coalitions supporting each party."[11] Examples of such elections include 1860, 1896, and 1936. By this standard, then, 1944 was not a "critical election" but a mere "maintaining election" that resulted in neither a transfer of power nor a major realignment in voter allegiance.

Overall, the literature on the Roosevelt-Dewey contest is relatively sparse, often comprising small parts of larger studies such as biographies and party histories. While a few episodes of the campaign, including FDR's health and Truman's vice presidential nomination, have garnered scholarly attention, only two published books exist that deal with the campaign in its entirety: *FDR, Dewey, and the Election of 1944* (2011), by David Jordan, and *Final Victory: FDR's Extraordinary World War II Presidential Campaign* (2012), by Stanley Weintraub. Moreover, few works focus in great detail on either Dewey or the contributions of his campaign. In fact, he is the subject of only one modern biography, Richard Norton Smith's *Thomas E. Dewey and His Times* (1982).

Unlike previous works, this study of the 1944 presidential campaign focuses on "politics as usual." This theme is incorporated in two ways. First, 1944 proved to be an ordinary election during an extraordinary time. There were parades, outdoor rallies, radio advertisements, newsreels, flashing cameras, celebrity endorsements, barbecues and rodeos, and balloons, flyers, placards, and pins. In other words, the election was typical, which made it remarkable. While the United States was fighting in a global war, over 56 percent of the voting-age population participated in free and fair elections at home. It was a remarkable demonstration of the American democratic process, establishing, as one newsmagazine noted shortly after the election, that the United States "could simultaneously fight a war and settle an election in [its] true tradition and spirit."[12]

It is this settling of "an election in true tradition and spirit" that is of major importance to this study. After all, if a campaign is merely about winners and losers, then 1944 does not really matter. However, if a campaign (as I argue) is something more, then the political twists and turns of 1944 are very important. According to political scientist Thomas M. Carsey in his *Campaign Dynamics* (2001), a campaign is ultimately a "struggle between candidates to provide new information to voters." Specifically, candidates attempt to "shape the information context within which voters make their decisions by battling to influence what is salient to voters when they cast their ballots. Through this process, the content of campaigns influences voting behavior."[13] Campaigns, then, are rivaling stories about the past, present, and future.

While the information voters have prior to the beginning of a campaign influences voting behavior, voters do not possess complete information. This information gap, Carsey notes, "creates uncertainty in the electoral process, and candidates try to reduce that uncertainty by providing additional information to voters over the course of a campaign."[14] The result is what Carsey calls "heresthetic change"—that is, changing the nature of the "issue space" for voters so they are encouraged to change which candidate they support. In other words, candidates seek to make the entire campaign revolve around a theme—war, peace, the economy, character, etc.—that plays to their strengths and their opponents' weaknesses. "The campaign becomes a struggle between candidates providing information to voters as they try to define for voters the important issues in that particular election."[15]

The wartime presidential campaign of 1944, like all other campaigns, was a serious and intense national conversation. At least two things contributed to make this campaign the "Hottest in Years."[16] One was the perceived closeness of the race in national polls. Indeed, while a March 1944 Office of Public Opinion Research (OPOR) survey showed the president enjoying an 81 percent approval rating on his handling of military and foreign affairs, Roosevelt and Dewey—as Chart 1 demonstrates—remained "evenly matched" in American Institute of Public Opinion (Gallup) polls throughout most of the year.[17]

Chart 1: Gallup Poll—Roosevelt vs. Dewey, 1944

DATE	POLL	RESULT	
May 20	Gallup	Roosevelt 51%	Dewey 49%
June 6	Gallup	Roosevelt 52%	Dewey 48%
Sept. 7	Gallup	Roosevelt 49%	Dewey 51%
Oct. 5	Gallup	Roosevelt 51%	Dewey 49%
Nov. 5	Gallup	Roosevelt 51.5%	Dewey 48.5%

SOURCE: George Gallup, "The Gallup Poll," *The Washington Post*, June 7, 1944, 19. George Gallup, "Roosevelt, Dewey Near Tie in Homestretch, Poll Shows," *The Washington Post*, October 6, 1944, 1. George Gallup, "Roosevelt Given Slight Advantage over Dewey in Final Gallup Report," *The Washington Post*, November 6, 1944, 1.

Electoral College projections also revealed a close race. It took 266 electoral votes to be elected president in 1944. According to Gallup on election eve, Roosevelt was assured 18 states and 165 electoral votes to Dewey's 10 states and 85 electoral votes. That left what Gallup called 20 "pivotal states," totaling 281 electoral votes, which remained too close to call (see Chart 2). While Roosevelt only needed to win 11 of those states to secure 292 electoral votes and victory, the state-by-state polling margins were extremely narrow. George Gallup, in his final preelection commentary, believed a Dewey victory was possible due to "the upward trend of Republican party strength, revealed in state and congressional elections of the last year" and to "a much greater intensity of feeling about this election" among Dewey voters.[18] Still, Gallup did not rule out a Roosevelt sweep in the Electoral College, noting that a shift of 1 percent in just two states—New York and Illinois—would result in another substantial Roosevelt victory.[19]

Chart 2: Gallup Poll—20 Pivotal State-by-State Projections, November 1944

STATE	ROOSEVELT %	DEWEY %
California	53	47
Maryland	53	47
Connecticut	52	48
Pennsylvania	51	49
Massachusetts	51	49
New Hampshire	51	49
Oklahoma	51	49
Oregon	51	49
Idaho	51	49
West Virginia	51	49
Delaware	51	49
New York	50	50
Missouri	49	51
New Mexico	49	51
Illinois	49	51
Maine	48	52
Ohio	48	52
New Jersey	48	52
Wyoming	47	53
Minnesota	47	53

SOURCE: George Gallup, "Roosevelt Given Slight Advantage over Dewey in Final Gallup Report," *The Washington Post*, November 6, 1944, 1.

Not surprisingly, what modern scholars call "issue space" became a major concern for both candidates. "Insofar as issues are important," political scientist Hadley Cantril observed that fall, "the outcome of the election will depend on what point the majority of people think we have reached on the continuum that runs from war to peace."[20] Thus, if the main issue (or theme) of the campaign was the war, then Roosevelt held a clear advantage. Indeed, a July 1944 *Fortune* poll revealed that if the war was "still going on at the time of the next presidential election," Roosevelt would garner 51 percent of support to Dewey's 42 percent.[21] Similarly, a Gallup poll released the previous month found that the two leading arguments for voting for Roosevelt were: "He has a wider first-hand knowledge of the war situation than his opponent and is therefore better fitted by experience to handle it" and "The middle of the war is no time to change administrations."[22]

However, polls revealed that Dewey benefited greatly when the main issue was domestic affairs—that is, "the immediate day-to-day, bread-and-butter problems of jobs, wages, and personal security."[23] For example, in a November 1943 OPOR poll, 53 percent of respondents indicated that postwar domestic problems, such as full employment and production, interested them more than potential postwar international problems, such as the creation of a new league of nations. Only 16 percent believed international affairs to be more important. Meanwhile, a Gallup poll conducted in August 1944 showed that 78 percent believed domestic problems would be the greatest task facing the next president. More troubling for Democrats was a *Fortune* poll in July 1944 that revealed voters chose Dewey over Roosevelt by almost ten points (49.6 percent to 40 percent) "if the war is over in both places, but the peace terms are not fully worked out."[24]

The nomination of a strong candidate by Republicans also fueled the intensity of the 1944 campaign. Democrats were clearly alarmed by Dewey's candidacy. Unlike Roosevelt's other Republican opponents—Herbert Hoover, Alf Landon, and even, arguably, Wendell Willkie—Dewey was, in fact, a fierce adversary. He was young, enjoyed a popular national reputation as a racket buster, and was an experienced modern campaigner. In late 1943, *Time* even described him as a "dragon slayer . . . armed with concentrations of modern heavy artillery, preceded by elaborate reconnaissance and followed by a staff of logistics experts. As man, District Attorney, or Governor, Tom Dewey is calm, neat, painstaking and deadly efficient."[25] Despite Harry Truman's widely accepted recollection of the campaign as "the easiest in which I ever participated," and that "The Republican candidates never had a chance," 1944 was a *real* campaign, chaotic and unpredictable, highly competitive and vigorously fought.[26]

Indeed, according to historian Robert Ferrell, "[O]nly [FDR] 'the champ,' the Democrats' greatest vote-getter since President Andrew Jackson ... could have assured victory. No other Democrat could have stood against Dewey and won."[27] Many Democrats at the time agreed—as a summer 1944 DNC study of Dewey's career indicated. "Today," the report noted, "he is one of the best [politicians] in the country, and he commands as slick a political machine as can be found anywhere."[28] Party leaders made it very clear to the faithful: "It was F.D.R. or the end of the Democratic era."[29] Recognizing the Dewey threat, the Roosevelt campaign sought from an early date to—as one Democratic memo instructed—"ridicule this nit wit out of the race."[30]

The other way the "politics as usual" theme is employed in this work is through a serious consideration of Dewey, who emerged as leader of the GOP at a critical time. The Republican Party experienced decline throughout most of the 1930s, lacking both popular national leadership and a unified strategy to combat the new Democratic majority. Complicating matters for the party was the lingering public presence of Herbert Hoover. Unlike most defeated presidents, Hoover refused to retreat from the public arena, sought to retain control over the party machinery, and continued to hold out hope for a political comeback. Thus, while Roosevelt afflicted the party from the outside, Hoover "embarrassed it from within."[31]

By the early 1940s, especially following Wendell Willkie's disappointing national loss in 1940, Republicans were demoralized and "split asunder by discord and misgivings."[32] The main fault line was between Willkie "liberals" and Robert Taft "conservatives." As the party's presidential nominee in 1940, Willkie, a former Democrat and political novice, supported most of the New Deal, as well as the president's foreign policy. This certainly did not endear him to conservatives, and neither did his neglect of the National Committee and his removal of key conservatives, including popular RNC chair John Hamilton, from the party leadership. Conservatives complained that under Willkie's leadership, the party, which "had boasted of a formidable and effective organization prepared to wage a real fight" at the beginning of the campaign, had become, by the end, "warped and weak ... [and] had reverted back to the dismal days of 1934."[33] By 1941, they were openly charging that "the party had been sabotaged by a candidate of Democratic faith on the Republican ticket."[34]

Taft, the son of former President William Howard Taft, was a senator from Ohio, first elected in 1938. According to one early Taft biographer, he "represented, if not always exactly, a Republican party that was essentially old-fashioned, essentially isolationist, and had its hopes and policies based in the past."[35] He was staunchly opposed to the New Deal and believed

Republicans should take a clear and confrontational stance against it. "There is only one way to beat the New Deal," Taft wrote in late 1942, "and that is head on. You can't outdeal them." After 1940, he was also unalterably opposed to Willkie (and his internationalism) and worked to destroy his influence in the party. "We are heading for a direct fight for control of the party machinery," he told a friend in late 1941. "I believe it would be fatal to the future of the Party if Willkie and [Henry] Luce . . . together with the wealthy crowd in the East, succeed in their [internationalist] aim."[36]

Dewey, in contrast, believed modern government to be a "sober, tough business" that required both competence and consensus.[37] "Good government," he told New Yorkers in 1942, "is not an abstraction. . . . It is made up of a team of live, active, vigorous men and women doing vital tasks with energy and intelligence."[38] Not surprisingly, he was criticized by both liberals and conservatives throughout most of his career for either "me too-ism" or for not promoting and standing on principles. Taft, for example, insisted that the governor possessed "no real courage to stand up against the crowd that wants to smear any Republican who takes a forthright position against the New Deal."[39] Willkie partisans, such as Russell Davenport, meanwhile, maintained that Dewey "gave himself over to the most reactionary elements in the party organization," and that unless his control over the party was "broken by a liberal and internationally minded leadership, the days of the Republican party are numbered."[40]

Dewey, of course, was not without political principles. Like most other Republicans, he stressed the importance of fostering "individual liberty as the only means to a society of opportunity and abundance." Furthermore, he insisted that all problems be handled "locally and voluntarily by community action, and by public opinion." If these proved insufficient, "then the solution is first to be attempted by local government, secondly by the state and lastly by federal action." This approach, Dewey argued, left the federal government "uncluttered with the vast detail of minor services . . . [and] free to devote its very best talents to the immense problems of world affairs, national defense, national fiscal management, national economic problems, agricultural stability and the broad social action which can only be handled by federal action."[41] Specifically, he believed in a middle way between the theory of laissez-faire of the 1920s, and the "creeping collectivism of the past few years."[42] "Government," he said in his Second Inaugural Address as governor in 1947, "can have both a head and a heart . . . it can be both progressive and solvent . . . [and] can serve the people without becoming their master."[43]

While a fierce partisan, Dewey resisted the polarization of American political parties that began with the New Deal. In his classic *The Age of Roosevelt: The Politics of Upheaval* (1960), Arthur M. Schlesinger Jr.

detailed the emergence of a "new politics" that set in motion greater ideological distinctions (and polarization) between the two leading parties. This
"new politics," embraced by Roosevelt early in his first term, stressed "issue-
driven coalitions" over traditional, "patron-based" and "service-oriented"
party organizations. The result was an interparty realignment in which, over
time, the Democratic Party became the distinctly liberal party, and the Republican Party the decisively conservative one.

Despite his youth and status as the first presidential candidate to be born
in the twentieth century, Dewey was very much a nineteenth-century man
in regard to party philosophy. Specifically, he echoed the mugwumps and
other reformers of the late 19th and early 20th centuries. "It is not the function of a political party to die fighting for obsolete slogans," he insisted in
1938, in his first race for governor. "It is not the function of political leadership to bark at the heels of political success. *It is the function of a political
party and it is the job of a political leader to seek positively to represent the
whole people in the solution of their daily problems* [italics added]."[44]

There were those in politics, he told students at Princeton University in
early 1950, who railed "at both parties, saying they represent nothing but a
choice between Tweedledee and Tweedledum." These people, Dewey insisted,
"have no experience in government and are either extreme reactionaries or
radicals who want a neat little party to carry out their special prejudices;
or these people are pseudo-intellectuals or just plain obstructionists." While
these "impractical theorists" demanded "that our parties be sharply divided,
one against the other, in interest, membership, and doctrine," Dewey believed
that it was actually the resemblances between the parties that constituted
"the very heart of the strength of the American political system." Americans,
he concluded, were "all members of the same family. The disparaging epi-
thets of those who want everything clear-cut and simple cannot erase the
stubborn fact that our objectives and interests as Americans are not neatly
opposed but are, and I hope always will be, mutual."[45]

Never optimistic about his chances of victory in 1944, Dewey waged a
competent and centrist campaign against Roosevelt in order to hold the
Republican Party together, and to transform it into a relevant alternative
within the postwar New Deal political order. His main objective, as Ford
Bond, Dewey's radio director, later observed, was to rebuild the Republican
Party "to be worthy of national trust." The party had not elected a president
for 16 years, during which many GOP voters had died and "little effort had
been made to acquaint new voters with the basic ideals of the party." Thus,
Bond insisted, "Every resource and energy was spent in the twin objective of
revitalizing the party and of winning the election." Dewey, then, did not offer
a simple return to the glory years of the party's ideological past but advanced

new policies that aimed to improve upon those of the Democratic majority.[46] For example, in a speech in San Francisco in 1944, Dewey advocated broadening and extending the benefits of social and economic legislation to more people. In doing this, Bond concluded, "he wasn't saying 'Elect a Republican administration and we will give you these [Democratic] things too.' He was giving voice to the American ideal. He was saying, in effect, 'You can have these things and Freedom too.'"[47]

Ultimately, Dewey was something that Roosevelt's other Republican opponents were not, and that was a party builder. A pragmatist, he accepted the social welfare legislation of the New Deal, while simultaneously expressing devotion to basic party traditions and rhetoric. An innovator, Dewey—even before Pearl Harbor—abandoned isolationism and acknowledged America's growing global responsibilities.[48] Believing that, without the existence of two or more internally diverse parties competing for support of the electorate and power in government, American liberties would be in danger, he chartered a cautious course and avoided ideological extremes. In doing so he rescued the party from collapse and laid the foundation for Republican presidential victories in the second half of the twentieth century. He was the youthful face of the party and an essential transition between Herbert Hoover in the 1920s and Dwight Eisenhower in the 1950s. In salvaging the GOP from Depression and war, he also maintained America's politics as usual—that is, the two-party system.

This study on the wartime presidential election of 1944 also examines the political landscape in the United States in the early 1940s, including the state of the Democratic and Republican parties and the rhetoric and strategies employed by both the Dewey and Roosevelt campaigns. Specifically, it details (1) the survival of partisanship in World War II America, (2) intraparty strife, (3) the leading domestic and foreign policy concerns facing the nation and politicians in the early 1940s, (4) the careers of the various Republican contenders for president in 1944, (5) the work of the two national nominating conventions, and (6) the fall campaign travels and everyday operations of both Dewey and Roosevelt and the often overlooked contributions of their feisty running mates, John W. Bricker and Harry S. Truman.

CHAPTER 1

The Triumph of Politics as Usual, 1941–1945

The Second World War was a watershed event in the history of the United States. It was, as journalist Haynes Johnson observed in the 1990s, "the crucible that forged modern America."[1] Between 1941 and 1945, the United States was changed from a nation of the Great Depression to one of opportunity and prosperity. It was a time of government growth, economic planning, population movement, and social reordering. It was also a time of fierce national debate and partisan division. Contrary to popular belief, World War II did not mute politics as usual in the United States. If anything, it amplified it. After all, at home, wartime changes—whether social, economic, or cultural—often required political responses, which, in turn, frequently sparked public controversies. For example, the United States was unprepared for war in 1941. Yet plants would have to be built to manufacture war goods, and supplies would have to be acquired to maintain those facilities. Furthermore, workers would have to be found to operate those plants—all the while maintaining domestic levels of consumption. Finally, wages and prices had to be brought under control in order to avoid ruinous inflation, and money had to be found to finance the entire war mobilization and production process. Such necessities were neither cheap nor easy and thus triggered much partisan discussion.[2]

Meanwhile, on the international front, desires for the prevention of future wars, and the postwar peace plans they spawned, also ignited partisan debate. Should the United States promote the creation of an international organization to foster peace after the war? How much authority would any such world body have? Would it undermine the sovereignty of the United States and the power of Congress to declare war and commit American forces to harm's way? Intricately connected to these questions was partisan blame for the failure to prevent the current war. For example, many Democrats exalted the fallen Woodrow Wilson and the failed League of Nations and criticized Republicans as post-Versailles saboteurs and backward-looking isolationists. World War II, then, did not interrupt American politics. Indeed, the war not only failed to bring about an end of partisan and ideological conflict, it also caused many new issues to emerge and altered existing political alignments.[3]

One early wartime issue was the very existence of partisanship itself. Some in politics and academia expressed reservations about democratic processes in time of war. Telling enough was the fact that most of these reservations were themselves political. For example, Albert Guerard, writing in the liberal *New Republic* in early 1943, argued that "If we choose to retain partisan labels, the Democrats, still nominally in power, are bound to suffer heavily.... For the Republicans will vote for all the essential war measures, and claim credit for their patriotism; but the Democrats alone will be blamed for the discomforts inevitably arising out of these measures."[4] The result, he predicted, would be a reaction at the ballot box in 1944 that would "engulf the Democratic Party, the New Deal, and with them much of our recent social progress."[5] Others feared that partisanship, with its petty political maneuvering and "carping criticism," might undermine the war effort both at home and abroad.[6]

Harold W. Dodds, president of Princeton University, disagreed. Political parties, he argued in an article for *The Yale Review* in the summer of 1942, were essential to both political liberty and national unity. "It is their struggles for power that activate government," Dodds noted. "Freedom of speech or opinion would be in vain without them to implement our liberties. There appears to be no alternative to elections except tyranny." Under the two-party system, he added, political parties tended to "dull the keen edges of issues on which people divide rather than to sharpen them by introducing new causes of disunity. It is in their interest to do so.... Each side wants to gain the support also of the independent middle-of-the-road voters not affiliated with it. As the two parties bid for votes their programs naturally move to the centre."[7]

Writing in his Marxist magazine, *Politics*, in early 1944, journalist Dwight Macdonald similarly argued that calls for national unity had dangerous implications, noting that "In the totalitarian nations politics has vanished completely, at least in the sense of open, institutionalized contests between various interest groups." As long as class societies exist, he concluded, the only hope of the submerged majority to change things for their good "will rest on political action, breaking through the fiction of organic unity between the lion and the lamb and setting class groups off openly against each other."[8]

For Republicans, as the opposition party, the issues of partisanship and public debate were very important. Certainly, many Republicans had been opposed to intervention prior to Pearl Harbor, but the Japanese attack had changed that. The United States was forced into war, former president Herbert Hoover, a leading non-interventionist, told reporters after the attack, and the country "must [now] fight with everything we have."[9] Even the prewar isolationist group, America First, which included members of all political stripes, dissolved in mid-December 1941, noting that "No good purpose can now be served by considering what might have been, had our objectives been attained.... We are at war. Today, though there may be many important subsidiary considerations, the primary objective is . . . victory."[10] Wartime opposition for Republicans, then, was not grounded in questions about the validity of the war but in the actual conduct of the war at home and abroad.

Still, Republicans feared that Roosevelt and the Democrats might exploit patriotic sentiment for either partisan or personal gain. Even the president himself had a reputation for seeking to discredit and silence his foreign policy critics—especially those who had had an isolationist background. According to historian Richard Steele, Roosevelt, in dealing with his foreign policy critics, was guided by an "intolerant, conspiratorial outlook" that led him to conclude too easily that "his long-standing political opponents had now aligned themselves with the nation's enemies, either to hurt him or to promote their own interest."[11]

Specifically, after 1939, Roosevelt equated anti-interventionism (and isolationism) with subversion and believed, as press reports in the early 1940s widely claimed, that Nazi agents and sympathizers, a fifth column, prepared the way for German armies by "boring from within" and "undermining the will and capacity of the democracies to resist."[12] Then, during the 1940 presidential campaign, Roosevelt linked Republicans with this threat, warning audiences that "something evil is happening in this country"—namely, the formation of an "unholy alliance" between Republicans and "the extreme reactionary and the extreme radical elements of this country." These elements were consistently critical of his administration, the president noted, but even more, they "hate democracy and Christianity as two phases of the same civilization. They oppose democracy because it is Christian. They oppose Christianity because it preaches democracy. Their objective is to prevent democracy from becoming strong and purposeful." While he was confident "that the rank and file of patriotic Republicans do not realize the nature of this threat," Roosevelt nevertheless insisted that many, even some of the party's leaders, had been drawn into such an alliance.[13]

Shortly after the 1940 election, Roosevelt added—in a letter to speechwriter Samuel Rosenman—that "too many" in the Republican Party were motivated by materialism and had thus come to think "in terms of appeasement of Hitler."[14] There existed, he said in his 1941 State of the Union message, "A small group of selfish men, who would clip the wings of the American eagle to feather their own nests. . . . Partisan groups . . . who wrap themselves in a false mantle of Americanism to promote their own economic, financial, or political advantage."[15]

Following Pearl Harbor, Roosevelt became justifiably more concerned with activity that could be deemed "seditious." Many of those who came to the attention of the administration were, in fact, "rabble-rousers" and unbalanced individuals—"the lunatic fringe," who, according to Roosevelt's attorney general, Francis Biddle, "were almost always anti-Semitic and often anti-Catholic." Still, Biddle recalled, Roosevelt "was not much interested in the theory of sedition, or in the constitutional right to criticize the government in wartime. He wanted this antiwar talk stopped." Indeed, the president frequently sent the attorney general "brief memoranda to which were attached notes about some of the scurrilous attacks on his leadership, with a notation: 'What about this?' or 'What are you doing to stop this?'"[16]

A nationwide speech by the chairman of the Democratic National Committee, Edward J. Flynn, in February 1942 seemed to confirm Republican fears. Flynn charged that Republicans were "not as much interested in the war as . . . [in] controlling the House of Representatives."[17] "[M]y feeling," he continued, "is that this crisis having occurred during a Democratic administration . . . is ours to direct . . . to an ultimate and complete victory." Looking ahead to the November midterm elections, he added: "I naturally feel that no misfortune except a major military defeat could befall this country to the extent involved in the election of a Congress hostile to the President. . . . We have not forgotten the obstacles thrown in the path of President Wilson after the first World War and the ultimate victims were people."[18]

Republicans were outraged by Flynn's comments. Congressman Joseph Martin, House minority leader and chairman of the Republican National Committee, accused the DNC chairman of "seeking a one-party system, and of wanting to 'liquidate' the Republican opposition."[19] "Republicans," he said, "will continue to give President Roosevelt one hundred per cent support to win the war. We will continue to put national safety above partisanship. Despite abuse or vilification . . . we will stand by the American right to offer any constructive appraisal or suggestion."[20]

Meanwhile, Republican senator Robert A. Taft of Ohio took up the issue in a speech on the floor of the Senate, arguing (even before Flynn's comments) that "there can be no doubt that criticism in time of war is essential to the maintenance of any kind of democratic government. . . . Of course, that criticism should not give any information to the enemy. But too many people desire to suppress criticism simply because they think that it will give some comfort to the enemy to know that there is such criticism. . . . Congress does have the job of reasonable criticism. I think it has the job of criticizing the conduct of the war when it is properly subject to criticism. [For example], the surprise at Hawaii should, in my opinion, be investigated by committees of Congress, and not left entirely to the executive department."[21]

A few months later, former president Herbert Hoover echoed Taft's sentiment in a speech before the Annual Assembly of the National Industrial Conference Board, Inc., in New York City. According to Hoover, "Criticism of the conduct of the war may rightly lead to criticism of public officials. In a democracy even the President is not immune from rightful criticism. . . . Patriotism is not devotion to a public servant. It is devotion to our country and its right aims. No public servant can be free of criticism if democracy is to continue to live."[22] Hoover's speech was well received from many quarters, and was, at Senator Taft's initiative, printed in the *Congressional Record.*[23]

Politics was not abandoned (or stifled) in World War II America. Politicians continued to bicker, issues continued to be debated, and elections continued to be held. Several things contributed to this triumph of politics. First, Congress, as historian Roland Young observed in a splendid 1956 study of the wartime body, continued to carry out its business under the usual paradigm—that is, the two chambers and their committees were organized according to parties.[24] Instead of centralizing control in a single, nonpartisan war committee, the Democratic-controlled Congress dispersed power over a wide number of standing committees and newly created investigation committees.[25] Thus organized, partisanship was inevitable. Second, the nation entered the war on the eve of the spring and fall midterm elections of 1942. As early as late 1941, then, politicians (even before Pearl Harbor) were positioning themselves for electoral success. And third, Republicans and Democrats viewed US entry into the war through very different lenses. These outlooks, in turn, impacted attitudes and actions toward future policy.

For example, many Republicans interpreted Pearl Harbor as the result of not only Japanese aggression and savagery but also administration ineptness. Indeed, on December 7, Senator Gerald Nye of North Dakota, upon learning of the Pearl Harbor attack earlier that day, accused the Roosevelt administration of "doing its utmost to provoke a quarrel with Japan." Another Republican prewar non-interventionist, Senator Arthur Vandenberg of Michigan, wrote in February 1942 that "it was the 'interventionists' (from the President down) who were constantly saying to the country 'this way lies peace': and it was the non-interventionists who were constantly saying to the country 'this way lies a war for which you are totally unprepared.'" In a letter to a constituent that September, Vandenberg added that Roosevelt's "final ultimatum to Japan two weeks ahead of Pearl Harbor (culminating these policies) made a Japanese attack inevitable."[26]

Democrats, meanwhile, construed Republican "isolationist" stances prior to Pearl Harbor as being responsible for America's lack of preparedness on December 7 and preferred to highlight those prewar views so as to discredit present-day Republican criticisms of Roosevelt's handling of the war. Indeed, when on December 11, Republican senator Charles W. Tobey of New Hampshire called for the removal of Secretary of the Navy Frank Knox and for a complete congressional investigation into the attack, Democratic senator Scott Lucas of Illinois publicly castigated the Republican for both his position and his timing.[27] "Oh! Shame on anyone at this hour—only 48 hours, no details, nothing—standing on the floor of the Senate, denouncing and condemning everything."[28] In so far as neglect was concerned, Lucas suggested Tobey reexamine his own Republican, non-interventionist record from the standpoint of defense. "You, Mr. Senator from New Hampshire, are no naval strategist," he declared. "The time has passed for you to continue the type of tactics you have employed in the Senate. If we had followed your advice, I hate to say where we would be today."[29]

Meanwhile, Democrat David Walsh of Massachusetts, chairman of the Senate Naval Affairs Committee, reminded his colleagues that "We must have confidence in our war President—not a Democratic President, not a New Deal President, but a war President serving in a new role which will mark his place in history." If there was a neglect of duty prior to Pearl Harbor, then Roosevelt, Walsh insisted, would "put his hands upon it and act in such a way as to retain the confidence of the American people."[30] In the House, Emanuel Celler of New York, a Democrat, went further than either Lucas or Walsh, declaring that Tobey and other Republican "isolationists" should apologize to the president for their prewar positions.[31]

These prewar Republican views, many Democrats believed, were open to electoral scrutiny. Indeed, in the nation's premiere election contest of 1942—the New York gubernatorial race—Democrat John J. Bennett accused his Republican opponent, Thomas Dewey, of being an advocate of "appeasement" before Pearl Harbor—someone who had deplored rearmament as a national policy, and who had opposed aid to America's allies.[32] Speaking in Buffalo, in late October, Bennett insisted that the prewar views of Republicans were electorally relevant, and that the war should not be "blithely" brushed aside as a campaign issue. After all, Bennett argued, "They [Republicans] are the ones who cried we would not be attacked, who thought Hitler should be left to go his way. They are the ones who needed the sacrifice of Pearl Harbor to blunt their criticisms. They are the ones who give the war only lip service." No, Bennett concluded, "The war is an issue. It is a moral issue and a political issue. It is a national issue and a State issue, a local issue and a personal issue."[33]

Political disputes, of course, ran multiple ways, and intraparty strife was also quite common. Within the Republican Party, for example, Thomas Dewey and Wendell Willkie were bitter rivals for control over the New York party apparatus in 1942, and then for the Republican presidential nomination in 1944. Both men were "moderate" to "liberal" and fought not only each other but also conservatives in the party such as Congressman Hamilton Fish of New York. Perhaps the most visible intraparty dispute, however, involved the Democrats in the New York gubernatorial campaign of 1942, where President Roosevelt supported one candidate for the nomination, and his former campaign strategist (and now bitter rival), James Farley, supported another. The result was a very nasty and public feud that no doubt contributed to Democratic losses in the state that November.

Still, interparty struggles between Republicans and Democrats continued to be the most prevalent form of political dispute during the war years. Both parties sought electoral advantages over the other and employed the usual partisan rhetoric to define themselves and their opponents. This was especially the case in the midterm elections of 1942—America's first major electoral battle since Pearl Harbor. In this rehearsal for the presidential election of 1944, the Republican Party, clearly concerned about appearing unpatriotic and harmful to the war effort (but not wanting to be sidelined by Democrats either), stressed two main themes.

The first was their present cooperation with the administration, especially as it related to the larger issues of the war and support for the troops. In an interview with the *New York Times* shortly after Pearl Harbor, Wendell

Willkie insisted that "We must recognize the fact that debate over our participation in the world conflict has ended. Japan brought it to a close, and Congress, reflecting the will of the people, has declared that a state of war exists. Our one job is to win that war."[34] In his speech accepting his party's nomination for governor of New York in August 1942, Thomas Dewey emphasized America's unity of purpose in the war. "Right now," he declared, "let me make plain one thing: the war in which America's young men are fighting and dying is not a political issue. At the induction center they do not ask your politics. On the beaches of France last week and in the steaming jungles of the Solomon Islands there were both Republicans and Democrats. They were fighting as plain Americans together."[35] Dewey also addressed Republican support for Roosevelt as commander-in-chief. That support, he insisted, was "full": "[E]very moment of every hour of every day, in all measures to win the war, we are supporting and will continue loyally to support our Commander in Chief."[36]

The second Republican theme was the need for honest and constructive criticism of the administration. Dewey stressed this issue too, noting in the spring of 1942 that "Many of us have criticized the administration severely. We shall continue to criticize the acts of the administration when we believe that criticism is helpful to our common effort. That is one of the very sources of the strength of a free republic. We should betray our country if we failed to make useful criticism."[37] On the eve of his victory that November, Dewey added that America was engaged not simply in a political campaign but in a vindication of freedom. "We have been proving," he said, "that with us democracy is alive and vigorous. We have dared to keep it vital even in the midst of total war. We have shown that even in the midst of such a struggle we still cherish and can make stronger our heritage of freedom."

Implicit in this critique, of course, was the familiar (and favorite) Republican charge that Roosevelt sought complete personal and political power. Specific Republican attacks, however, usually manifested themselves in the form of condemning the conduct of the war. One of the more explosive indictments of the administration came in September 1942 from Clare Booth Luce of Connecticut, running in her first successful bid for Congress. Luce took the administration to task for waging what she called a "soft war." Speaking before the Connecticut state GOP convention, the 39-year-old writer insisted that "while the Administration and many of its appointees have talked a tough war, so far, unhappily, they have fought a soft one. A soft war is an improperly conducted one." Luce went on, then, to detail several characteristics of this "soft war," including chaos and confusion in Washington, lack of a unified economic command, petty partisanship, the raising of false issues (such as "isolationism"), and the creation of an artificial "scarcity of patriotism."[38]

That fall, the Democratic Party suffered serious electoral setbacks. In the House of Representatives, Republicans added 47 seats, giving them a total of 209 seats to 222 for the Democrats and making 1942 the most successful election for Republicans since they lost control in 1930. Meanwhile in the Senate, the GOP picked up 9 seats, leaving the Democrats with a working majority of only 21. In statewide races, the picture looked just as bleak for Democrats. Republicans won the governorships in the "big and potent" states of California, New York, Ohio, and Michigan, giving GOP governors a total population of 76 million to govern—a clear Electoral College majority.[38] Speaking extemporaneously to supporters after his New York victory, a jubilant Thomas Dewey spoke for many Republicans when he declared: "We have proven that our system of government is so good that we can make changes even in total war to strengthen the conduct of that war. We have shown our enemies that they don't even begin to understand the stuff democracy is made of."[40]

CHAPTER 2

Thomas Dewey and the Dilemmas
of Republican Wartime Opposition

The 1930s decade was a difficult one for the Republican Party. Associated with economic depression and the unpopular Herbert Hoover, Republicans witnessed their majority status erode at all levels of government. The election of Franklin Roosevelt, a Democrat, to the presidency in 1932 did little to improve Republican prospects. Upon entering office in March 1933, Roosevelt launched the New Deal, his series of bold economic reforms to combat the Great Depression, instilling hope and courage in the American people. The Great Depression, then, unleashed great political upheaval. New voters (that is, groups outside the core electorate) were mobilized, while many old ones, dissatisfied with the Republicans, converted (or switched allegiances) to the Democrats. Ultimately, an interparty realignment was established in which the Democratic Party became the distinctly liberal party and the Republican Party the decisively conservative one. The 1930s decade, then, was a bleak one for Republicans. Indeed, they faced multiple challenges, including blame for the Depression, minority party status, and lack of a coherent and positive response to the New Deal.

According to Angus Campbell, Philip Converse, Warren Miller, and Donald Stokes in their classic *The American Voter* (1960), the Depression era witnessed a major partisan realignment—"the conversion of erstwhile Republicans" to Democrats.[1] Generally, they observed, party identification in the United States was stable and "not readily disturbed by passing events and personalities." Only in the most extreme of circumstances—an economic depression, for example—was party loyalty affected by politics. Examining national election data from the 1930s through the 1950s, Campbell and his colleagues presented a sophisticated analysis of party identification and concluded that, in the 1930s, a partisan realignment occurred when three Republican groups who were impacted the most by the events of that decade switched their party allegiance.[2]

The first group included young voters who came of age in the 1920s and never developed a strong sense of party identification. Not surprisingly, they quickly abandoned the majority party, the Republican Party, once severe economic crisis began. A second group included those voters who benefited from New Deal policies and thus began identifying with the Democratic Party. Employing data from a 1952 study, Campbell and company noted that many voters continued to interpret the policies of the 1930s in highly personal terms. For example, "A sales clerk in Pittsburgh says she was a Republican until Mr. Hoover's Administration, now she is a Democrat. 'My husband [she told the study] was a government employee and we got the cuts in pay under Hoover. We lost our house on account of that.'"[3] The third group of voters, meanwhile, included minorities, especially Jews and blacks. In the case of Jewish voters, the authors speculated that it was the rise of Nazi Germany, and the Roosevelt administration's opposition to it, that contributed to the partisan shift.

In *The Responsible Electorate* (1966), V.O. Key added that government action and campaign oratory played a key role in a two-way realignment. Prior to Roosevelt's New Deal, he argued, the federal government "had been a remote authority with a limited range of activity" that affected few, including operating the postal system, improving rivers and harbors, and maintaining a small military force. The New Deal, with its large-scale measures for unemployment relief, public works, and social security, changed those priorities and made the federal government "an institution that affected the lives and fortunes of most, if not all, citizens."[4] Initially, he insisted, "persons of all classes deserted the Republicans [in 1932] to vote for Franklin D. Roosevelt and a change." Then, as the decade progressed and the New Deal unfolded, persons of upper-class status and conservative disposition were drawn from Democratic postures to the Republican ranks.[5] Governmental actions and political rhetoric, he concluded, heightened "polarization along class and occupational lines," and thus party switching was common in both directions.

Republicans were also challenged by the mobilization of new, Democratic-leaning voters. According to Samuel Lubell, in *The Future of American Politics* (1952), the "Roosevelt revolution" of the 1930s rested upon "the revolt of the city"—the influx of previously uninvolved groups, including "women, young people, and the foreign-stock, urban, working class."[6] Republicans, he noted, had long been laboring on the wrong side of the national birthrate. During the 1930s, 21 million people reached voting age, the majority of whom were children of the immigrant poor. Their parents had come to the United States some 28 million strong between 1890 and 1914 and had settled in Atlantic seaboard cities. They habitually voted Democratic. These urban minorities received little support from Republicans in the 1920s, while the Democratic Party began appealing to them as early as 1928. Then, in the 1930s, Lubell concluded, Roosevelt awakened them "to a consciousness of the power in their numbers ... [and] extended to them the warming hand of recognition, through patronage and protective legislation."[7]

Unfamiliar with minorities' status and unable to articulate a single response to the New Deal, Republicans soon descended into factionalism, confusion, and further defeat. The main fault line was between those, such as former president Hoover, who wanted to intensify the party's anti–New Deal message, and pragmatic officeholders who believed it was imperative to compete with the New Deal for the support of the masses.[8] In 1934, the Republican National Committee, under conservative, pro-Hoover leadership, organized that year's national midterm campaign to attack Roosevelt and his policies. The result was disaster. Instead of gaining seats in Congress—as was customary for a party out of power during midterm elections—the GOP lost 19 seats in the House of Representatives and 10 in the Senate.

Two years later, Republicans nominated a moderate for president, Governor Alfred M. Landon of Kansas, who sought to distance himself from northeastern moneyed interests and Old Guard Republicanism, and to identify instead with his own rural American roots. Unfortunately, according to Landon biographer Donald McCoy, he was "overshadowed in tone and coverage by those less moderate than he," including Hoover and even his own vice presidential running mate, Frank Knox.[9] Landon himself later recalled that "much of the ground I covered in the closing weeks of the campaign was discredited because of the Liberty League, Economy League, etc. One trouble was that I had no one ... to pick up the progressive and moderate side of my speeches."[10]

However, not all of Landon's speeches were as "progressive" as he remembered. For example, speaking in Milwaukee in late September, he condemned the Social Security Act as "unjust, unworkable, stupidly drafted and wastefully financed." In Baltimore, he even insisted that "New Deal policies would lead to the guillotine."[11] Reflecting the divisions within his own party, Landon ultimately "found himself in the uneasy position of advancing many contradictions in his campaign."[12] He symbolized frugality in government but favored government programs of such dimensions that he would have been, like Roosevelt, unable to achieve a balanced budget. He also denounced the president's relief policies but "took considerable pains to offer his assurances that he would continue relief."[13] Writing in the *New York Herald Tribune* shortly before the election, Walter Lippmann observed: "There are as yet no signs that the Republican party has found an issue on which it can unite. In fact, there are many signs which indicate that the schism which rent it in 1912, was healed in 1920, and broke out again in 1932, is deeper than ever."[14]

On Election Day, Roosevelt routed Landon, receiving a record-breaking 60.8 percent of the popular vote. Republicans were repudiated, disheartened, and divided. When the Seventy-Fifth Congress convened in early 1937, at the apogee of Democratic strength, only 17 Republicans sat in the Senate, and 89 in the House of Representatives. "We Republicans," Arthur Pound of the *Atlantic Monthly* observed shortly after Landon's defeat, "if we are to devise a brand of conservatism with a chance of winning the nation back to the Republican party, must recognize that it will require elements beyond wealth in the present and fear of the future."[15]

Republicans in fact rebounded in the 1938 midterm elections, picking up 75 seats in the House and 7 in the Senate. Much of this success, however, was grounded in Democratic misfortunes, including Roosevelt's plan to pack the Supreme Court in 1937, labor strife in the automobile and steel industries, and the deepening of the Depression. Although still in the minority in Congress, Republicans were lifted by the president's second-term problems. The outbreak of World War II in 1939, however, thwarted Republican hopes for winning the White House in 1940. While the party's presidential nominee, Wendell Willkie, made the election relatively close (falling 5 million votes short of FDR), many conservatives, including Hoover, deemed him a moderate and internationalist, and too far removed from the GOP's fundamental beliefs. Indeed, Hoover, in analyzing the 1940 returns to a friend, noted that Willkie—in appealing to New Dealers, independents, and anti–New Deal Democrats—had actually run behind regular Republican candidates in statewide races by some 1 to 2 million votes.[16]

Willkie vehemently disagreed with such assessments. In a letter to The *Washington Post* reporter Mark Sullivan in late November, Willkie pointed out that he had carried both Michigan and Indiana, while the Republican governors there failed to win reelection. Furthermore, he ran ahead of the Republican gubernatorial candidate in Kansas, as well as the candidate for the US Senate in New York. "I appreciate," he wrote, "that there is a very aggressive propaganda being carried on by certain leaders . . . but I really am quite anxious about this . . . because I think it would be almost tragic if the Republican Party falls back into the old-guard reactionaries in the belief that it could have won if that had been its program in 1940."[17] "The 1940 election result," historian Lewis Gould concluded, "produced a permanent sense of grievance" within the party's conservative base.[18]

Republicans also lacked serious and popular direction. Out of power at all levels, the party did not have a single leader or voice the way Democrats did in the person of the President of the United States. The only leader closely associated with the party was the nation's only living former president, the unpopular Hoover, age 66 in 1940. Unlike most previous former presidents, he refused to allow "himself to rust in inactivity" and took to radio and print "to direct a few well-placed shots at the New Deal administration."[19]

Not surprisingly, Republicans suffered from an identity crisis—particularly as it related to foreign policy. Although isolationism—defined variously as "antipathy toward Europe and things European (particularly military alliances, power politics, and wars), belief in the invulnerability and suzerainty of the United States in the Western Hemisphere, [and] a fervidly nationalistic desire to preserve American freedom of action"—cut across party lines, it was most widely associated with the Republican Party.[20] It had been Republicans who led the fight against Woodrow Wilson's beloved League of Nations after World War I, and it had been Republicans, in the years immediately prior to Pearl Harbor, who were the most vocal "non-interventionists" and members of such "isolationist" organizations as America First. That did not mean, of course, that all, or even most, within the GOP were isolationists. They were not. Still, as with most other issues, Republicans were divided along several fine lines when it came to foreign policy.

First, there were the staunch "isolationists." "Isolationist" was a word often used by wartime Democrats to describe most prewar Republicans. It was a word that denoted not only "non-involvement" in world affairs but also pro-Axis sympathies. Democrats pointed to two things to justify this label. One was Republican opposition to the League of Nations and the Treaty of Versailles at the end of World War I. And the other—hinting at German support—was Republican opposition to American aid to the Allies of World War II prior to Pearl Harbor. In reality, of course, support and/or opposition for both issues was much more complex and bipartisan.

Many Republicans, then, resented being singled out for their pre–Pearl Harbor "isolationist" views. In a letter to Ohio governor John W. Bricker in the fall of 1944, Herbert Hoover complained that "If the Democratic Party has been so devoted to the League of Nations, why did not Mr. Roosevelt with his rubberstamp Senate join it [in 1933]?"[21] The RNC, meanwhile, compiled and published a list of FDR's own "isolationist" statements from the 1930s—including the president's October 30, 1940, campaign, which pledged that "Your boys are not going to be sent into any foreign wars. . . . The purpose of our defense is defense"—and concluded that "Republicans who were out of power after 1933 can scarcely be blamed for the isolationism of Franklin Roosevelt."[22]

Most Republicans were not isolationists in the strictest sense, that is, they did not call for the United States to retire to America after the war and to take no interest in the actions or problems of other nations. Nevertheless, a small fringe—including Gerald L.K. Smith, editor of the monthly *The Cross and the Flag* and founder of the new America First Party, and New York congressman Hamilton Fish—who opposed any kind of revived or rejuvenated postwar "league of nations." Furthermore, many in this small group of staunch "isolationists" never fully reconciled themselves to American military involvement in the Second World War.

Some party leaders, then, worried that the GOP might be used by Nazi appeasers in the United States as a vehicle for a negotiated settlement with the Axis powers. Speaking at the fifty-sixth annual Lincoln Dinner in New York on February 12, 1942, Thomas Dewey, the leading Republican candidate for New York governor that fall, warned of an "American Cliveden set in Washington and other cities . . . [that was] scheming to end the war short of military victory." While appeasers were present in both parties, Dewey noted, "history teaches that they all may attempt to sneak into the party of the opposition. They may even attempt to use it to achieve their cowardly end."[23]

A second group of "isolationists" were those Republicans like former president Hoover, who favored American participation in world affairs, but who had opposed American intervention in World War II before Pearl Harbor. This group of "non-interventionists" genuinely believed that the United States would be able to achieve greater influence on future peace if it remained out of the war. They were not isolationists in the strictest sense, and after Pearl Harbor, this group immediately expressed support for both the president and the war effort. They also endorsed the idea of some kind of postwar international organization. As Michigan's Republican senator Arthur Vandenberg, a symbol of pre–Pearl Harbor non-intervention in the Senate, later observed, "My convictions regarding international cooperation and collective security for peace took firm form on the afternoon of the Pearl Harbor attack. That day ended isolationism for any realist."[24]

Then there were those within the party who, in early 1941, had endorsed Roosevelt's Lend-Lease plan for assisting the Allies and accepted the growing likelihood that the United States would be required to enter the war. Furthermore, these Republican "internationalists" sought to "convince Americans to join a world peace organization and thereby promote equality among all peoples, regardless of race, color, or nationality."[25] Specifically, most in this group advocated, first, the immediate creation of an Allied organization to address war problems and, second, the transformation of that Allied organization into a world state to settle postwar problems and keep future peace. Led by Wendell Willkie, these internationalists were described by their more conservative critics as "Republican Pollyannas who want to compete with Henry Wallace."[26]

By late 1941, and with American entry into World War II, the Republican Party was in desperate need of leadership. It found it in New York's Thomas Dewey. Overall, Dewey possessed name recognition and broad, national appeal as a racket buster. He was also young, articulate, and pragmatic—believing the GOP had to build upon the progressive tradition of Theodore Roosevelt if it wanted to be successful in the future.[27] Thus, he accepted a role for government in assuring "relief for the needy," fair wages, and the protection of "the very young and the old, the sick and the infirm, from economic and social injustice."[28] Most importantly, Dewey demonstrated great skill in spanning the rhetorical gap between conservatives and liberals in the party, often appealing to both groups. Although ultimately unsuccessful in his quest for national office, Dewey played a key role in stimulating and directing the Republican Party's return to electoral prominence in the second half of the twentieth century.

Born in the small town of Owosso, Michigan, on March 24, 1902, Dewey came from a comfortable Midwestern home. His father, George, was a local newspaper editor and Republican leader, who instilled in his only child the value of hard work, and an interest in politics and writing. "Politics, thanks to my father," Dewey later wrote, "was as natural a part of our home as eating and sleeping." The Dewey family frequently welcomed Republican candidates for state office into their home, including Congressman Joseph W. Fordney (1899–1923), whom young Dewey called "Uncle Chase." "Our visitors never seemed to object to the presence of a boy in the room," he recalled, "and I spent many days and evenings listening to the great men talk about such faraway subjects as legislation in the Congress and foreign affairs."[29]

Meanwhile, Dewey's mother, Annie, was an efficient manager of the family home and a very powerful influence over her son. It was from his mother that Dewey learned thrift, tidiness, and perfectionism. Indeed, Dewey was a model boy. He had perfect attendance at school, was never tardy, and learned quickly. He was also a very determined youth. In fact, his persistence was legendary in the community. For example, when told by his high school principal that he should stay home for a few days after a football injury left him limping and with one arm in a sling, Dewey replied, "Oh no, that would spoil my perfect attendance record." When the principal consoled that he could at least go home to bed after classes, Dewey retorted, "And miss football practice. I wouldn't do that either—the boys might think I was a quitter."[30] He was such an exemplary child, one journalist later observed, "that his schoolmates looked upon him with suspicion and frank disapproval."[31]

Years later, as he was running for president, Dewey tried to downplay this "boy scout image," instructing his mother when dealing with reporters "to skip, if possible, any reference to my having never missed a day in school or been tardy. It is hard for people to understand and many will not believe it. Probably it should be just omitted and if anyone raises the question themselves, you might just pass it off by saying I was just very healthy and happened to have my childhood illnesses during the summer."[32]

In high school, Dewey was involved in a number of activities, including band, chorus, yearbook, and drama. He also enjoyed arguing and was a member of the debating team, where he excelled. He possessed both an inquisitive mind and a passion for facts. "He took nothing on faith," *Look* magazine observed in 1944. "He demanded proof . . . and had little time for sloppy or mediocre thinking and was pretty frank about it."[33] According to one classmate, he exhausted every side of an issue and would "always see right through to the best answer. Sometimes I think he kept on arguing just to see how many things he could say on a subject. And he always won, just always."[34] Indeed, next to his 1919 senior picture in the school yearbook, *Spic*, was the quote: "First in the council hall to steer the state, And ever-foremost in a tongue debate."[35]

From 1919 to 1923, Dewey attended the University of Michigan, where he studied music and had hopes of becoming an opera singer. Dewey's voice was actually quite good, New York music critic Deems Taylor recalled, but he lacked a singer's temperament. In what also would come to characterize his political performances, Dewey sang "too intelligently" and with "not enough impulse."[36] Still, his musical studies helped him, as one early admirer noted, to develop "a speaking voice and diction which could coo and could roar."[37] Convinced that he could never "set the opera world on fire," Dewey ultimately turned to the law, and in 1925, graduated from the Columbia University School of Law in New York. Shortly thereafter he passed the bar and began practicing law with the firm of Larkin, Rathbone and Perry on New York's lower Broadway. Then, in June 1928, Dewey married Frances Eileen Hutt, a young and pretty opera singer from Sapulpa, Oklahoma.

It was during this time too that Dewey became involved in New York politics. In 1937, when he ran for district attorney, he told reporters that "I'm frankly a novice at this business." He had hoped to live above political battle, he explained, but the crime and corruption he saw forced him into the arena. "The issue of decency and having a place where your wife and children would want to live [are] more important than ... the desires of any man alive."[38] In fact, Dewey was far from a novice at politics. In 1925, at the age of 23, he became assistant district leader to the Republican captain of the Tenth Assembly District in Manhattan. In 1931, he served as the governor of the Young Republican Club of New York, and in 1932, he managed his patron George Z. Medalie's unsuccessful bid for the US Senate.

In New York City during the 1930s, Dewey built a national reputation for himself as a tough, racket-busting district attorney, successfully prosecuting Lucky Luciano, Legs Diamond, and Jimmy Hines. In 1937, he was even loosely "portrayed" by actor Humphrey Bogart in the MGM film *The Marked Woman,* a fictionalized account of the Luciano case.[39] In 1938, Dewey ran for New York governor but narrowly lost to popular incumbent Herbert Lehman. By then, he had received the attention of national Republicans, including the nation's only living former president, Herbert Hoover. In a confidential letter to a friend in October 1939, Hoover admitted that he thought "very highly—very highly indeed—of that young man" and expressed strong support for Dewey "as the best bet in sight" for the Republican presidential nomination in 1940.[40] However, despite an early front-runner status (and victory in every contested primary), Dewey's nomination bid ultimately fell short of victory. His youth (he was only 38 years of age in 1940) and inexperience (he had never held a statewide office)—combined with the outbreak of World War II in Europe—wrecked his convention drive, and the Republican nomination went instead to Wendell Willkie.

Disappointed by that loss, Dewey was buoyed by Hoover, who increasingly, if informally, came to advise the young New Yorker on political strategy. Hoover understood that a deep and fundamental shift had occurred in American life since the New Deal. It was, he noted in a letter to Dewey in July 1940, "a time of effervescent public moods, of short distance thought instead of long distance deliberation, of rapid shifts to meet emergencies of the moment rather than the deeper currents of national life." This changing pattern of American life, Hoover continued, had resulted in "a substantial realignment of our political parties" and threatened the very existence of the Republican Party and a two-party system in the United States. It was up to young party leaders such as Dewey, the former president wrote, "to stay alert and active in public life." According to Hoover, Dewey—an "outstanding person . . . [who had a] fundamental sense of the long view rather than the transitory"—would bear much of that great responsibility.[41]

In 1941, Dewey enhanced his national image by participating in the first cross-country, fact-finding, and fund-raising tour for USO clubs. He found that many state-side soldiers did not have "a simple, clean place where they could wash up and get a night's sleep in decent surroundings." Soldiers also lacked entertainment, as many public places refused to welcome them. Dewey was especially disturbed by a sign on a public swimming pool in one town that he visited that read, "No dogs or soldiers allowed." Upon returning to New York, he recommended the construction of USO rest and recreation buildings across the country. His tour raised $15 million for the USO—nearly $5 million more than projected.[42]

Meanwhile, Dewey offered tepid support for Lend-Lease, calling for "every possible aid to Great Britain short of war" but adding, somewhat clumsily, that the Lend-Lease Bill itself "would bring an end to free Government in the United States and would abolish Congress for all practical purposes."[43] However, less than a month later, at a Lincoln Day dinner in Washington, Dewey—perhaps with eyes on a Gallup poll that showed 68 percent of Americans approved of the president's plan—clarified his position, announcing: "I believe our party stands out almost unanimously for all-out aid to the heroic people of Britain. With some necessary reservations of power to the people through Congress, I am satisfied the House [Lend-Lease] Bill will be adopted. Speaking for myself alone, I hope it will be."[44]

Then, in January 1942, while speaking before the Economic Club of New York, Dewey acknowledged that the Pearl Harbor disaster was the result not merely of two Pacific commanders unaware of danger but of an America where "many saw the danger but no one acted on it to the limit, and no one to an adequate degree. No one of us can claim exemption from that." The country, he said, must move beyond a "pre–Pearl Harbor state of mind."[45] Still, Dewey, as one historian observed, "was too proud and too much a partisan to do public penance for past [isolationist] misjudgments."[46] Thus, he soon found himself to be the subject of much criticism from his old pre-convention rival in 1940, Wendell Willkie.

Willkie alienated Dewey and many other Republicans in the spring of 1942 with his refusal to forgive past non-interventionist stands and to categorize all Republicans who had disagreed with the Roosevelt foreign policy as "isolationists." Delivering the commencement address at Union College in May 1942, the former chief of a utility corporation—with an eye toward the approaching midterm elections—called upon the graduates to "choose leaders who have principles and the courage to state them plainly. Not men who examine each shift of sentiment and watch the polls of public opinion to learn where they stand. I beg of you, vote for straight-out men—not wobblers."[47]

Willkie was especially critical of Dewey, toward whom the above Union College remarks were no doubt directed. Willkie's dislike of Dewey was grounded in two things. First, he distrusted Dewey's recent conversion to internationalism and believed the former district attorney would become a rallying point for isolationists after the war. And second, Willkie wanted to become the Republican nominee for president in 1944, and he viewed Dewey as his chief rival. Like any other contender, he sought to discredit and eliminate possible threats to his candidacy. As a matter of fact, Willkie's foreign policy views were not that different from those of Dewey, Hoover, and Landon. Certainly, he was more of an idealist, but he was no more of an internationalist. Willkie genuinely wanted to reform the Republican Party, and he desperately wanted to become president. His passion, mixed with ambition and poor political skills, combined to distance him from those who were actually quite close to him on most issues.

Dewey's views on foreign policy had in fact developed significantly since 1940, when—during his first campaign for the presidency—he had advocated "avoiding entangling alliances and upholding the Monroe Doctrine."[48] Dewey was annoyed, then, by Willkie's constant sniping in the spring of 1942 and believed the former party standard-bearer was attempting to corner him on the issues and sabotage his New York gubernatorial campaign later that year—if not blatantly challenge him for the office.[49] "Our friend Wendell is out to do me dirt," he confided to his mother that April. "I am not as worried as I ought to be, probably."[50] Most Republicans, like Dewey, had been non-interventionists, and after Pearl Harbor, they resented criticism from officials within the Roosevelt administration, as well as among Willkie Republicans, that they had been "isolationists."

Herbert Hoover decided to confront the issue directly, and on May 20, in his first major speech after US entry into the war, the former president warned against what he called the "high priests" of intolerance, who "have concluded that all those who were opposed to war before Pearl Harbor cannot possibly be patriotic Americans ever. Or at least they are under suspicion as being appeasers, compromisers, various obnoxious bipeds, reptiles, and

Cliveden sets, Nazis sympathizers and Sixth Columnists. Yet 75 per cent of the American people were opposed to the war before the attack on Pearl Harbor. Nevertheless this 75 per cent who are now in outer darkness are willingly sacrificing their sons, their brothers, their husbands, and they are working and paying without murmur."[51]

After the speech, Hoover privately observed that it had raised the hair of those who had organized for the midterm elections to defeat all Republican representatives and senators who had been pre–Pearl Harbor non-interventionists. "This group," Hoover complained, "is an unnatural combination of the reactionaries and the left-wingers who, for entirely different points of view, worked to get the country into war—and want a monopoly of patriotism now."[52] Dewey, who maintained a frequent correspondence with Hoover, agreed. In a letter to the former president a few days after the speech, Dewey compared Hoover's efforts to those of Theodore Roosevelt in World War I. "As I understand it," Dewey wrote, "Theodore Roosevelt did more to help the Republican Party in 1918 . . . by stumping the country in aid of the war effort. I think your speech has started such a movement for 1942." The speech itself, Dewey insisted, was "magnificent" and "a political ten strike as far as the Republican Party is concerned."[53]

In an effort to pacify Willkie and to forestall an expected Democratic "isolation" attack that fall, Dewey launched his own effort in May to shore up his internationalist credentials. Dewey was not an isolationist, but he had been a militant enough non-interventionist in 1940 to be labeled that June by the *New York Daily News* as "an isolationist, meaning that if elected he will be 100 percent for arming to the teeth for defense of this country, but against buying any further into Europe's war."[54] Dewey now made three major steps to change that image.[55] First, he announced his support for an anti-isolation resolution sponsored by Willkie (and adopted by the RNC's national meeting in Chicago in April). Moreover, he promised to promote it at the Republican State Convention in Albany in June.

Second, in a speech before a Republican women's club on May 9, Dewey acknowledged the mistakes of America's post–World War I foreign policy. "In retrospect," he admitted, "we can see now that the period between the two wars was an unreal truce. The world tried to live on borrowed time and borrowed money without facing its problems. The United States played a decisive role in the war, [and] then withdrew from an equally decisive role in the peace. We were half in and half out of the affairs of the rest of the world." As to the current war and the coming "peace," Dewey noted that "It will be impossible to put back into their bottle the genii which have been released. National and racial aspirations, long subdued, have been awakened. The hopes of hundreds of millions of people all over the world are on the march. The victory at arms will be only the beginning."[56]

And third, on May 22, Dewey, with great drama, highlighted his opposition to Republican representative Hamilton Fish of New York's 26th Congressional District. Fish, age 54, was the grandson of President Ulysses S. Grant's secretary of state and his namesake. First elected to Congress in 1920, Fish was a vocal critic of the New Deal, a committed anticommunist, and a staunch "isolationist." Prior to Pearl Harbor, Fish, who was voted "the least useful member of the House" in a 1940 poll of Washington correspondents, dismissed Roosevelt's preparedness efforts as "phony" and accused the administration of spreading "war hysteria."[57] While the isolationist propaganda Fish supported often bordered on being pro-German, critics conceded that the congressman was "in no sense a fifth columnist"—just "a dupe of Hitlerism."[58] During the 1940 presidential campaign, Roosevelt often denounced Fish—along with "isolationist" Republican congressmen Joseph Martin and Bruce Barton—as "Martin, Barton, and Fish." Fish, who lived until 1991, later recalled that "I know he [Roosevelt] hated me, but I don't really believe in hate. So now I don't hate Roosevelt—but frankly I despise him."[59]

Fish was a problem for Dewey not only because he was a fellow New York Republican but also because Dewey (like FDR) was a registered voter in Fish's district. Perhaps hoping to goad Fish into a public confrontation, Dewey privately expressed his opposition to the congressman's reelection in conversations with state party leaders for several months. On May 22, Fish took action and telephoned the gubernatorial candidate, inquiring of his loyalties in the upcoming primary fight. The conversation was anything but cordial. Dewey informed the congressman that he was, in fact, "unalterably opposed" to his reelection. "Your office was used by our enemies," Dewey charged, and remaining "in the race would be 'a terrible disservice' to the party."[60] Fish countered that his vigilance against communism made him an asset in the House—"a claim Dewey dismissed with a contemptuous snort."[61] Fish then retorted that a man Dewey's age should be fighting in the war. He also suggested that, if Dewey continued to oppose him, he and his friends would launch a personal attack against the Republican hopeful, and "that if he [Fish] were defeated for renomination he would then become an independent candidate for Governor against the Republican nominee."[62] That, Dewey replied, was "about as complete a case of blackmail as I have ever heard." No, Fish concluded, it was simply counsel "not to butt into my district."[63] Later that day Dewey assembled reporters and released a statement about his exchange with Fish, including the details of their conversation.

Dewey's strategy seemed to work. Returning to New York from a vacation at his Rushville, Indiana, farm on May 23, Willkie expressed "delight" at Dewey's support for his anti-isolation resolution. "It was also pleasing," Willkie added, "to read that Mr. Dewey has publicly joined those who have been opposing the nomination of Hamilton Fish. Although Mr. Dewey does not say on what grounds his opposition is based, I am quite sure it must be because of Mr. Fish's diehard isolation position."[64]

A few days later, Dewey stumbled. Speaking extemporaneously before a largely pro-Fish audience, Dewey, in endorsing Fish's opponent, Augustus W. Bennet, declared—at least according to the *New York Times*—that he was "opposed to the Congressman *not for his views,* but because of the misuse of his office by friends he has had [italics added]."[65] Willkie was deeply concerned by the statement and told reporters a few days later that Fish's views and record—not his friends—were the most important questions. According to Willkie, Fish "is and was a sincere and outspoken advocate of policies which would confine the United States, as far as international affairs, to a non-participation in the affairs of the world."[66] The following day, a Willkie supporter, Helen P. Simpson, the widow of a former New York County Republican leader, signed a relatively large advertisement against Dewey in the *Times*. The advertisement asked, "Why don't you attack Mr. Fish's views?" and concluded that "You do not measure up, Mr. Dewey! We have not time to wait for you to learn. We must have leaders whose past record shows we can trust them to the end. Your record is not clear."[67]

Shaken by the controversy, Dewey moved quickly to clarify his comments, issuing a statement on June 15 that sought to reconstruct the speech from notes taken by one of his aides, Paul E. Lockwood. In his statement Dewey correctly noted that no stenographer had been present, and that Lockwood had taken notes, as was his practice for all of the candidate's extemporaneous remarks. According to Dewey, Lockwood's notes contained the correct wording of the controversial remarks: "This is *even more* than a matter of views. I am opposed to the Representative from this district *not for his views only* but because of the misuse of his office and the associates he has had [italics added]"[68] Dewey's version of the speech was no doubt correct. He was not an isolationist, and he had nothing to gain by contradicting Willkie, whom he had been courting and trying to appease for several weeks. The damage was done, however. Suspicion of Dewey among internationalists continued well past the midterm election and into 1944.

A few days later, on June 30, 1942, Dewey apparently composed (or had composed) an anonymous, and ultimately unsent, letter to Willkie. Writing merely as "delegate to the 1940 convention," Dewey warned that now that Willkie was a candidate again, he would have to defend certain "isolationist statements" of his own made in 1940. "I think that most people would like to forget about the past," the letter continued, "but you have set the standard for looking backward." The letter ended by urging Willkie to stay out of the New York race—"Most of your real friends would deplore a contest between you and Mr. Dewey. You are working for the same ends . . . unity in the war and the building of a better world after the victory."[69] As it turned out, Willkie did not challenge Dewey for governor. Instead, the former party standard-bearer departed the country on a 50-day journey around the world. Clearly relieved, Dewey wrote home to his mother in late July that there had been "no trouble from my fat friend for some time. I hear he is going to Russia before the Republican Convention, so he will be where he belongs, and I hope he stays there until Christmas."[70]

In November 1942, Dewey finally achieved his first statewide electoral success, winning the New York gubernatorial race and securing that office for Republicans for the first time in 30 years. From his headquarters in Manhattan, Dewey issued a statement on the importance of the Republican gains. "This election," he said, "has one simple meaning. . . . The fact that one party lost and the other party won is not important. We are not here tonight to celebrate a party victory. We are all of us interested in only one victory—total, uncompromising, crushing victory over our country's enemies. If this election has any meaning, it is that the American people are pledged with all their hearts and souls to that end, and to that end only." The country, he concluded, must "now put aside all rivalries" and, in all things related to achieving victory in the war, remain united in "unswerving loyalty to our Commander in Chief."[71] Privately, an appreciative Dewey, looking at his stack of congratulatory telegrams following his remarks, told intimates, "Gee, this is a glorious day."[72]

Dewey was undoubtedly the big winner of the 1942 midterm elections and deemed by many as the front-runner for the Republican nomination in 1944. "As a result of his election," James Hagerty argued in the *New York Times* that November, Dewey was now in a position for a "Presidential Coup," occupying in the Republican party a station "comparable to that which President Roosevelt held in the Democratic party in 1930."[73] Today, Dewey's name does not generate much excitement or, for that matter, recognition. In the 1930s and 1940s, however, he was a major political force and a young man on the rise. As Dewey addressed supporters in the lobby of the Roosevelt Hotel on election night, one enthusiastic partisan cheered: "This makes you the next President of the United States!"[74]

CHAPTER 3

Franklin Roosevelt and the
Challenges of the Democratic Majority

The early 1940s marked a low point in the Roosevelt administration. The war was going badly, and the president seemed unable to effectively and efficiently handle domestic affairs. In a January 1943 Gallup survey, 60 percent responded that they were dissatisfied with the way the government had conducted the war effort at home the previous year. Complaints included "should have shown more foresight and acted sooner on rationing of scarce goods," "should have tightened up government efficiency," "should have dealt more firmly with labor unions and strikes," and "should have given the public more information about war problems—less 'sugar coating' of bad news."[1] Indeed, Roosevelt's efforts at mobilizing the economy for war—through the creation of new (and bickering) "alphabet agencies" and the implementation of wage restrictions and price controls—only alienated voters (especially farmers and industrial workers) and had resulted in dramatic losses for his party in the 1942 midterm elections. According to *Time*, just days after the election, "The New Deal, on shaky ground since 1938, had now clearly fallen from its crest; if the conservative elements of the Democratic Party were eliminated, it would virtually become a minority party."[2] "Everywhere we have gone," one reporter later observed, "the one complaint of the kindred souls that we find is that the Democratic organization is shot to hell, and that the caliber of the local candidates who are running as Democrats is slightly less than zero-zero. The day where they can ride in on Roosevelt's shirt-tails has gone. . . . I want to vote for Roosevelt [in 1944], but if he is elected my recommendation is this: he ought to fire everybody below the rank of vice president and start again. . . . [T]here is too much dead wood around Washington after 12 years. . . . [I]f he is going to secure his place in the history books at the page where he is in my book, he had damned well better clean house and get some new blood."[3]

Most politicos and analysts were confounded by the 1942 midterm results. Gallup had predicted that Democrats stood to lose (at the most) one seat and that they had the potential to gain nineteen. Democrats were shocked and alarmed. "No man can say," *Time* magazine noted a few days later, "exactly when one political movement dies and another is born. But anyone who looked last week could see that Franklin Roosevelt's New Deal was sick, with ailments that could not lightly be thrown off." "Unless we can reverse this political tide," one Democratic congressman declared in late November, "the Democratic Party faces defeat in 1944. I don't know whether we can dam it up or not; we are in a bad way."[4]

Although Democrats maintained their majorities in both houses of Congress, Republicans gained 47 seats in the House of Representatives (reducing the Democratic majority to only 9 seats) and added 7 seats in the Senate (leaving Democrats with a working majority of 21). As the Seventy-Ninth Congress convened in January 1943, Roosevelt faced serious challenges to his leadership. The narrowness of Democratic majorities in the new Congress allowed Republicans and conservative southern Democrats (who filled more than half of the Democratic seats in Congress) to join forces and dominate the legislative agenda. Writing to House Republican leader Joe Martin of Massachusetts a few days after the midterm election, Herbert Hoover noted that the Republican gains gave Congress two great opportunities: "to insist upon a reorganization of the war agencies so as to stop this blundering delay and this loss of lives in this war" and "to stop the use of war measures to permanently collectivize this country."[5] Throughout 1943, then, Congress frustrated and defeated much of the administration's domestic agenda. Increasingly, the Democrats, like the Republicans, were divided over both domestic and foreign policy concerns.

This intraparty strife, of course, was not unusual and in fact gave testimony—in stark contrast to the twenty-first-century ideological polarization of the two main parties—to the fact that there existed within each party a wide and varied ideological spectrum. This was especially true of the Democratic Party. The so-called Roosevelt coalition that had thrust Democrats into power in 1932 and had maintained that majority since, included white southern conservatives, blacks, northeastern liberals, and midwestern farmers. Not surprisingly, the Democratic Party was riddled with internal division by the early 1940s. The main lines of contention were drawn between southern conservatives and northern liberals over civil rights, war mobilization, the New Deal, and the power of organized labor and its role in the party.

America's entry into the Second World War constituted a major turning point in American race relations. During the course of the 1930s and 1940s, black expectations (and power) rose, while white hostility in some quarters outside the South slowly diminished. In 1932, Franklin Roosevelt became the first Democrat since Franklin Pierce in 1852 to win the presidency with a majority of the popular vote. That majority, however, did not include blacks, most of whom still voted—if at all—Republican. Despite the fact that Roosevelt failed to push for civil rights legislation in his first term, a black majority—for the very first time—voted for the Democratic Party in the next presidential election, and black voters became a part of the Roosevelt coalition.[6]

Although blacks had supported Roosevelt in record numbers in his landslide 1936 victory, very little concerning race changed in the administration, and the Democratic Party—as revealed by its failure to adopt a civil rights plank in its party platform in 1940—seemed slow, if not unwilling, to move on civil rights. Particularly frustrating to many blacks was the administration's refusal to push for an end of discrimination in the armed services.

In 1940, Roosevelt, seeking an unprecedented third term, was challenged by Republican Wendell Willkie, a Wall Street lawyer and former Democrat who actively sought black support. At the Republican National Convention in Philadelphia that summer, Willkie presided over the writing of the strongest civil rights party platform plank in American history up to that time. Republicans supported federal antilynching legislation and protection of blacks' right to vote. Furthermore, the party promised to end discrimination in the military, the civil service, and all other branches of the government. Fearful of losing black support (yet mindful of divisions within his own party), Roosevelt sought to counter the Willkie campaign by announcing in October the appointment of several prominent black leaders to high-ranking positions within the military's bureaucracy—a move, the president hoped, that would demonstrate his desire to end discrimination in the military.[7]

Roosevelt won that November, but his margin of victory (5 million votes) was much smaller than in 1936 (11 million votes).[8] Indeed, with many middle-class whites and farmers returning to the Republican fold, the president owed his narrow, but crucial, victories in Illinois, Kentucky, New Jersey, New York, Ohio, Pennsylvania, and Tennessee to black support. In early 1941, the NAACP—well aware now of its electoral importance to the administration—increased its calls for an end of discrimination in the armed services (and actually made plans for a march on Washington later that year). Fearful of both a public protest and an open break with black constituents, the president, in late June, issued Executive Order 8802, which stipulated that all employers, unions, and government agencies concerned with vocational training must provide for the full and equitable participation of all workers in defense agencies, without discrimination. To administer the ruling, Roosevelt established a Committee on Fair Employment Practices (FEPC) to investigate complaints.

Meanwhile, many white Democratic leaders in the South were angry and alarmed over both the growing tide toward civil rights and the administration's response to it. In March 1943, Louisiana governor Sam H. Jones published an essay in *The Saturday Evening Post*, criticizing "New Deal democrats" as "illustrious white agitators" pursuing "the mongrelization of the South." According to Jones, the New Deal had undermined the foundations of the "Solid South"—namely, states' rights and "the race question"—and had thus inaugurated a new day in the South in which voters "vote men rather than labels. . . . We may support a Democrat, a Southern Democrat, a Republican, or a Mr. No-Party-At-All, but you can be sure that he is going to be a man prepared to speak and act our language."[9]

Then, in the summer of 1944, the United States Supreme Court ruled in *Smith vs. Allwright* that the Democratic white primary in the South was unconstitutional. Although the Constitution prohibited states from denying the vote on account of race, white southerners, since the end of Reconstruction in the 1870s, had advanced the theory that the Democratic Party was a private association and, as such, could discriminate in any way it chose.[10] Since there was no substantive Republican presence in the South, the Democratic primary functioned as the election, and as a result, the Court ruled, was in violation of the Fifteenth Amendment. The Supreme Court's ruling in *Smith vs. Allwright*, V.O. Key observed in 1949, "precipitated a crisis in southern politics." "It is obvious," former Alabama governor Frank Dixon anxiously wrote his state party chairman, "that the only thing that has held the Democratic Party together in the South for many years past has been the thing which caused its strength in the first place, namely, white supremacy. . . . [Now], through forced registration of negroes in this state, the Democratic Party will become anathema to white people in the South."[11]

In Arkansas, Governor Homer Adkins reaffirmed that the Democratic Party was a white man's party and called upon the state party to change its rules to circumvent the Court's decision. Mississippi congressman John Rankin, meanwhile, "warned legislators in his state to take action against the 'communistic drive . . . to destroy white supremacy in the South.'"[12] Not surprisingly, one immediate impact of the Court's decision was an interjection of race into the political campaigns of 1944—especially among the Democrats who had been "progressive" in the past.

Southern frustration with the president also manifested itself in a short-lived challenge to FDR's nomination to a fourth term, as represented by the "Texas Regulars," who in the summer of 1944 temporarily took control of the state's Democratic organization. The Regulars not only resented *Smith*, but also (and more importantly) the administration's efforts at war mobilization, which, critics claimed, encouraged big government, higher taxes, and bureaucratic inefficiency and waste.

Democratic divisions over race delighted many Republicans. Writing to Thomas Dewey in early June 1944, Alf Landon, the 1936 GOP standard-bearer, expressed hope that the Texas controversy had "all the earmarks of being the most important political development of our generation"—a development, he believed, that would "insure the election of a Republican president." The Democratic fight in Texas, Landon observed, was a "real fight to the finish and not a sham battle" that represented a larger "movement in the South to take back control of the Democratic party from the C.I.O."[13] Dewey was not as optimistic, however, writing to Landon on June 6 that "We still have a long row to hoe."[14] In the end, of course, Dewey was right. Roosevelt was too popular—with an 80 percent Gallup approval rating in the region in 1943—to lose the South. "The southern boys will support Roosevelt," a young Navy pilot from Connecticut named George Herbert Walker Bush, wrote home to his family the following September. "The ones I've talked with seem to think he's some sort of a god—I don't believe they look too closely at what the New Deal administration has done or has not done."[15]

Another divisive issue within the Democratic Party in the early 1940s was the New Deal. Despite Roosevelt's attempted party purge of 1938, conservatives remained active in the Democratic Party, especially in the South. Conservatives as a whole, of course—regardless of party—were associated with individualism and a fierce resistance to the New Deal. Specifically, they believed that the New Deal, along with the war, was responsible for the creation of a "domestic superstate" and a partially controlled economy.[16] Furthermore, conservatives feared that rising bureaucracy and "omnipotent government" would, in turn, lead to an American totalitarianism. Mass society, bureaucracy, and mediocrity, they believed, "were robbing the individual, as citizen, as employee, as consumer and human being, of individuality" and freedom.[17]

Conservative books published during the war called attention to those concerns. For example, in his 1944 *The Road to Serfdom*, Friedrich Hayek, an Austrian-born professor of economics at the London School of Economics, argued that economic planning—that is, "planning against competition"—leads to dictatorship. "Economic control," he wrote, "is not merely control of a sector of human life which can be separated from the rest; it is the control of the means for all our ends." Whoever controlled the means also determined which ends were to be served, and which values were to be rated higher and lower—"in short, what men should believe and strive for." Instead of collectivism, Hayek favored making "as much use as possible of the spontaneous forces of society, and resort as little as possible to coercion." Thus individualism became the supreme value and could not be "reconciled with the supremacy of one single person to which the whole of society must be entirely and permanently subordinated."[18]

Meanwhile, Ludwig von Mises, an Austrian economist living in the United States, argued in *Omnipotent Government: The Rise of the Total State and Total War*, also published in 1944, that the roots of Nazi totalitarianism (and thus World War II) were grounded in the post–World War I German ideology of etatism (or "trend toward government control of business"). Nazism, he insisted, was not a product of capitalism but of government control. This control characterized Nazi Germany, and it was the quest to enhance that government control that led to war in 1939. "A nation's policy, von Mises wrote, "forms an integral whole. Foreign policy and domestic policy are closely linked together; they are but one system; they condition each other." Since the further a nation "goes on the road toward public regulation and regimentation, the more it is pushed toward economic isolation," it should be no surprise that Nazi Germany sought Lebensraum and, ultimately, world hegemony. With its national sovereignty hindered by international division of labor and free trade, Nazi Germany went on the attack, seeking to control all economies so as to be in control and to not be challenged by free trade and democracy.[19]

The works of Hayek and von Mises—along with those of Isabel Paterson (*The God of the Machine*, 1943) and Garet Garrett (*The Revolution Was*, 1944), to name only a few—were clear indictments of FDR and the New Deal and opened the door to another, more popular, concern that had obvious implications for politics and interpretations of the war at home: totalitarianism. "A self-conscious ideology with both the desire and the ability to maintain absolute power and control over its politically fragmented population," "totalitarianism" was a word imported from Europe that was first applied to Mussolini's Italy, and then to Hitler's Germany, in the mid-1930s.[20] By the start of the Second World War in 1939, some anti-Communist observers (including liberals) in the United States began using the term "totalitarianism" to describe the Soviet Union, which, by that time, had signed a nonaggression pact with Hitler and had participated in the invasion and division of Poland.

According to historians Les Adler and Thomas Paterson in a 1970 essay on *The Merger of Nazi Germany and Soviet Russia in the American Image of Totalitarianism*, "Soviet secretiveness, censorship, unconcern for public opinion, purges, ideological purification, and frenzied denunciation of enemies in the 1930s seemed to echo characteristics of the Nazi regime." Many Americans, they noted, blurred the ideological differences between Communism and fascism and tended to believe that totalitarian methods overrode the role of ideology in shaping political forms."[21] Thus, even after Hitler turned against Stalin in the summer of 1941, many Americans still viewed the two ideologies "as denials of human freedom and tolerance, saw Germany and Russia as international aggressors, and pictured Hitler and Stalin as evil comrades." "The American people," The *Wall Street Journal* observed that June, "know that the principal difference between Mr. Hitler and Mr. Stalin is the size of their respective mustaches."[22] In a *Fortune* magazine poll conducted in October 1941, 35 percent of those surveyed thought Germany and the Soviet Union equally bad, while 32 percent believed that, while there was not much choice between the two, the Soviet Union was slightly better. Roosevelt's decision to extend Lend-Lease aid to the Soviet Union that fall (1941) was met with fierce opposition, especially from conservatives.[23]

After the United States joined the war effort with Great Britain and the Soviet Union in December 1941, an effort was made by the administration, as well as those in academia and media, to stress "common cause" within the Grand Alliance. For example, Joseph E. Davies, a friend of FDR and former US ambassador to the Soviet Union (1937–1938), argued in his 1941 *Mission to Moscow* that "the Russia of Lenin and Trotsky—the Russia of the Bolshevik Revolution—no longer exists." Communism there had proven to be inefficient, and after a long and sometimes cruel process, the Soviet Union transformed into "a system of state socialism operating on capitalistic principles [which is] steadily and irresistibly swinging to the right." Even if Communism did survive inside the Soviet Union, Davies concluded, it was not a threat to the United States. Stalin was neither a revolutionary nor a bloody tyrant—"A child would like to sit in his lap and a dog would sidle up to him"—but a leader attempting to create an egalitarian society in which all men would be governed according to ethical principles—"the same principle of the 'brotherhood of man' which Jesus preached."[24] Similarly, Foster Rhea Dulles's *The Road to Teheran: The Story of Russia and America, 1781–1943* (1944) attempted to demonstrate the absence of conflict between the two nations as well as their common revolutionary pasts and anti-imperialist stands. Even Wendell Willkie, the Republican presidential nominee in 1940, in his 1943 best seller *One World* wrote of a "new Russia" that would neither "eat us [nor] seduce us."[25] It was somewhat of an intellectual stretch, however, and many Americans—both liberal and conservative—continued to be skeptical of Communist Russia.

Not all Americans, of course, were so easily convinced "that the fires of war had purified the Stalinist dictatorship," and they demanded a more realistic view of the Soviet Union.[26] A foreign book to have tremendous impact in the United States during the war (and later upon the postwar American conservative movement) was Arthur Koestler's novel *Darkness at Noon*, published in 1941. Koestler was a Hungarian and former Marxist, who became disillusioned with Stalin and the purges of the late 1930s. The book eventually went through several editions, and by the mid-1940s was an anticommunist classic. However, as historian John Lewis Gaddis observed in the early 1970s, while "antipathy for communism remained strong within the United States throughout the war. . . . Americans directed this hostility against *their own communists,* not Russian ones [italics added]."[27] Indeed, with the expansion of government power during the New Deal and World War II, some Americans became convinced that some form of collectivism, including communism, might develop indigenously in the United States.[28] As 1944 approached, the Republican Party sought to capitalize on this concern and reach out to conservatives regardless of party label.

In a speech before the New Jersey Taxpayers Association in January 1944, Democratic senator Harry Byrd of Virginia, speaking for many conservative Democrats around the country, warned of dictatorship and financial ruin. Government bureaucracy, the 57-year-old presidential hopeful said, "has overflowed from Washington and [with its 3,063,379 paid employees] entrenched [itself] in every nook and corner of America." Setting aside the tremendous costs ($8,000,000,000 in annual salaries, and $100,000,000 in travel expenses), Byrd then explored bureaucracy's "sinister implications as affecting the American way of life and our form of Government." The present "Frankenstein of Federal bureaucracy" was, he declared, a dictatorship—a dictatorship born not out of war but out of the New Deal. New Dealers, he insisted, had abandoned government of the people, by the people, and for the people, and replaced it with "a group of theorists who think the people do not know what is best for them, and that these theorists are the only people fit to rule the nation. Under war powers they [now] have the authority to do what they always dreamed of—to take complete control of the fortunes and conduct of every citizen in the United States; to use them like bricks and mortar to build a new system of government."[29]

Insisting that he was (and would remain) a "Constitutional Jefferson Democrat," Byrd then criticized Roosevelt by name. The president, he said, had abandoned the party platform on which he was elected in 1932, and—after ten years of vast New Deal spending and "boondoggling"—had now put the country's economic future at risk. To preserve "our American way of life," Byrd concluded, there were "a few simple truths" that must be observed.[30] One was "that the people must support the Government, and not the Government the people." Whenever the federal government supported the people, he explained, "we must go to State Socialism or even something worse." The other truth was "that what you spend you must pay." Yet the Roosevelt administration was spending public money "on the assumption that money borrowed and spent is a means to promote prosperity" and that it never had to be repaid. That, Byrd insisted, was absurd and would soon "bankrupt our nation."[31]

Republicans hoped to reap the benefit of this division too. Writing to John W. Bricker in October 1943, Herbert Hoover insisted that "our job [going into 1944] is to secure the support of the Jeffersonian wing of the Democratic Party, not try for the New Dealers—whom we can never get."[32] Indeed, in the fall of 1944, the Constitutional Democrats of North Carolina mailed letters to doctors and dentists in the state, advocating a Republican presidential victory that fall. Their specific concern was "the New Deal's determination to socialize the medical profession."[33] According to the letter's author, E.S. Dillard, the state manager and treasurer of the organization, a New Deal victory in the 1944 election would set back the medical community "not less than a quarter of a century."

These cracks in the Democratic coalition were not new. Back in 1940, two sister publications within the Patriot News Company in Harrisburg, Pennsylvania—*The Patriot* and *The Evening News*—issued a widely distributed editorial that articulated the growing concerns of many conservative Democrats. Insisting that the New Deal had drifted "further and further away from Jeffersonian Democratic principles," the editorial indicted the Roosevelt administration along several lines, especially its "endless lend and spend policies and the mistaken and mischievous notion that a people can spend their way back to prosperity." Other grievances highlighted included "The readiness to borrow and boost the National debt to the stratosphere"; "Indifference to the importance of thrift in and out of government"; "Encouragement, if not stimulation, of class feeling"; "Alarming and extravagant growth in bureaucracy"; "Drift toward nationalization of industry and state socialism"; and the "Attempt to pack the Supreme Court."[34] Republicans were hopeful, then, that many such conservative Democrats—in the North and upper South—would support the GOP in 1944.

While conservatives within the Democratic Party were growing increasingly frustrated with the Roosevelt administration, so too were liberals. During a press conference in December 1943, the president announced that the New Deal slogan was no longer relevant and that what was needed was a "Dr. Win-the-War." When pressed later by reporters to explain the comment, Roosevelt added that Dr. New Deal had treated an internally sick nation during the Depression. After Pearl Harbor, Dr. Win-the-War had to be consulted to fight a new crisis, an external infection that threatened the nation's very survival.[35] Liberals were outraged. In a confidential report to Roosevelt in early 1944, Samuel Rosenman informed the president that most Americans supported a federal commitment to full employment and the expansion of social security programs. Furthermore, many in the administration believed that Democratic losses in the 1942 midterms were the result of lack of interest among Democratic voters and that an abandonment of the New Deal, even as a slogan, could generate greater electoral apathy in 1944.

Roosevelt, however, saw it differently. His articulation of "Dr. Win-the-War" was grounded in his keen observations of World War I politics. For example, in 1918, Roosevelt, then serving as assistant secretary of the Navy under President Wilson, noted that British prime minister David Lloyd George's popular support was based "on the sole issue of winning the war. The Conservatives who used to despise him as a demagogue; the Liberals who used to fear him as a radical; and most of the Labor people who now look upon him as a reactionary, may hate him just as much as ever and be unwilling after the war to trust reconstruction to his hands, but they will stand by him just as long as his administration keeps the winning of the war as its only political aim."[36] It was this understanding that shaped Roosevelt's approach to the later years of the New Deal, the war, and the 1944 election.

Roosevelt was, in fact, a very pragmatic politician. He was, as he himself noted in his 1932 book, *Looking Forward*, interested in applying what worked to solve a particular problem at hand. In 1933, during the dark days of the Great Depression, the New Deal was his tool. By the early 1940s, however, the United States was not in an economic depression but a global war, and

"Dr. New Deal" was not equipped to handle that crisis. The Second World War required an all-out Allied victory and, thus, the emergence of what Roosevelt called "Dr. Win-the-War," characterized by military construction, troop deployments, and wartime domestic controls. As early as November 1942, in a speech to the *New York Herald Tribune* Forum, Roosevelt had noted as much. During a time of war, he said, "the American people know that the one all-important job before them is fighting and working to win. *Therefore, of necessity, while long-range social and economic problems are by no means forgotten, they are a little like books which for the moment we have laid aside in order that we might get out the old atlas to learn the geography of the battle areas* [italics added]."[37] The New Deal was not dead during the war, just dormant, and by all indications, Roosevelt planned to incorporate it into a postwar atmosphere of peace.

Indeed, earlier in 1943, Roosevelt's National Resources Planning Board (NRPB), established in 1939, published two reports that highlighted the administration's commitment to liberal policy innovation in the tradition of the New Deal. The first, *Security, Work, and Relief Policies,* "exhaustively scrutinized American public assistance requirements and programs. Emphasizing 'serious maladjustments' in the nation's economy, the report concluded that 'the need for public aid will be both large and persistent for some time to come.'" Specifically, it "urged comprehensive government programs to assure 'access to minimum security for all our people'" in the postwar era. The second document, *National Resources Development, Report for 1943, Part I. Post-War Plan and Program,* meanwhile, provided the NRPB with recommendations for postwar reconversion and prosperity. Calling for a larger government responsibility for economic development and stability, the report proposed a "new [economic] bill of rights" and advocated full employment in a "dynamic expanding economy with increasingly higher standards of living."[38]

It was in that vein, in the summer of 1943, that the president delivered a fireside chat outlining his postwar plan for American military personnel—a plan that would eventually become known as the G.I. Bill.[39] Addressing the nation from the White House on July 28, Roosevelt announced that, in the postwar years, returning soldiers should be entitled to several things, including (1) a mustering-out pay sufficient enough to cover expenses in the transition between military and civilian employment; (2) unemployment insurance; (3) an opportunity to get further education or trade training at the cost of the government; (4) improved and liberalized provisions for hospitalization, rehabilitation, and medical care; and (5) pensions for disabled members of the services. "There is one great fear in the heart of any serviceman," First Lady Eleanor Roosevelt wrote the following summer, "and it is not that he will be killed or maimed but that when he is finally allowed to go home and piece together what he can of life, he will be made to feel he has been a sucker for the sacrifice he has made."[40] The president agreed and was committed to ensuring that American veterans would "not be demobilized into an environment of inflation and unemployment, to a place on a bread line, or on a corner selling apples. We must, this time, have plans ready—instead of waiting to do a hasty, inefficient, and ill-considered job at the last moment."[41]

Although some in Washington (and around the country) criticized Roosevelt's fireside chat of July 28 as a "campaign speech," his plan was overall well received. Private Leon Rosenbloom of Camp Swift, Texas, wrote the president on July 29, calling the speech "excellent." The father of a serviceman from New Jersey also expressed support and admonished Roosevelt to "take good care of your health, sir, as our Country needs you—these dreadful days—we have never for one moment lost faith in you and never shall." A resident from San Francisco added that the speech was "inspiring, stimulating, and challenging." W. Floyd Deacon of Grapevine, Texas, however, disagreed. Writing the president on July 31, Deacon expressed his disapproval of Roosevelt's "boondoggling in our nation and in the world" and extended his best wishes to "when you return to private life at the end of 1944. Happiness will reign again when your New Deal is remembered as a nightmare."[42]

Then, a few months later on January 11, 1944, President Roosevelt delivered his Eleventh Annual State of the Union Address, unveiling what one scholar has recently called "the Second Bill of Rights." Struggling with the flu and under doctor's orders to stay in the White House, Roosevelt delivered the speech in absentia, sending a paper copy to Capitol Hill instead. Then, at 9:00 p.m., the president—fearing that the newspapers would not give the undelivered speech full attention—read his message to the nation over the radio. He was, the president explained to his listeners, under doctor's orders to rest and remain indoors. In what was perhaps the most radical speech of his presidency, he argued that "true individual freedom cannot exist without economic security and independence. 'Necessitous men are not free men,'" he said. "People who are hungry and out of a job are the stuff of which dictatorships are made." The president then articulated a "second Bill of Rights under which a new basis of security and prosperity can be established for all—regardless of station, race, or creed." It included the right to a useful and vital job; the right to earn enough to provide adequate food and clothing and recreation; the right of farmers to raise and sell their products for a decent return; the right of businessmen to trade in an atmosphere of freedom from unfair competition and domination by monopolies at home or abroad; the right of every family to a comfortable home; the right of all to adequate medical care; the right to adequate protection from the economic fears of old age, sickness, accident, and unemployment; and the right to a good education. These rights, he insisted, spelled security and after the war must be implemented. "America's own rightful place in the world depends in large part upon how fully these and similar rights have been carried into practice for our citizens. For unless there is security here at home there cannot be lasting peace in the world."[43] With this bold and high-minded speech, Roosevelt, subtly but surely, kicked off his bid for a fourth term. Dr. New Deal and Dr. Win-the-War had become one.

CHAPTER 4

Mackinac and the Making of a Republican Foreign Policy

A major issue of partisan division during World War II was rival visions of a postwar world. The Japanese attack on Pearl Harbor in December 1941 dealt a devastating blow to isolationism in the United States. In a Gallup poll the previous summer, only 38 percent of Americans questioned wanted the United States to join a league of nations after the war while 39 percent objected. By the summer of 1942, those numbers had dramatically changed, with 73 percent in favor and 27 percent opposed.[1] According to historian Robert Divine in his *Second Chance: The Triumph of Internationalism in America during World War II* (1971), the lessons of war, coupled with the ceaseless activity of internationalist pressure groups such as the Committee to Study the Organization of Peace, had finally crippled isolationism and convinced many Americans that the United States had to play an active role in the postwar world. But what kind of role would that be? "Internationalism" was subject to various meanings, and its advocates, regardless of political party, were often in disagreement as to the purpose of American involvement in the war and the nature of the peace that would follow. One group, including Clarence Streit, Henry Wallace, and Sumner Welles, subscribed to the Wilsonian tenets of "progressive internationalism," with the hope that the war would usher in a period of worldwide social reform and the belief that peace should be founded on the equality of all nations. Other internationalists, meanwhile, contended that such views were overly idealistic. According to this more "conservative" and "realistic" group, including Walter Lippmann, H.J. Taylor, and John Foster Dulles, Americans "should understand the limitations upon world order imposed by nationalism, and recognize that peace could be attained only by agreement among the big powers."[2] Sensing a growing curiosity among the American people, publishers and magazine editors produced an outpouring of books and articles dealing with the postwar world.[3] As a result, by the end of 1944, a voluminous literature of postwar international relations had emerged, and Americans now had a chance to read and discuss every possible approach to the future peace.[4]

Republicans had done well in the 1942 midterms, but their success was grounded in public dissatisfaction with Roosevelt and domestic issues. Foreign policy—specifically as it related to a postwar world organization—continued to be a problem for the GOP. Many party leaders worried from a practical perspective that Republicans were, on foreign policy at least, emitting signals in all directions and thus bewildering the American public.[5] "From the people I see of all kinds all over the country," Thomas Dewey wrote Alf Landon in June 1943, "I think there is a very unfortunate and yet genuine confusion about the position of the Republican Party in international affairs."[6] It was time, he believed—if the GOP hoped to be competitive in the next year's presidential election—for Republicans to unite and articulate a single, internationalist vision of postwar American foreign policy.

Republicans promoted at least four general (and leading) postwar plans. The first advocated winning and settling the war before articulating any specific details for an "Association of Nations." A fierce proponent of this approach was former president Herbert Hoover. In late 1942, Hoover, along with career diplomat Hugh Gibson, offered a complex analysis of war, peace, and the postwar era in the best-selling *The Problems of Lasting Peace*. According to Hoover and Gibson, there should be a clear distinction between the "cooling off" (or transition) period after the war and the establishment of a world organization. In a major speech in Chicago on December 16, Hoover expanded on his collaboration with Gibson, especially as it related to a "cooling off" or transitional period after the war. "The essence of my proposal," Hoover declared, "is that we have no armistice, no general peace conference, such as Versailles. But that we set the peace making in two stages."[7] The first stage was what Hoover called an instant "conditional peace." This involved—as he and Gibson had articulated in *The Problems of Lasting* Peace—total disarmament of the enemy, the designation of provisional boundaries of nations, the removal of economic blockades, famine and pestilence relief, and the immediate call of freely chosen elective constitutional assemblies in the liberated and enemy countries. "With these minimums," Hoover asserted, "the world could move forward."[8]

Hoover's second and final stage in this "new approach to peace making" was "that the world should take time to cool off and work one by one" to find solutions for those problems that require time for deliberation, such as disarmament, reparations, intergovernmental debts, the punishment of war crimes, and the "building of international machinery to preserve peace." These problems, Hoover concluded, "must have time for the cooling of war revenge and hatred. Many of them must have time for the development of world opinion and adherence. They should be separated from each other for solution and each saved on its merits."[9]

Another Republican postwar plan, espoused by Minnesota governor Harold Stassen, called for the incorporation of the United States into an international state. Stassen unveiled his "Blueprint for a World Government" in May 1943. Described by Taft as "fantastic, dangerous, and impractical," Stassen's plan—based loosely on Clarence Streit's *Union Now* (1939)—embraced the creation of an association of sovereign nations that would be organized as a single-house parliament and was devoted to, among other things, establishing a world code of justice and building a "United Nations Legion," consisting of air, naval, and land forces capable of enforcing the code of justice, supporting the administration of international areas, and insuring the continued disarmament of probationary areas.[10]

A third plan that many Republicans seemed to endorse (at least in part) was one spelled out by journalist Walter Lippmann in his 1943 book, *US Foreign Policy: Shield of the Republic*. Lippmann called for the Allies (the United States, Great Britain, the Soviet Union, and China) to preserve international order—policing the world as the Congress of Vienna in Europe had after the wars of Napoleon in the early nineteenth century—and to serve as a nucleus for a more general postwar association of nations. The next year, Lippmann followed up with *US War Aims* (1944), which offered a scathing indictment of Wilsonian collective security. According to Lippmann, a former Wilson associate, the principles of the late Democratic president—outlined in his Fourteen Points speech of 1918—were a series of prohibitions grounded on the assumptions that national sovereignty was on the eve of yielding to world government. Thus, Wilsonian principles "forbid nation states to do the things which they have always done to defend their interests and to preserve their integrity."[11]

Although not opposed to international organizations, Lippmann argued that the United States must not repeat the error of counting upon a "league of nations" to establish peace. That was the responsibility of the victors. Specifically, peace could be achieved by maintaining the combined defenses of the Atlantic nations, by continuing the great coalition with the Soviet Union and with China, and by making it impossible for Germany and Japan to undo the settlement of this war and to separate the victors.[12] Any universal body that should exist must function primarily as a facilitator of intercourse among the nations already at peace. "Let us not be so naïve as to think that the great issues of war and peace . . . will or can be settled by public debates and public voting in an international assembly."[13] The responsibility for preventing war, Lippmann concluded, was with the great military states themselves. There was, he wrote, no escape from that reality.

Another substantive postwar plan supported by many Republicans was John Foster Dulles's "Six Pillars of Peace" (1943), a plan that even President Roosevelt privately endorsed as "splendid."[14] Dulles, age 55 in 1943, was the grandson of John Watson Foster, who had served as President Benjamin Harrison's secretary of state from 1892 to 1893, and the nephew of Robert Lansing, who had served as President Woodrow Wilson's secretary of state from 1915 to 1920. In 1908, Dulles, at the age of 20, graduated from Princeton University, where he had taken a course on constitutional government taught by Woodrow Wilson. Following graduation, he pursued postgraduate studies in international relations at the Sorbonne, and in 1909 he enrolled in George Washington University Law School. He passed the bar exam in 1911, and with assistance from his grandfather John W. Foster, Dulles was hired by the Wall Street firm of Sullivan and Cromwell, where he would stay until 1950.[15] Then, in 1937, the tall, stooped, and bespectacled Dulles met young Thomas Dewey. The two men were neighbors in the Woolworth Building in New York when, that May over lunch, they began a mutually beneficial friendship that would last until Dulles's death in the late 1950s.

At lunch in May 1937, Dulles informed the young prosecutor and rising New York Republican that the senior litigation man at Sullivan and Cromwell was in poor health and was likely to retire soon. Dulles wanted to see him replaced by someone "both youthful and poised, [and] capable of top-notch research and courtroom hypnosis"—someone like Dewey. Although Dewey did not take Dulles's job offer (he ran unsuccessfully for governor in 1938 instead), the two became close associates, and as Dewey contemplated higher national office, he sought advice from Dulles on foreign affairs. An admirer of his old professor Woodrow Wilson, Dulles nevertheless embraced the young New York Republican, and in turn Dewey, who was inexperienced in the field of international relations, drank, as Dewey biographer Richard Norton Smith observed, "deeply from the Dulles cup." Dulles himself later described Dewey as the "aptest pupil" he ever had.[16]

In early 1941, Dulles was named chair of the Federal Council of Churches' one- hundred member Commission to Study the Basis of a Just and Durable Peace, and in 1943, he formulated an ethical "Statement of Political Propositions" upon "which world order must be based"—the so-called Six Pillars of Peace.[17] Reflecting Dulles's personal ideology and conviction that "Christians should, as citizens, seek to translate their beliefs into realities," the statement's "underlying premise was that 'disregard for moral law brings affliction,' and 'we must find a way to bring into ordered harmony the interdependent life of the nations.' Its underlying purpose was to outline 'six areas within which national interdependence is demonstrated, and where, accordingly, international collaboration needs to be organized.'"[18] Specifically, these "Six Pillars of Peace" included (1) organized political collaboration (including regional pacts) between the Allies and subsequent regional others, (2) multilateral economic agreements based upon liberal trade principles, (3) a standing international body to adapt a global peace treaty to changing conditions, (4) the promotion of the ultimate autonomy of subject peoples, (5) international control of armaments, and (6) the international recognition of spiritual and intellectual liberty.[19]

In the spring of 1943 Dulles presented the "Six Pillars" to President Roosevelt, who professed interest in making "some public reference" to it "at some near future date."[20] Having hoped for an immediate endorsement, Dulles was disappointed and privately railed against the Roosevelt administration's lack of "competence to deal with the problem of bringing this war to an acceptable end and making quick and orderly transition to some better postwar order."[21]

Dewey endorsed the principles of the Six Pillars, believing Dulles's plan to be the kind of plan necessary to bring about a just and durable peace—that is, one that was "concrete, though not specific."[22] Still, with the GOP lacking consensus on foreign policy issues, Harrison Spangler, the newly elected Republican national committee chairman, announced in May 1943 that a foreign policy conference was to be held that fall on Mackinac Island in Lake Michigan. The origins of the Mackinac Conference were grounded in the formation, in May 1943, of a pro-Willkie, anti-isolationist, extra-party organization called the Republican Post-war Policy Association. Not wanting to be upstaged and fearing disunity on foreign policy as the 1944 presidential election approached, Spangler—a friendly acquaintance of Dewey, who had been a compromise choice as chairman in late 1942—invited 49 Republican congressmen, governors (including Dewey), and RNC members. Wendell Willkie, who did not hold public office, was not invited, and neither were senators Joseph Ball of Minnesota and Harold Burton of Ohio, both of whom had been advocating the creation of a United Nations Organization for months.

The so-called Ball Resolution was introduced in the Senate in March 1943. Overall, it called for the immediate creation of an inter-allied organization to be already in place when the war ended, and, in the meantime, to deal with current war problems. The proposal was met with wide criticism from both sides of the aisle. Senator Alben Barkley, Senate majority leader and Democrat from Kentucky, questioned the need for a wartime organization while Senator Arthur Vandenberg, Republican from Michigan, argued: "I think the first job is to win the war; and though I concur in the belief that we must have a large measure of post-war cooperation, I am unwilling to do *anything* which might disunite the *war* effort by premature peace efforts."[23]

The real star at Mackinac that September was Dewey, who made headlines upon his arrival when, during a news conference with reporters, he proposed continuing the military alliance with Great Britain into the postwar period. According to the governor, such an alliance was "very likely and in our interests." The United States, he continued, had "had a *de facto* alliance with Great Britain ever since the War of 1812. In the two principal cases since when war was made on Great Britain, we went to her defense. The American people never before had such a shock as they had when they realized that Germany might capture the British fleet. You remember as well as I how everyone was chilled."[24] Furthermore, Dewey, echoing Roosevelt's Four Policemen concept, "hoped" that the Soviet Union and China would join in this postwar partnership—which, he insisted, would never interfere with American sovereignty. Citing John Foster Dulles's "Six Pillars of Peace" as his inspiration, Dewey concluded that the "time had come . . . for America to abandon selfish nationalism and assume new international obligations."[25]

The *New York Times* reported the next day that Dewey's words had "had an electric effect among the others gathered at the conference" and marked his definite rise "into the class of advanced Republican thinkers on international affairs—vying with Wendell L. Willkie and some others who have taken such positions."[26] The *Chicago Tribune*, however, was not so impressed. "Gov. Dewey Goes Anti-American" was its editorial headline. "The Governor," the paper fumed, "is a tragic example of a man who was not quite big enough to rise above his immediate environment." He had now, the editorial concluded, lost millions of Republicans voters, who, in light of his recent statements, had "no recourse but to repudiate him as a deserter."[27]

Alf Landon, meanwhile, privately called Dewey's remarks "bad" and warned that any such alliance "would simply mean turning all the rest of the world against us."[28] Herbert Hoover concurred, writing Landon in late September that he was "sorry that Dewey got off on this line. It was not helpful to either him or the country."[29] Not content to privately seethe, however, Hoover (along with Hugh Gibson) wrote an essay for *Collier's* in November entitled "The Futility of Military Alliances." Although he never mentioned Dewey by name, Hoover sought, as the title of the article suggested, to discredit the "various proposals" that had "recently been made" calling for an immediate British-American military alliance. "Military alliances have produced many wars," Hoover and Gibson wrote, "but never a lasting peace."[30]

Dewey was pleased by the "splash" he made at Mackinac, but in a letter to his mother a few days later, he confessed that "it was all an accident," and that he had not intended to make any news. Still, he found public reaction to be positive, and—perhaps with an eye on the next year's presidential election—welcomed the personal attack from the *Chicago Tribune.* Their statement, he confided to his mother, "has been quite satisfactory to me. The support of that paper may be useful in Illinois, though I am not sure of it. Unless it is against you, however, it is a terrific liability in other states."[31]

Meanwhile, the actual task of drafting a foreign policy model to be presented at Mackinac fell to Senator Vandenberg. "I am hunting for the middle ground," Vandenberg wrote a friend, "between those extremists at one end of the line who would cheerfully give America away and those extremists at the other end of the line who would attempt a total isolation which has come to be an impossibility."[32] Vandenberg's advance resolution was submitted to Dewey and a few others for review before the conference began in early September. Dewey carefully scrutinized the proposals, urging Vandenberg to "use more specific language when discussing Republican obligations toward future world peace."[33] Overall, Vandenberg's plan, approved by the Mackinac Conference on September 8, followed closely the senator's own resolution then before the Senate. Overall, the Mackinac Declaration called for "responsible participation by the United States in a *post-war* cooperative organization among *sovereign nations* to prevent military aggression and to offer permanent peace with organized justice in a free world [italics added]."[34] Writing to Vandenberg after the conference, Dewey congratulated the senator "on a great job of conciliating the divergent views not only of your committee but of the whole Council. . . . The Party should be grateful to you indeed for a major contribution to its welfare as well as that of the country."[35] Hoover agreed, believing Mackinac strengthened Republicans by demonstrating "to the country that we had leadership and cohesion in the Party."[36] Even Willkie called it "a very distinct step in the right direction."[37] The Republican Party was now on record, with the war still in progress, as supporting the principle of international organization. As historian Robert Divine noted in the early 1970s, "It was the most important step yet taken toward American involvement in a future international organization."[38]

CHAPTER 5

Democrats and the Postwar World

Franklin Roosevelt was 61 years old in 1943 and in increasingly poor health. He had been elected president of the United States three times and would be asking for yet another term in 1944. He was, without doubt, one of the greatest politicians in American history. Born in 1882, Roosevelt enjoyed great privilege as a young man, traveling the world and being educated in schools like Groton and Harvard. Like Thomas Dewey, Roosevelt attended Columbia Law School, but unlike his future Republican rival, he did not graduate—dropping out in 1907 after passing the New York Bar Exam. The following year he began working—like another future rival, Wendell Willkie—on Wall Street as a corporate lawyer. Roosevelt got his start in politics in 1910 when, from his highly Republican district around Hyde Park, he ran for and was elected to the New York State Senate. When the Democrats, under Woodrow Wilson, returned to national power in 1913, Roosevelt was appointed assistant secretary of the Navy (1913–1920), a position his Republican cousin Theodore had once held and one that he would hold through the First World War. Roosevelt's rise on the national scene occurred in 1920 when, at the age of 38, he was selected to be the vice presidential candidate for the Democratic ticket led by Governor James Cox of Ohio.

The 1920 presidential campaign left a deep imprint on Roosevelt and the Democratic Party and was referenced repeatedly by both in the early 1940s—especially as it related to foreign affairs. In 1920, the First World War had recently ended, and a worn and gravely ill President Wilson was attempting to lead the United States out of its isolationist past and into a new awareness of international responsibility. Specifically, Wilson (through the Treaty of Versailles of 1919) had called for the establishment of an international organization grounded in the principle of collective security—the League of Nations. This attempt was challenged (and ultimately thwarted) by Republicans and some Democrats, who feared America's sovereignty would be compromised. The 1920 campaign, then, centered on this question: Would the United States ratify the Treaty of Versailles and join the League of Nations?

The Republican ticket of Warren Harding and Calvin Coolidge, promising a "return to normalcy," was evasive on the question. Indeed, Roosevelt later recalled that Harding was so vague "that citizens of diametrically opposite opinions could join in his support and praise. He was given at least lip-service by League of Nations supporters, by the bitterest League opponents, and by those who talked of the creation of some entirely new association of nations."[1] FDR and the Democratic Party's standard-bearer, James Cox, were, however, unflinching in their support for ratification and the League. Democrats, Roosevelt insisted that fall, offered "a treaty of peace, which, to make it a real treaty for a real peace MUST include a League of Nations; because this peace treaty; if our best and bravest are not to have died in vain, must be no thinly disguised armistice. . . . 'Peace' must mean peace that will last."[2] In his acceptance speech for the vice presidential nomination that summer, FDR outlined what would continue to be his critique of Republican foreign policy for the next 25 years. Speaking in Hyde Park on August 9, 1920, he dismissed as "trifling men" those who, "in the heat of political rivalry," sought to "manufacture political advantage out of a nationally conducted struggle."[3]

The Cox-Roosevelt ticket, along with Democrats nationwide, went down in defeat in a landslide that November. In control at all levels, Republicans—despite some campaign talk to the contrary—ultimately voted down the Versailles Treaty in the Senate and prevented the United States from joining the League of Nations. At the end of the decade, in an essay for *Foreign Affairs* entitled "Our Foreign Policy," Roosevelt lamented that the Harding administration—and the subsequent Coolidge one—had failed to live up to the Wilsonian promise and to give "great constructive aid . . . in the task of solving the grave problems facing the whole earth . . ." Furthermore, he charged, "the outside world almost unanimously views us with less good will today than at any previous period."[4]

By then, of course, tragedy had stricken Roosevelt's life. In July 1921, while vacationing in Campobello, he became ill with polio and never walked again. Over the course of the 1920s, he worked to regain his health and in

1928 was elected governor of New York. Four years later, in the midst of the Great Depression, Roosevelt was elected president of the United States. In 1936 he was reelected in a landslide, and in 1940 he sought and won an unprecedented third term.

A revival of Woodrow Wilson studies coincided with the surge of public support for US entry into some form of world association after the war. "The Woodrow Wilson Foundation, almost totally inactive in the 1930s, came to life again during the war. At their twentieth annual board meeting in 1942, the directors took note of 'a nation-wide return to the broad ideals of international cooperation and organization presented to the world by Woodrow Wilson.'"[5] That same year, the American Council of Public Affairs published a collection of Wilson's speeches entitled *Wilson's Ideals*. In his introduction, editor Saul Padover portrayed Wilson as a prophet rejected in his lifetime but vindicated by the present crisis:

> If he had not been defeated in his struggle to secure permanent peace and the rights of nations, there would be no Armageddon today. If Wilson had not been defeated [by Republicans in the Senate], France would still be a nation, and Norway, and Holland, and Czechoslovakia, and Italy would be free; Greece would not be a charnel house; Poland would not be depopulated; Yugoslavia would not be a shambles. Because Wilson lost the battle for peace, millions of men have already died, and millions more will yet die.[6]

Yet, Padover concluded, his work was not in vain: "There can be no doubt as to the [military] outcome [of this war], but this time the peace, too, will be won and won essentially on the basis of Wilson's ideals. There can be no other durable peace but a democratic and cooperative peace, as Wilson had envisioned it."[7]

The year 1944—with the coming presidential election and the rise of interest in a postwar organization—witnessed the publication of a number of other Woodrow Wilson and League of Nations studies. "Nearly all the authors were sympathetic to Wilson, treating him as a man whose tragedy was live before his time."[8] A very popular work, published at the beginning of the year, was Gerald Johnson's *Woodrow Wilson: The Unforgettable Figure Who Has Returned to Haunt Us*, a pictorial biography that stressed the people's failure to understand the prophetic vision of their president. According to Johnson, an editorial writer for *The Baltimore Sun*, Wilson had many faults. He was "arrogant, bullheaded, puritanical, icy, or blistering on occasion, sometimes appearing to be self-righteous, frightfully candid, learned, and impatient of ignorance, with a faculty of being right in a most irritating way."[9] But that was not all, Johnson concluded:

> If that were all, then Wilson being down would stay down. But he doesn't. For the past two years, especially, he has haunted our minds like a bad conscience. Americans are thinking and talking of Wilson more than they are of some political leaders who consider themselves very much alive. Men have begun to examine him again and they find an interesting thing. His faults stuck out; they did not drive in. His bitterest enemy never called him weak. If he was right, then the rest of us were wrong, terribly wrong. Why should Wilson's memory return to trouble us in the hour of our agony? We repudiated, dismissed and buried him long ago; why will he not stay dead? He will not be dismissed, he will not be ignored, he haunts us by night and by day. Is he, in a sense, the conscience of America?"[10]

Then there was J. Eugene Harley's eulogistic *Woodrow Wilson Still Lives*, which told the familiar story of how isolationists frustrated Wilson's postwar vision of international cooperation. Harley, a professor of political science at the University of Southern California, described Wilson's ideals as "forming 'a veritable Rock of Gibraltar' and 'a strong rallying point for all who think of the days of peace and reconstruction ahead.'"[11] Similarly, Karl Schriftgiesser's hard-hitting and popular biography of Senator Henry Cabot Lodge—Wilson's Republican nemesis—entitled *The Gentleman from Massachusetts*, depicted Wilson as a man of vision and principle. Lodge, in contrast, was portrayed as "a man filled with a venomous hatred of Wilson," while the defeat of the League of Nations in the Senate was treated as "a conspiracy hatched at Theodore Roosevelt's sickbed and carried out against the national interest for partisan and personal motives."[12] Early in World War I, Schriftgiesser observed, "Lodge had wanted a League of Nations. When it came, it was the gift of a Democratic President, the gift of a man who his closest friend [former president Theodore Roosevelt] deeply hated and for whom he himself had built up a hatred equally intense. For that reason, and because he wanted to bring back his party into power, he fought to the bitter end."[13]

The deceased president made it into not only thousands of pages of print but also a Hollywood film. Darryl F. Zanuck's Oscar-winning screenplay, *Wilson* (1944), a Twentieth Century Fox production, became an immediate and critical success, starring Alexander Knox (nominated for an Oscar as "Best Actor") in the lead role. In the film's final scene, Wilson stood in the ornate President's Room in the US Capitol Building and bade his cabinet farewell. The date was supposed to be March 4, 1921, Wilson's last day in office. A grandfather clock, reading three minutes until noon, ticked loudly in the background. Then, John Barton Payne, secretary of the interior, approached Wilson and asked: "Mr. President, now that the United States has rejected the League, can we ever hope for peace—a real understanding among nations?" Knox's Wilson thoughtfully replied:

> Yes. I am not one of those who has the slightest anxiety about the eventual triumph of the things I've stood for. The fight has just begun. You and I may not live to see it finished, but that doesn't matter. The ideals of the League are not dead just because a few obstructive men now in the saddle say they are. The dream of a world united against the awful wastes of war is too deeply imbedded in the hearts of men everywhere.... I'll even make this concession to Providence—it may come about in a better way than we proposed.[14]

With one minute of the Wilson presidency remaining, Senator Lodge and his Republican cohorts marched into the room and reported that the Sixty-Eighth Congress was ready to adjourn. Wilson glared at his archrival and replied coldly: "The President has nothing further to communicate." The clock then struck noon, Wilson slowly exited the room, and with "My Country 'Tis of Thee" playing in the background, the film credits began to roll. Watching a private showing of *Wilson* at the White House in early September 1944, President Roosevelt was inspired. Impressed by some of the quotations, he asked aide William Hassett to look them up for future reference in the presidential campaign.[15]

Like Republicans, however, Democrats were also divided over postwar planning. Although they were in general agreement on the war and internationalism (that is, they believed in the war effort and in an active role for America in the postwar era), Democrats were increasingly divided over what the world should look like after the defeat of the Axis Powers. For example, to those on the left such as Henry Wallace and the editors of *The Nation* and *The New Republic*, the war offered America a chance to establish a New Deal for the world—an opportunity, as the vice president described it in the spring of 1941, to organize the postwar world around "the eradication of human suffering and poverty."[16]

Wallace expanded upon this idea in *The Century of the Common Man* (1943). A compilation of Wallace's wartime speeches, the book's central theme was the importance (and necessity) of strong domestic programs in keeping the postwar peace. "We now know," Wallace wrote, "that the modern world must be recognized for what it is—an economic unit—and that wise arrangements must be made so that trade will be encouraged. The foundations of democracy can be rendered safe only when people everywhere have an opportunity to work and buy and sell with a reasonable assurance that they will be able to enjoy the fruits of their works."[17] The defeat of Germany and Japan, then, was only half the battle. Complete victory, he insisted, depended on the willingness of the United States to build a world in which human and material resources were used to the utmost and translated into real wealth and a higher standard of living. Furthermore, "Certain minimum standards of food, clothing, and shelter ought to be established, and arrangements ought to be made to guarantee that no one shall fall below those standards."[18] These guarantees, then, would usher in what Wallace called the "democracy of the common man," characterized by a promotion of equality of economic opportunity, free education, and minority and women's rights. In this democratic world community, the vice president concluded, "there will be a place for everyone—the worker, the farmer, the business man, the housewife, the doctor, the salesman, the teacher, the student, the store clerk, the taxi driver, the preacher, the engineer—all the millions who make up our world."[19]

In contrast, southern conservatives within the party, such as Senator Harry Byrd of Virginia, were skeptical of such idealistic designs. "The President of the United States," Byrd told the New Jersey Taxpayers Association in January 1944, "has declared for four freedoms. I am for all freedoms provided these freedoms come up from the people themselves. The Vice President of the United States, not satisfied with only four freedoms, has added seven more freedoms to apply to the inhabitants of all the world." Missing from all of these freedoms, Byrd concluded, were two freedoms vital to the American home front—"one is the freedom from bureaucracy and the other is the freedom of private enterprise."[20]

While Republicans articulated a postwar foreign policy at Mackinac in 1943, the Roosevelt administration—facing a divided party in Congress—continued to struggle with developing its own detailed and long-range plan for the postwar world. Certainly, the Roosevelt administration wanted to tread lightly on this issue and not antagonize the Soviet Union to the point of making a separate peace with Germany. Furthermore, the White House was concerned with public opinion and did not want to do anything that might undermine domestic unity and the prosecution of the war. Shortly after Pearl Harbor, the State Department, led by Cordell Hull of Tennessee, was assigned the task of developing concrete war aims—including considerations of not only world organization but also treatment of the defeated Axis Powers. In regards to world organization, Hull, a neo-Wilsonian internationalist and sure-footed devotee to collective security who wanted to avoid the mistakes of 1919 and 1920, established in early 1942 the Advisory Committee on Postwar Foreign Policy to formulate a blueprint for peace and to help generate a public opinion favorable to the idea of world organization. It included representatives from the State, War, Navy, Treasury, and Agriculture Departments, the White House, the Board of Economic Warfare, the general public, and both Democrats and Republicans in Congress. Hull, however, continued to move cautiously, focusing not on specific plans but on educating the American people on the merits of any such international body.

Meanwhile, over the course of 1942, the Roosevelt administration quietly embraced Hoover's "cooling off" articulated in *The Problems of Lasting Peace*. For example, in a widely acclaimed Memorial Day speech at the Arlington National Amphitheatre, Undersecretary of State Sumner Welles—ten days after receiving an advance copy of Hoover's book—distinguished between immediate postwar peace concerns and, on the other hand, final peace terms to be determined and entered into after the passing of a "period of social and economic chaos which will come inevitably upon the termination of the present war, and after the completion of the initial and gigantic task of relief, of reconstruction and of rehabilitation which will confront the [Allies] at the time of the Armistice."[21] At a press conference the following year, Roosevelt himself—without ever acknowledging Hoover—told reporters:

> People are awfully . . . immature when they talk about "after the war." They have the idea, because of certain precedents, that when the last shot is fired in one area . . . there will be an immediate peace conference, or if all the areas stop shooting that there will be immediately a peace conference; there will be a great treaty signed between all the Nations of the world.
>
> I think that it is a pretty fair guess to say that there will be a *transition period* [italics added]. You have to remember that most of the world is pretty well shell-shocked now. . . . And I think that for the good of humanity perhaps it might be good before we start writing the fair copy of what is going to happen later on, that we should catch our breaths. . . .
>
> And so I rather look forward to a period of transition between the firing of the last shot and the signing of a formal agreement or treaty. Obviously, there are certain things that will happen during that transition period. One of them is the maintenance of peace . . . by . . . the victors.[22]

Writing to a friend a few days after Roosevelt's remarks, Hoover noted that the president had adopted his line and added with satisfaction that "The newspapers here comment on the fact that it is my proposal."[23]

Then, on March 14, 1943, Republican senator Joseph Ball of Minnesota introduced in the Senate the bipartisan Ball-Burton-Hatch-Hill Resolution (B2H2), which called for "an organization of the United Nations" with authority "to provide for the assembly and maintenance of a United Nations military force and to suppress by immediate use of such force any future attempt at military aggression by any nation."[24] Without input and leadership from the White House—Roosevelt was not as enthusiastic about collective security as Hull—and with both Democrats and Republicans divided along several ideological lines, the resolution soon stalled. Then, on September 21, 1943, shortly after Republicans met at Mackinac, the US House of Representatives overwhelmingly passed the Fulbright Resolution, named after freshman Arkansas Democrat J. William Fulbright, expressing support for the creation of "appropriate international machinery with power adequate to establish and to maintain a just and lasting peace among the nations of the world, and as favoring the participation of the United States therein."[25]

In early November the Senate finally followed suit and passed a similar United Nations resolution, the Connally Resolution—named after its sponsor, Democrat Tom Connally of Texas—that recognized "the necessity of there being established at the earliest practicable date a general international organization, based on the principle of the sovereign equality of all peace-loving states, and open to membership by all such states, large and small, for the maintenance of international peace and security."[26] In both the House and Senate resolutions—as well as in the subsequent joint resolution—the supporters of B2H2 failed to secure explicit reference to military force. For his part, Ball was determined to make it a central issue in the upcoming presidential campaign.

Franklin Roosevelt, though an "internationalist" and public supporter of collective security rhetoric, never had any intention of limiting US freedom of action within the context of a postwar collective security organization.[27] According to political scientist Willard Range, Roosevelt held few deep convictions regarding the details or structure of the machinery of collective security.[28] His chief interest and goal was cooperative action by states for the maintenance of peace and not the search for proper vehicles and methods to apply that principle. He was, nevertheless, willing to accept almost anything in the way of machinery so long as it produced the desired end of cooperative action. Thus, he allowed Hull and Democrats in Congress to proceed with a United Nations plan in 1943 and 1944. Roosevelt's own cooperative preference, however, remained a traditional balance of power, spheres of interest, realpolitik. As he revealed publicly at Tehran in December 1943, the president wanted Big Power guardianship over not only the policing of the defeated Axis powers but also all important postwar decisions. Specifically, he envisioned the world divided into four spheres of influence, each dominated and policed by its most powerful resident—Great Britain, China, the United States, and the Soviet Union.

Another foreign policy problem facing the Roosevelt administration by 1944 was the question of postwar Germany. Would it, as Gerald Swope, president of General Electric and a friend of FDR, suggested in a *New York Times* article in September 1943, be broken up, slapped with economic controls, and purged of its "Prussian military clique"? Or, would it, as Secretary of State Cordell Hull envisioned, be unified and have a strong self-supporting economy that would help "restore sanity to its society and empower the rebuilding of Europe"?[29] Franklin Roosevelt believed himself to have a special understanding of German politics and psychology. As historian Michael Beschloss observed in a recent study on this subject, no other American president had had more early experience on German soil than FDR. As a youth, his family traveled to Germany frequently, even enrolling him in a local school to learn the language. In 1901, he and his mother had tea with Wilhelm II aboard the Kaiser's yacht. Then, in 1919, shortly after World War I, Roosevelt, as assistant secretary of the Navy, once again returned to Germany, this time with his wife, Eleanor, to visit the ancient fortress at Ehrenbreitstein on the Rhine and Mosel Rivers.

This experience deeply influenced the president. According to Beschloss, he believed that "the Germans were a 'misguided' people 'subjected to the rule of a [Prussian] military caste' and 'led along a path they could not understand.'" Like the author of *Is Germany Incurable?*, a popular book published in 1943 by New York psychiatrist Richard Brickner, Roosevelt believed German society to be "paranoid" and "megalomaniac." In late 1943, the president told Hull that Germany should be divided into three or more states with Prussia—which he incorrectly perceived to be a great haven for Nazism—totally disarmed and completely isolated. Of those closest to the president, Secretary of the Treasury Henry Morgenthau, a secular Jew and longtime friend and Hyde Park neighbor of FDR, had perhaps the most influence with the president—at least on this issue.[30]

In January 1944, after early indications of a Jewish Holocaust, Morgenthau approached the president about creating a War Refugee Board "to forestall the plan of the Nazis to exterminate all Jews and other minorities."[31] Roosevelt—not wanting congressional hearings on government inaction and fearful of losing Jewish votes to an acceptable Republican such as Thomas Dewey who, as early as September 1943, called for "immediate action" by the United States to prevent "Europeans governments infected with bigotry and sadism from destroying large groups of the Jewish people and other persecuted minorities"—agreed.[32] A few months later, in the spring of 1944, Morgenthau proposed another plan to the president, one for postwar Germany. Overall, the Morgenthau Plan called for all heavy German industry to be destroyed. Germany's plants and equipment, labor, and other assets would be given to the Soviet Union and other Nazi victims. There would be no reparations, but the Allies would draw up a list of "arch-criminals of the war" who, once apprehended, would be "put to death forthwith by firing squads."[33] Finally, reflecting the president's own views of Prussian militarism, all German aircraft, military uniforms, bands, and parades would be outlawed. The War Department was hostile to Morgenthau's proposal, considering it dangerous and naïve. The big question, however, was what FDR thought of the plan.

CHAPTER 6

John W. Bricker and the Conservative Republicans

Many conservative Republicans were not happy with either Willkie or Dewey and, in the lead-up to 1944, turned elsewhere. One name often mentioned by both Washington insiders and conservatives was "Mr. Republican," the son of former president William Howard Taft, Senator Robert A. Taft of Ohio. Taft, age 55, was a freshman senator, elected in 1938, and the chief conservative spokesman within the Republican Party. Like Thomas Dewey, he had made a serious and ultimately unsuccessful run for the Republican nomination in 1940. Taft was certainly the favorite of most conservatives for 1944. Indeed, in an essay for *The Saturday Evening Post* published in 1943, Taft eloquently articulated many of their domestic concerns. "The Administration which is elected in 1944," he wrote, "will have the power to make over America. We have had to tear our business and economic structure to pieces in the interest of war production. It must be made over for peace production either on the basis of individual freedom or on the basis of Government control. We have had to surrender many individual rights and submit temporarily to Fascistlike regulation." The winner of 1944, Taft continued, "will determine whether these controls are permanent or whether the multiple freedoms intended by our Constitution and Bill of Rights are restored to our people as the basis of liberty."[1]

On foreign affairs, Taft preferred to wait until war's end before articulating any ideas about a new world institution. Writing to Ohio governor John W. Bricker that summer, Taft noted that "We can all agree that the United Nations [i.e. the Allies] are going to have to police the world for some years after the war, furnish relief to Europe if we have any food left ourselves, and set up a sound economic basis for future prosperity. We ought to be able to postpone any fight about Leagues of Nations, sovereignty, and international states until long after the 1944 election."[2]

Ultimately, Taft—to the great disappointment of many conservatives—decided against a presidential bid. There were a number of reasons for his decision. First, Roosevelt, as commander-in-chief, would be difficult to defeat in wartime. Furthermore, the president enjoyed "a tremendous publicity organization" and was a master at defending his policies and cutting "the ground out from under our feet."[3] Taft was optimistic at times, though. For example, in September 1943, he wrote a friend that he was "sure that we would win [in 1944] overwhelmingly on domestic issues. The President has lost his popularity, and there is no enthusiasm for him, but this is balanced somewhat by the Commander-in-Chief argument that the war is going well and he should be allowed to finish it. I think we can beat him in Ohio, war or no war, but I am not sure about the east. However, it looks to me as if the war would be over, in which case we ought to win, or if it is not over, it will be because of serious reverses, and the people may feel that a change might just as well be made."[4] Still, according to biographer James T. Patterson, "Taft was more cautious about predicting Republican victory in 1944 than he had ever been or ever was to be in his entire career."[5]

Second, Taft was up for reelection to the US Senate in 1944 and faced stiff Democratic resistance. If he tried for the presidency and failed, he might, he feared, lose his Senate seat.[6] And third, Ohio's other outspoken conservative Republican, Governor John W. Bricker, won reelection to a third term in 1942 and was already building a campaign organization. Taft liked the 50-year-old Bricker and thought him to be the only contender expressing "in forthright terms the sentiment of the Republicans against the New Deal."[7] In fact, in June 1943, Taft wrote Bricker in response to a newspaper article that suggested his recent Grove City speech on foreign policy was tantamount to a presidential candidacy announcement. Taft assured the governor that such talk was "silly" and that he only "intended to make speeches from time to time, explaining the policies which I think the Republicans ought to follow, largely in order to combat the foolish ideas which Willkie is spreading around."[8]

With Taft out of the race, many conservatives—united in their opposition to Wendell Willkie—rallied behind the Ohio governor. John William Bricker wanted to be president of the United States, and in November 1943, he announced his candidacy for the 1944 Republican nomination. "Confusion and distrust reign throughout the land," he declared. "We need not alone a change of Administration but a change of the philosophy of government held by many new dealers."[9] "Your announcement," Alf Landon wrote him a few days later, "had a good wallop to it and it is one of the best things I have read in a long time."[10] Hoover was also encouraging, writing in early 1944 that "I just want you to know that I receive many signs that the tide is turning in your direction."[11]

Overall, Bricker was a contender with several political advantages. First, he was an attractive governor from the Midwest. Ohio had produced seven Republican presidents since the end of the Civil War, and Bricker—the only Republican in Ohio's history to be elected to three terms as governor—had proven himself a natural vote-getter. Born in a log cabin in Madison County, Ohio, in 1893, Bricker had a reputation as a "plain, homespun, common-sense fellow" who, as a youth, had attended a little red schoolhouse near Columbus and helped his German-Scottish-Irish father husk corn. In 1912, he enrolled at Ohio State University, receiving a Bachelor of Arts degree four years later and, ultimately, a law degree. The First World War, however, interrupted his graduate studies. In 1917, after being turned down for military service due to an irregular heartbeat, Bricker sought other ways to serve, working first as an athletic director to the 329th Infantry, 82nd Division, at Camp Sherman, Ohio, and later as chaplain. After the war, he returned to Ohio, passed the bar, and began practicing law in Columbus. In 1938, after two terms as attorney general, Bricker was elected governor on a program of cleaning up state government. As governor, he was "ruggedly honest, intensely sincere," and hardworking. "There is a saying," *The American Mercury* observed in May 1943, "that any man who can carry Ohio, Michigan, and Indiana can be elected President of the United States. If this is true, then John William Bricker could be elected today; for there seems little doubt that he could carry these states against Roosevelt."[12]

A second advantage for Bricker were his solid anti–New Deal, conservative credentials. On his first day as governor in 1939, he had fired four thousand officeholders in the state and by the early 1940s could boast that, in spite of greatly increased public services, Ohio had fewer state employees—22,000 in all—than it had just a few short years earlier. In contrast, he complained, "we've got 90,000 Federal employees in Ohio. What do they do? I ask you, what do they do? We haven't asked deferment for a single State employee, yet thousands of these Federal jobholders are being kept out of the Army!" A top priority in a Bricker presidency, he told a reporter, would be a drastic decrease in the number of federal employees. He wanted to be president, he said, not to save the world but to "defeat that bunch of rascals" and "fumigate Washington."[13]

Third, Bricker did not have a prewar "isolationist" record. In fact, he had been so busy "running Ohio" that he had not gotten involved in any of the postwar planning debates. He did not have time for that fight, he once explained, but insisted that his first concern would be simply "to make America strong."

Fourth, he had strong support in the South. In October 1943, former president Hoover advised Bricker "that gaining the support of conservative states' rights southerners was a key to victory. He wrote to the governor: 'It seems to me our job is to secure the support of the Jeffersonian wing of the Democratic Party, not try for the New Dealers—whom we can never get.'"[14] Bricker agreed and in late 1943 traveled to the South and met with community leaders in several states, including the Virginia Chamber of Commerce.

And fifth, Bricker was—aside from Willkie—the only Republican who had officially announced his candidacy. Other possibilities, including New York governor Thomas Dewey, General Douglas MacArthur, and Minnesota governor Harold Stassen (in service in the Pacific), all insisted that they neither wanted the nomination nor were seeking it. If Bricker was in fact the only conservative in the race and the liberal Willkie, who had strong opposition within the party, could be outmaneuvered, the Ohio governor had every reason to believe that his chances of becoming the party's nominee were very strong.

If Bricker was a contender with many advantages—and he was—then he was also a candidate with many flaws—flaws that ultimately proved his undoing. One problem with Bricker was that he was a virtual unknown outside of the Midwest. Furthermore, he was perceived to be an intellectual lightweight, who was vague on most issues, especially those relating to foreign policy. That image did not help the governor, when in a response to a reporter's question, in the spring of 1943, on postwar planning, he admitted: "I don't know anything about how the postwar world should be organized. I have never been to Europe. How can I know where the boundary between Russia and Poland should be? How can I know what kind of government France should have? . . . If I should be elected President, I'll get the best advice I can from people who know something about the rest of the world, and I'll do the best I can."[15] While such statements were a part of the governor's overall "down-home" appeal in Ohio, he was seeking to move from the governor's mansion to the White House, and as such, his remarks were shallow, naïve, and insufficient. Then, in March 1943, Bricker's "pre-candidacy" was dealt a serious blow when the great Kansas journalist William Allen White dismissed the governor as "an honest Harding" who, like the late president, "hopes to get by without saying anything, without getting on either side of the momentous questions of the hour—domestic or foreign." He was, White continued, the candidate of "the same forces in the Republican Party that gathered around Taft in 1912 and that nominated Harding in a 'smoke filled room' in 1920." Those forces must be resisted in 1944. The nation, he concluded, required a man with the leadership to "say who he is, what he is and why."[16]

The harm inflicted by White's article was compounded by Bricker's failure to respond adequately.[17] In early April 1943, just a few weeks after White's scathing piece, Bricker delivered what was supposed to be a major foreign policy address before the Political Science Academy in New York City. It was a dismal failure. According to Bricker biographer Richard O. Davies, "His speech amounted to nothing more than another set of familiar, if nonspecific, generalizations about the dangers to American freedom posed by an incursive federal bureaucracy. Not only was his speech lacking in specific policy statements and laden with trite generalizations, but he uncharacteristically suffered from a first-class case of stage fright. His delivery was uncertain and tentative." Furthermore, his remarks "only reinforced the growing perception that he lacked a grasp of the major issues." Bricker did not help his case when, on January 1, 1944—in opening his official drive for the nomination—he delivered a nationally broadcast radio address that, amazingly, failed to address any foreign policy issues. The governor promised instead to focus upon "whether the place of the individual in society shall be strengthened or whether he shall become more and more dependent upon organized government."[18]

Bricker was further disabled by his failure to build a strong organization capable of coordinating the multiple demands of a campaign. In late 1943, Bricker's campaign manager resigned after a dispute with his boss. Though a new manager was selected, the Bricker campaign continued to be perceived as loose, inefficient, and uncertain and thus frightened away many potential financial supporters. In addition, complaints began to surface about mail going unanswered. John B. Hollister, a former Willkie supporter and advisor to Bricker, complained to the campaign in January 1944 that people—especially donors and national committeemen—needed to be flattered and that such "loose ends should be picked up." "[T]here is," he argued, "nothing more unflattering than failure to answer a letter."[19] Robert Taft, an early supporter of Bricker, believed the governor made a strategic error in not actively participating in the primaries. "Bricker could have been nominated," Taft reflected to a friend in 1944, "if he had started six months earlier.... He should have gone into [the] Wisconsin [primary], and I believe he could have taken all the Dewey delegates and made himself the anti-Willkie candidate."[20] In the end, Bricker's star never rose. His campaign lacked depth, organization, momentum, and ultimately, popular support.

The problems with Bricker led many conservatives to rally behind General Douglas MacArthur, the 64-year-old commander of the Southwest Pacific Area Theater. MacArthur was an attractive presidential possibility for several reasons. First, he had an impressive military background and reputation. A 1903 graduate of West Point, he subsequently served as a member of the Army's General Staff (1913–1917), brigadier general of the 84th Infantry Brigade (1917–1918), superintendent of West Point (1919–1922), Army chief of staff (1930–1935), military advisor to the Philippines (1935–1941), and commander of all US forces in East Asia (1941–1942). Since early 1942, MacArthur had been waging an offensive against Japanese forces in the southwest Pacific, using "highly successful 'leapfrog' flanking envelopments with combined air, land, and sea forces."[21] From Australia, his base of operations, MacArthur had "leapfrogged" along the New Guinea coastline and by the summer of 1944—following Admiral Chester Nimitz's victories in Saipan, Tinian, and Guam—was poised to retake the Philippines.

In addition, MacArthur was very popular—a Roper poll conducted for *Fortune* magazine in 1942 revealed that the general had an approval rating of 57.3 percent. MacArthur's popularity was grounded not only in his military successes but also in his public utterances and ability to control the news. For example, "in 1943, he said of Corregidor, the doomed Philippine fortress from which he had escaped by PT boat the year before: 'Until we lift our flag from its dust, we stand unredeemed before mankind. Until we claim again the ghastly remains of its last garrison, we can but stand humble supplicants before Almighty God. There lies our Holy Grail.'"[22] In addition, he granted interviews only to those reporters who agreed to depict his speech and actions in very favorable and extravagant terms. Altogether, this led many Republicans, including Senator Arthur Vandenberg of Michigan, to believe that he was the only Republican capable of defeating Roosevelt in a wartime presidential campaign.

At the same time, MacArthur had conservative credentials. Although never an isolationist, MacArthur's rout of the Bonus Army in Washington DC in 1932, as well as his frequent clashes with President Roosevelt over Army appropriations in the mid-1930s, endeared him to many conservatives. Equally important was the fact that he seemed to be willing to accept a draft for the Republican nomination. In the spring of 1943, Senator Vandenberg met with two of MacArthur's aides in Washington and expressed vigorous support for the general. To the senator's surprise, he shortly thereafter received a confidential letter from MacArthur, dated April 13, 1943, which read: "I am most grateful to you for your complete attitude of friendship. I only hope that I can some day reciprocate. There is much that I would like to say to you which circumstances prevent. In the meanwhile I want you to know the absolute confidence I would feel in your experienced and wise mentorship. MacArthur."[23] In his diary, Vandenberg expressed amazement at the message, and its potential historical worth, and concluded, "'Mac' certainly is not 'running away' from *anything*. It is typical of his forthright courage."[24]

Vandenberg, independently of the general, then proceeded to quietly organize a draft movement for MacArthur—"quietly," he believed, being essential to success. Writing in his diary in September 1943, Vandenberg noted:

> I think it is desperately important that there should be no signs whatever of any centrally organized activity. It seems to me that the American people are rapidly coming to understand what the General is up against in the Far East [a reference to the Roosevelt-Churchill decision to fight the war in Europe first and the subsequent shortage of men and materials in the Southwest Pacific]. These people can easily martyrize him into a completely irresistible figure. So it seems to me more important than ever that we should give our own "commander-in-chief" no possible excuse upon which to hang his own political reprisals. It is obvious on every hand that the movement [for MacArthur] is making solid headway in all directions.... *I cling to the basic thought that if MacArthur can be nominated it will be as the result of a ground swell and not as the result of any ordinary preconvention political activities* [italics added].[25]

As it turned out, prudence and subtlety were not characteristics of either MacArthur or many of his congressional supporters. Against Vandenberg's protests, the general, who had made no public statement expressing interest in the presidency, was entered into both the Wisconsin and New Hampshire primaries, where he performed poorly—even coming in last in New Hampshire. In Illinois, MacArthur supporters won their only primary victory, with their candidate, running unopposed, receiving 76 percent of the vote.[26] The result of all this visible draft activity was—just as Vandenberg had feared—increased scrutiny of the old soldier. Indeed, in January 1944, The *American Mercury* published a scathing article entitled, "General MacArthur: Fact and Legend," which was subsequently printed in the *Army Library Bulletin*. The article identified the general with "Old Guard Republican" isolationists and attempted to tear down—by separating "fact from fancy"—hero worship of MacArthur.[27] Then, in mid-April 1944, came the death nail of MacArthur's unofficial candidacy.

On April 14, Republican congressman A.L. Miller of Nebraska, a MacArthur supporter, disclosed that he had written to the general about the presidential race and had received a reply.[28] He then released to the press his correspondence (two letters) with the Pacific commander. "I was shocked," Vandenberg later recalled, "that he should have ever written the letters which Miller made public."[29] In Miller's first letter, the congressman railed against the Roosevelt administration and asserted "that unless this New Deal can be stopped this time, our American way of life is forever doomed." MacArthur replied, expressing his agreement "unreservedly" and calling Miller's arguments "complete wisdom and statesmanship." In the second letter, which MacArthur called "scholarly," Miller warned that "a 'monarchy' was being established in the United States by 'left-wingers and New Dealism.'"[30] A few days later, on April 29, an embarrassed MacArthur released a statement from his headquarters in New Guinea, requesting that "no action be taken that would link my name in any way to the nomination. I do not covet it nor would I accept it."[31] "The MacArthur adventure," as Vandenberg described the draft movement, was over.

CHAPTER 7

The Fall of Wendell Willkie

While conservative Republicans continued their search, liberal Republicans once again placed their faith in the 52-year-old Wendell Willkie. A native of Indiana, Willkie had made his fortune in New York as a Wall Street lawyer and head of the utility giant Commonwealth and Southern. Although he was a former Democrat who had never been elected to public office, Republicans embraced him as their nominee in 1940. Energetic, husky-voiced, spontaneous, fiercely independent, and sincere, the liberal, anti–New Dealer Willkie was the GOP's "alien savior" at a time when the party was weak, in despair, and "in the mood for the miraculous."[1] Willkie waged a vigorous campaign against Roosevelt's third term bid but, in the end, was unsuccessful, and a disappointment. Although widely read and very prolific, as a novice to national campaigns he made many mistakes in 1940 and often came across as disorganized, unprepared, and shallow. Furthermore, the Republican Party had a long history of treating its unsuccessful presidential candidates harshly. Unlike the Democrats, Republicans had never nominated an unsuccessful presidential nominee a second time.[2] Finally, a Willkie comeback was complicated by his bold and courageous defense of Lend-Lease in early 1941, which alienated him from many in the GOP base. Thus, Willkie, who desperately wanted another attempt at the presidency, faced a long and difficult road to the Republican nomination in 1944.

After his post–Pearl Harbor tour around the world, Willkie returned to the United States in late October 1942 and began working on the book *One World*. Published in 1943, the book chronicled Willkie's recent 49-day, 31,000-mile trip around the world, including his visits to the Soviet Union, China, and the Middle East as well as his meetings with leaders such as Joseph Stalin and Chiang Kai-shek. In addition, the book was an internationalist lecture. "There are no distant points in the world any longer," Willkie wrote. "I learned by this trip that the myriad of millions of human beings of the Far East are as close to us as Los Angeles is to New York by the fastest trains. I cannot escape the conviction that in the future what concerns them must concern us, almost as much as the problems of the people of California concern the people of New York. Our thinking in the future must be worldwide."[3] Alarmed by a lack of articulated Allied war aims, he warned that a war without purpose is a war without victory and that there must be open discussions among the nations and within nations.

Overall, Willkie laid out three specific proposals concerning the postwar world. First, he advocated the creation of a common council of the Allied nations of World War II—or as he called them, the "United Nations"—in which all planned together and devised future economic cooperation strategies, administrative strategies for the defeated Axis nations, and organizational strategies to deal with the multiple problems accompanying the victorious Allied nations in the war's aftermath. Failure to create such a council and to achieve those strategies, he wrote, would result in our "moving from one expediency to another, sowing the seeds of future discontents—racial, religious, political—not alone among the peoples we seek to free, but even among the United Nations themselves."[4]

Second, Willkie insisted that the Allies must agree that World War II was a war of liberation, "giving to all peoples freedom to govern themselves as soon as they are able, and the economic freedom on which all lasting self-government inevitably rests."[5] Both of these aspects of freedom, he wrote, must be emphasized in the postwar era lest the victors will have won neither the peace nor the war. And third, Willkie argued that the United States must play an active and constructive role in the postwar and increasingly interdependent world.

Although the book was an instant best seller and Willkie was popularly hailed as the "Best Qualified [Republican] on World Affairs," not everyone was impressed. For example, Herbert Hoover's biographer Eugene Lyons dismissed *One World* as a "drug-counter success"—"a hasty, breezy, and extraordinarily superficial travelogue, without the redeeming quality of humility." Willkie, he continued, hopped from land to land, soaking up half-truths with all the ardor of an adolescent tourist. In due time, the volume may be viewed by historians of our epoch as a curious testament to American innocence in world politics."[6] Senator Robert Taft of Ohio, meanwhile, privately noted that while the book served the purpose of advertising Willkie, it was overall "a pretty poor book when it comes down to expressing any ideas of value."[7]

Then, in the summer of 1943, while touring the country and promoting his book, Willkie opened his drive for the Republican nomination. That fall, he made appearances throughout the West and South, but with little impact. A poll taken among the party rank and file for The *Republican* magazine in early 1944 revealed that the "'average Republican leader' was willing to have the United States join a worldwide organization dedicated to keeping the peace and promoting economic cooperation. This average Republican, however, was against extensive disarmament after the war, the surrender of island outposts, and the 'idea of Uncle Sam masquerading as an international Santa Claus.'"[8] A Gallup poll in February showed Willkie a distant second to Dewey (45 percent to 21 percent) among Republican voters. Then, in March, Dewey's lead in Gallup increased to 50 percent, while Willkie remained in second place with a steady 21 percent. Furthermore, in a separate Gallup study, Willkie's unfavorable rating (43 percent) was almost as high as his favorable vote.[9] The decline of Willkie's political fortunes in early 1944 was related to several things.

For one, he lacked political finesse and, as a result, was often perceived to be lecturing, rather than leading, the party. A former Democrat, he even on one occasion addressed his audience as "You Republicans." In November 1943, the *Omaha World-Herald* observed that Republicans "mistrust [Willkie] as another 'big cock of the roost,' stubbornly bent on having his own way, with contempt for all others whether of high degree or low, if you are not as smart as he is."[10] *Time* magazine, meanwhile, referred to him as a "Moose on the Loose" and described his manner at a fall dinner for freshmen GOP congressmen in Washington as "aggressive" and "truculent." According to the report, "Willkie told Congressmen he could have the Presidential nomination if he wanted it; he was ready to go over their heads to the people."

In reality, Willkie had little choice but to try and appeal to voters in the 1944 primaries. In late 1942, Republican leaders hostile to Willkie took control of the Republican National Committee. Herbert Hoover, still a powerful voice within the GOP, had led the way. Willkie's choice for chairman of the RNC was Fred Baker of Washington, a long shot for the position at best. Most anti-Willkie Republicans, meanwhile, rallied behind Werner Schroeder, the Republican national committeeman from Illinois. While Schroeder had the votes to win the chairmanship, Hoover did not want a confrontation with the Willkie forces that might weaken the party going into 1944. Quietly and shrewdly, then, Hoover orchestrated the rise of a "compromise" candidate, Harrison Spangler of Iowa. In fact, for Hoover, Schroeder had been a decoy from the very beginning. According to Gary Dean Best, in his excellent two-volume study on Hoover's post-presidency, "the strategy had apparently been to block Willkie's candidate [Baker] with Schroeder and then offer Spangler as a compromise."[11] This, Hoover believed, would make the Willkie forces feel as if they had accomplished a major victory, but the RNC would still be firmly in the hands of anti-Willkie forces. "Spangler's election tickles my funnybone in many places," Hoover wrote a friend a few days later. "Willkie fell into a complete trap, and is just now beginning to awake to it."[12]

The presidential primary in the first half of the twentieth century was not what it is today. Originally—dating back to the early 1830s and the rise of the second party system—no primaries were held. Instead, delegates to a national convention were selected by state party conventions whose own delegates were chosen by local conventions. By the 1870s, party bosses and political machines reigned supreme. In the early 1900s, Progressive reformers began to champion the direct election of candidates and the bringing to an end of corrupt machine politics. In 1910, Oregon became the first state to establish a presidential primary in which the delegates to the National Convention were required to support (at the convention) the winner of the primary. By 1944, nearly 15 states had adopted the presidential primary.

Willkie had no real primary challengers in 1944. Bricker was waging a traditional preconvention campaign, courting party state party leaders, while New York governor Dewey, former Minnesota governor Harold Stassen, and General Douglas MacArthur all repeatedly insisted they were not running. Thus, Willkie hoped to use the Republican primaries to demonstrate popular support, and—armed with that support—move on to the convention in June and force his nomination on party leaders. Although his obstacles were great, Willkie did have at least one asset that he hoped might carry him successfully through the primary season: the youth vote. According to a spring 1943 Gallup survey, Willkie's greatest support came from voters under the age of 30.[13]

Speaking with reporters in Portland, Oregon, on February 14, Willkie announced that he was in fact a candidate for the nomination, and that he had entered the New Hampshire, Oregon, Wisconsin, and Nebraska primaries. "I believe," he said, "that the question of who is to be the Republican Presidential nominee in 1944 should be decided by the rank and the file of the

80 POLITICS AS USUAL

Republican party. I believe also that the people also should have opportunity to hear fully the views of the candidates. I will express my views fully on the issues."[14]

The last part of 1943 and the early months of 1944 were hard for Willkie. He was under attack from various directions and had made some unfortunate gaffes. For example, in late 1943, he made news by refusing to shake hands with Vice President Henry Wallace at the *New York Herald Tribune* Forum. Then there was the meeting of New Jersey Republican women, where Willkie jumped on a table—knocking over a pitcher of water in the process—and blew kisses into the crowd. "Willkie is being hysterical," Thomas Dewey wrote to a supporter, "and the most conspicuous characteristic of his peregrinations to date is that they have not been successful."[15] Indeed, a Gallup poll from October 1943 found the leading complaints against Willkie to be "too changeable," "talks too much," "judgments are not sound," and "too much like FDR." Tellingly, his internationalist position was not mentioned by those polled.[16]

The nation's first primary was held in New Hampshire on March 14. Willkie, who delivered only one pre-primary speech in the state, won six of the state's eleven delegates to the Republican National Convention that summer. Dewey, meanwhile, won only two. Three delegates remained unpledged. Willkie, however, had anticipated winning at least nine delegates and was disappointed at the results. Still, he pressed on to Wisconsin.

The Wisconsin primary, scheduled for April 4, was not the most advantageous place for Willkie to make his stand. The state had a strong isolationist background and fell within the circulation territory of Colonel Robert R. McCormick's prewar non-interventionist *Chicago Tribune*. The paper was fiercely opposed to Willkie's candidacy, often referring to the Indiana native as "the barefoot boy from Wall Street." McCormick, who had served as a delegate to the Republican National Convention in 1940, had been the sole dissenter to Willkie's otherwise unanimous nomination on the sixth ballot. He cast his vote instead for Dewey. Since Mackinac, however, McCormick had cooled on Dewey and, in 1944, openly endorsed General MacArthur. Willkie, however, believed that a strong showing in the Midwest, a section of the country where he had least support, would enhance his position at the Republican National Convention that June. As he had in the fall of 1940, Willkie set out to personally convince voters, embarking on a grueling 12-day, 1,500-mile trek across the state in March.[17]

In Wisconsin, Willkie touched upon several themes meant to bolster his candidacy. One was that the Republican Party had a long tradition of mavericks "fighting within the party for the things they believed to be right."

The implication was that by being a maverick he was in fact being a typical Republican "in the true Lincoln tradition." Speaking at the GOP birthplace of Ripon on March 20, Willkie identified himself with Gilded Age "Liberal Republicans" such as Horace Greeley, who in the 1870s had fought the corruption of the Ulysses S. Grant administration. He also compared himself to Theodore Roosevelt and the Progressives who bolted the GOP in 1912. The chief function of a political party, Willkie declared (in a clear slap at Thomas Dewey), was to stand for principles instead of serving as a vehicle for men who simply wanted power.[18]

Another Willkie theme in Wisconsin was that the Republican Party, strong in the Midwest, needed to expand its appeal to the two coasts. The 1944 election, Willkie argued in a speech in Green Bay on March 21, would be determined by the industrial centers in the East and West. To cut down the Democratic vote in those areas, he continued, the party must give recognition (through a strong and progressive party platform) to the fact that America does not stand alone in the world. "Any Republican candidate . . . of the school of thought of the *Chicago Tribune* will be overwhelmingly defeated," Willkie declared. "In the industrial centers there is open resentment against that school of thought of narrow nationalism, economic toryism and opposition to social advances. They will overwhelmingly oppose the Republican party or any party having any connection with that doctrine."[19] Contrary to charges that he had made "some kind of deal with the Administration to keep Mr. Roosevelt in office," Willkie insisted that his main objective was "to make the Republican party worthy of removing Mr. Roosevelt from office." The GOP, he added in a speech at Beloit College a few days later, must not evade the issues or attempt to capitalize on the forces of discontent. That, he said, would be a fatal mistake, and Republicans would suffer the same defeat as Democrats in 1864.[20]

In addition, Willkie stressed postwar international cooperation. A few weeks before the Wisconsin primary, *Foreign Affairs* magazine published an essay by Willkie entitled "Our Sovereignty: Shall We Use It?" in which the presidential hopeful argued that if the United States was to avoid another world war, "we shall have to give up the idea that sovereignty is something simply to be conserved . . . and accept the idea that it is an active force to be used." According to Willkie, the United States entering into a "League of United Nations" was analogous to American automobile drivers yielding to traffic laws. "Many of us remember," he wrote, "when there were so few motorcars that each driver was left free to make his own rules of the road. It was generally understood that a good citizen behind the wheel of a two-cylinder runabout would slow down on corners and either stop or make as little noise as possible when he encountered a horse. Beyond that, if he didn't deliberately run into people, 'reckless driving' meant only that he would break a spring or his own neck." But as time passed and roads became filled with powerful automobiles, there had to be a surrendering of sovereignty. "A man," he wrote, "could no longer make his own rules of the road." Instead, Americans had to obey such things as traffic lights and traffic police. And all of this, he noted, was for good. After all, it was "the red and green lights" that gave "us freedom to use our automobiles."[21]

Similarly, Willkie concluded, "The highways of the world are now crowded." There were, he wrote, no empty seas, no air spaces yet to be traversed, and no land where the rights and interests of many peoples do not meet and clash. The world was increasingly interdependent, and thus "The United States or any other nation cannot make the rules of the road all by itself." This did not mean he favored the abolition of sovereignty. On the contrary, Willkie insisted American sovereignty had to be used in joining with other nations for security in order to save American sovereignty. Responding to critics of his essay who claimed he would "boondoggle" the world and give away America's substance if elected president, Willkie reassured five hundred students at Beloit in late March: "That is so foolish. Certainly no one would expect Wendell Willkie to give away the substance of our nation. I did not get where I am by being a nut."[22]

Then, on March 28, in speeches at La Crosse and Wisconsin Rapids, Willkie unveiled his final theme. Responding to the *Chicago Tribune*, which a few days earlier had asserted that "Willkie is not so stupid as to think he has a chance of getting the Republican nomination" and asked, "What game is Willkie up to?" Willkie declared: "If I have no other reason to ask for your good will, I am entitled to at least some of your support for the enemies I have made. I have the most valuable list of enemies of any public or quasi-public figure in America." He then listed Gerald L.K. Smith (of the America First Party) and Colonel McCormick (of the *Chicago Tribune*) and declared their opposition to him to be a great compliment. "Gerald Smith before Pearl Harbor said that there was no occasion to build an army in face of the threat to our freedom," Willkie continued. "In those days Hitler had conquered Western Europe, and any man with any foresight at all saw that Great Britain was the outpost of our freedom. Every one of those who held that position then oppose me today. Gerald L.K. Smith and Colonel McCormick, how proud I am that they are against me!"[23]

The end of Willkie's drive for the presidency came on April 4, the day of the Wisconsin primary. Although he was the only candidate to personally campaign in the state, he came in last. Dewey smashed him, receiving 17 of Wisconsin's 24 delegates. Willkie, meanwhile, failed to win a single delegate. Conservatives were ecstatic. "[T]he people of Wisconsin have spoken," declared the *Chicago Tribune*. "As citizens they are for America and an American newspaper. . . . Our long, bitter fight to save this country is heading toward a triumphant conclusion." The Wisconsin primary, the paper concluded, was a vindication of "American First" principles, and a repudiation of "internationalism and un-Americanism."[24] Many Democrats agreed. Writing to a friend in the Justice Department, Clyde Eastus, a US attorney in the Northern District of Texas, gleefully predicted that since "the Republicans have turned Isolationists . . . [and] have made up their minds to nominate a boy named Dewey for President," Roosevelt "will carry every state in the American Union."[25]

Speaking in Omaha, Nebraska, the day after his humiliating loss, Willkie officially withdrew from the race. "The result of the primary," he told a startled audience, "is naturally disappointing. . . . It is obvious now that I cannot be nominated. Therefore, I am asking my friends to desist from any activity toward that end and not to present my name at the convention. I earnestly hope," he concluded, "that the Republicans will nominate a candidate and write a platform which really represents the views which I have advocated and which I believe are shared by millions of Americans."[26] Willkie then shook the hands of well-wishers, boarded a train, and returned to New York. "From today on Mr. Willkie can be dismissed as a minor nuisance," crowed the *Chicago Tribune*. The Rochester *Democrat and Chronicle*, meanwhile, predicted that Willkie's demise would "raise Mr. Dewey's stock almost prohibitively beyond the reach of other candidates." The *Kansas City Star* agreed, observing that a Dewey "stampede" was now underway, and that Dewey was "as certain of being the GOP nominee as President Roosevelt is to be the Democratic candidate."[27]

Willkie's defeat in Wisconsin was related to several things. As Willkie biographer Donald Bruce Johnson observed: "He was not always cordial to party workers upon whom he was dependent; he was uncompromising in his charges that his opponents represented reaction in contrast to his brand of liberalism; and most important, he bitterly criticized his own party members. No matter how valid his comments may have been, they smacked to party regulars of disloyalty to the party as a whole."[28] Willkie's great failure, journalist Eugene Lyons observed that summer, was in party leadership. "He has scolded and threatened and hinted at revolt if he is not renominated. But he has made no attempt to bring together Republican factions, to reconcile conflicting viewpoints. His guiding purpose . . . has been to slug the Republican Party into submission rather than to win it over."[29] "Of course he was talking at the party from the outside," Thomas Dewey later remarked. "Gosh, you like to have a fellow who identifies himself with the party if he expects to be its spokesman, its leader. . . . He'd been a Democrat until 1940, and had never got over it."[30]

Finally, many Republicans, as polling data indicated, simply disagreed with the Hoosier on most issues. This was true not only in the area of foreign affairs, but also domestic issues. For example, on February 3, 1944, Willkie delivered a speech in New York on "Our Domestic Economic, and Fiscal Policy in Relation to Our Well-Being at Home and Abroad," in which he advocated dramatic tax increases to help pay for the war while it was still being waged.[31] The speech was originally written by a Willkie advisor named John W. Hanes, who, in the first draft, called for lower taxes. Willkie read the speech, and believing the "lower the taxes" theme was unrealistic, changed it to include a 16-billion-dollar tax increase. Hanes protested that such a proposal would kill Willkie off politically—to which the candidate replied, "Johnny, you said this was the time for a speech on taxation, and I am making it."[32] The speech, which did not offer any specifics on how these extra billions would be obtained, was a disaster, and Willkie found himself roundly criticized by business Republicans who had supported him in 1940. Although hailed by journalist Arthur Krock and many others as "courageous," Willkie's proposal was actually both unnecessary and unproductive. For example, Congress had already debated and voted on the issue. His vague but controversial remarks, then, came too late to have an impact in Congress, offered no specific solutions, and alienated his base. "The only certainty," author Eugene Lyons observed that summer, "was that in the process [Willkie] had made himself the favorite Republican candidate of New Dealers who will vote Democratic if Roosevelt runs again."[33]

CHAPTER 8

Thomas Dewey and the Struggle for Republican Consensus

The collapse of the Willkie bid cleared the way for Dewey's drive toward the nomination. Throughout 1943 and early 1944, the governor insisted that "I am not and shall not become a candidate for the Republican nomination. I have important work to do here in New York and I want to do it."[1] He had good reason to be a reluctant candidate. The conventional wisdom was that FDR was unbeatable in 1944. Should Dewey win the nomination and then lose the general election, his national political career would come to a humiliating end. Indeed, no losing Republican had ever secured the presidential nomination a second time. Dewey, who wanted to be president someday, faced great political risk. Perhaps, Don Wharton of *Look* magazine speculated that spring, 1948 would be a better year for the governor to launch a campaign for president. Even if he waited until 1952, Wharton noted, Dewey would only be 50 years old. Time was on his side.

Still, the nomination was apparently very much on his mind. In his private correspondence with confidants such as Hoover and Landon, Dewey—as early as August 1943—closely followed Willkie's political movements and contemplated convention strategy. While Dewey was unquestionably ambitious, he was also incredibly loyal to his party. In November, Landon—who had been giving Dewey information on another potential rival (and a Willkie ally), Minnesota governor Harold Stassen—reassured a sympathetic Republican that Dewey's statements disavowing a presidential bid were hollow. According to Landon, "No man in public life is big enough to refuse the call of his party. . . . When he entered public service he became the servant of the people and he is subject to their call. . . . I do not recall any man in our political history who has refused the call of duty of his party to serve his country. So, I don't care what Dewey says and whether he means it or not. What is the use of quibbling over that?"[2] Speculation regarding a Dewey candidacy continued to mount through 1943, and into early 1944. "Like Topsy," one aide wrote the governor the previous May, "it 'just growed.'"[3]

While it is not possible to determine precisely when Dewey made the decision to seek the Republican nomination in 1944, it is clear that by the fall of 1943 he was heavily involved in discussions about the convention. For example, in a letter to Hoover on October 16, Dewey wondered if it would not be viewed as presumptuous—as Hoover had suggested in a letter the day before—to telephone California's new and popular Governor Earl Warren, and encourage him to head and choose the convention delegation from his state. Warren, Dewey wrote, "plans to come here in about a month and I anticipate having a good talk with him then. . . . [However, if] you feel that a call now is necessary and would not risk being more harm than good, do let me know and I will do the necessary."[4]

The following month, Dewey again found himself preoccupied with convention concerns—this time an idea by Herbert Hoover to have the nominating convention in September rather than June. Hoover, in a letter to RNC chair Harrison Spangler, had argued that presidential campaigns never officially got underway until after Labor Day, and that the interregnum from June to September was "a useless and often degenerating period" in which the candidate "is subjected to criticisms and argument which he cannot reply to adequately. He can do nothing effective until the campaign opens. If he could deliver his speech on Sept. first, then he is on the way by the fifteenth to the real campaign."[5] Dewey, who had been forwarded a copy of the letter, responded to Hoover a few days later. While he promised the former president to "give the idea of a late convention very intensive study," Dewey's mind nevertheless appeared set: "It had never seemed to me that the outs [i.e. the opposition] gained by a late, short campaign," he wrote. "That is what beat us in NY for 20 yrs."[6] The real turning point of Dewey's interest in the nomination, however, may have been a Lumbermens Mutual Casualty Company study of the delegates to the 1940 Republican National Convention, released in February 1944. According to the report, 75–88 percent of 1940s delegates now found Dewey to be "the far favorite" for the 1944 nomination.

Dewey stood out from other possible contenders for a number of reasons. First, he was young—only 42 in 1944—and an energetic and experienced campaigner. "If Dewey has learned anything in his five campaigns," journalist Forrest Davis wrote in the summer of 1944, "it is a sense of pace and balance. Hence, [the campaign against FDR] will be a game of thrust and parry, flanking the opposition at its weakest, refusing action on its strong points."[7]

Dewey also had a flair for the dramatic, and a pleasing baritone voice that came across effectively on radio. In fact, in 1937, when running for district attorney of New York County, he, as one journalist observed, "chilled the marrow of the big town's voters. A menacing new story of crime and politics appeared each week. New Yorkers, dining at home or abroad, taxi drivers huddled at their stands, and little groups in taverns cringed as [Dewey's] cold, precise voice announced: 'Tonight I am going to talk about murder committed by gangsters, abetted by politicians. I am going to name names.'"[8] The Marxist publication *New Masses*, fearing Dewey's growing appeal, observed that the "racket buster par excellence is already nearly as important in the popular imagination as Dick Tracy. An ex-choir boy flaying the devils of corruption in the wicked city is always sure-fire in the countryside, and Dewey is no exception."[9] Dewey won that campaign, and in 1944, many Republicans (and Democrats alike) believed him to be more than capable to take on FDR.

In addition, Dewey, who already had a national reputation as a tough New York City crime fighter, was the governor of New York, an office that seemed to breed presidential nominees. Indeed, over the course of the past one hundred years, eight governors of New York had won their party's nomination, and four had actually won the ultimate prize.[10] His mere occupancy of that office, then, made him a perpetual object of presidential consideration. In early November 1943, Dewey made the front cover of *Time* magazine. Under his picture was the caption, "The next biggest job is good training for the biggest."[11]

Republicans were especially enthusiastic about Dewey's position, and the potential that held for 1944. After all, New York had 47 electoral votes, and only three presidents since the Civil War had been elected without them (Grant in 1868, Hayes in 1876, and Wilson in 1916). Since Republicans had made recent gains in the western states, a victory in New York (and a few other eastern states), some pundits believed, could return Republicans to national power in 1944. Regardless, no one was better suited to challenge Roosevelt in the East than Dewey. If he could not defeat the president in New York and its neighboring states, the conventional wisdom ran, nobody could.[12]

Dewey, however, was more than a mere occupant. He had, after only two years in office, built a solid record of achievement as governor. For example, he set aside $163,000,000 as a postwar job fund for returning soldiers, cleaned up the state's mental health system, fought vigorously for farmers and higher food production, reformed and lowered taxes, and greatly improved the state police system.[13] He also won praise for making several notable black appointments to state government, including Francis Rivers as justice of the City Court in New York.[14] Rivers, a graduate of Columbia Law School and a former aide to Dewey, was the first black attorney to hold such a high judicial post in the state.[15]

Furthermore, the governor had a reputation for intelligence, efficiency, and getting things done. Herbert Brownell, Dewey's campaign manager, later recalled: "He assembled a first-rate staff about him and always had a practical goal: getting someone convicted or a bill passed through the legislature. Although I would not describe him as a political visionary, he knew what needed to be done. He was a true reformer and not a self-interested politician, and he had the zeal and ability to surmount opposition to his reform efforts. This didn't make him popular with those people he had to deal with, but it did make him effective."[16]

Finally, Dewey was an effective party leader, who, since his rise as special prosecutor in 1935, had built his own very powerful statewide Republican machine. This machine, a 1944 DNC report on Dewey disapprovingly but correctly observed, was a "straight Dewey organization" completely geared to his personal fortunes." Most of the men around Dewey in 1944—the so-called swimming-hole cabinet—were, in fact, the same men who had been with him since the mid-1930s. They were relatively young, very talented, and extremely loyal to the governor. Throughout 1943 and early 1944, they too encouraged Dewey's presidential ambitions.

One such advisor was the amiable, hardworking Paul Lockwood, Dewey's political secretary. It was Lockwood who brushed aside talk of Dewey waiting until 1948 to seek the nomination. "Destiny," Lockwood explained, "waits on no man. By 1948, an Eisenhower will come out of the war. This is Dewey's year." Then there was Edwin F. Jaeckle, a 48-year-old lawyer from Buffalo, who had joined with Dewey in the DA's close but ultimately unsuccessful bid for governor in 1938. "I was not Dewey's man," Jaeckle later recalled. "Nor was he mine. Events brought us together. We were a very strong combination. There was a mutual respect. I was like a trainer with a good horse."[17] The shrewd, indiscreet, tough-talking Jaeckle had become chairman of the State Republican Committee in 1940 and was one of Dewey's top political strategists on the eve of the 1944 presidential campaign.

Another important advisor to Dewey was 39-year-old Yale law graduate and Nebraska native Herbert Brownell. Dewey and Brownell met in New York in 1930 in a Young Republican Club, where the two were active in reform politics. Specifically, they were opposed to New York's corrupt mayor, James J. ("Jimmy") Walker, who was under investigation for bribery, and the local Democratic organization, Tammany Hall. In those days, Brownell later remembered, the state Republican Party "was almost an appendage of Tammany Hall, and its reputation was hardly much better." However, in 1931, a group of young Republicans, including Brownell and Dewey, rebelled "against the moribund city Republican organization" and supported the investigation into Walker. Brownell even ran for the state legislature to sponsor legislation needed by the investigating committee and chose Dewey as his campaign manager. Although Brownell, who had the support of the former governor and 1928 Democratic presidential nominee, Al Smith, narrowly lost the general election, the experience taught him that through strong organization and intense canvassing, the tightly controlled Tammany district could eventually be won by a Republican. That 1931 campaign also launched the political career of Dewey, who with his "mellifluous voice" introduced Brownell on the campaign stump and garnered the attention of the press. In 1942, Brownell, by now a state assemblyman, returned the favor and managed Dewey's successful bid for governor.

There also was J. Russell Sprague, a 58-year-old national committeeman from New York and a member of the Dewey team since 1940. For years he had been the GOP boss of Nassau County, Long Island. He now served as the governor's fund-raising chief. Despite Sprague's having little experience in national politics, Drew Pearson of The *Washington Post* described him as "smooth as the oysters his father used to hoist from Long Island sound."[18] Other Dewey men included John Burton, a professional researcher and state budget director; Elliott Bell, a college friend and neighbor who served as financial advisor; James Hagerty, press secretary; and John Foster Dulles, foreign policy advisor. Together, Team Dewey worked steadily behind the scenes, beginning in October 1943, to promote the governor and to engineer a draft.[19]

While Dewey wanted to be the Republican nominee for president in 1944, he did not want an open primary fight. He was, according to historian Michael Anderson, a "consensus politician" who "harbored an almost obsessive concern over the appearance of party unity. He wanted to gain the nomination . . . by working behind the scenes, and wanted to directly control any effort exerted on his behalf." Furthermore, Dewey believed "that individual contests in time of war could serve only to disunite the Republican

Party" and thus both weaken the party's chances for victory in November and undermine the party's success in office should it prevail.[20] So when supporters in Wisconsin made an effort to place the governor's name on the primary ballot in April, Dewey on February 23, 1944, sent a telegram to the 25 delegates earnestly requesting that "those petitions be not filed." He then added, "I want to make it entirely clear that any use of my name meets my strongest disapproval."[21]

Unlike today, nominating conventions in the first half of the twentieth century (and through 1968) were more than giant pep rallies. Uncertainty loomed in most conventions (as most delegates were uncommitted) and all sorts of smoke-filled, backroom political maneuverings. Almost always there was surprise. For example, in 1940, Dewey had long been the leading contender for the presidential nomination among Republicans, only to be surpassed by a last-minute convention surge for the largely unknown Wendell Willkie, who, just days earlier, had not even been regarded as a serious candidate. Nominating conventions, then, did the hard work of *selecting* nominees, and it was in that context that Dewey and his managers maneuvered cautiously in late 1943 and early 1944.

Dewey did not want to be just any other candidate—as he had been in 1940—but an acclaimed leader who was called upon by his party in a time of need. In fact, he had taken the same approach in his bids for governor in 1938 and 1942. It was his reputation and popularity as a racket buster, and not any organizational connections, that catapulted him to those nominations. In New York, then, he owed his office to no single group and was therefore able to govern "with no personal axes to grind or obligations to fulfill."[22] This was the approach he hoped to employ in 1944.

By late fall 1943, Dewey's advisors, without any "official" support—"He never gave a nod and he never gave me a no," Jaeckle later recalled—were meeting to consider strategies and to take a more active role in pursuing delegates outside of New York.[23] By spring 1944, former president Herbert Hoover, after dining with the governor in late March, observed privately that Dewey "has agents in practically every state who were actively working for his nomination and keeping him in touch with the situation throughout the country." Furthermore, Dewey "approached everything . . . from the obvious mental point of view that he was going to be the Republican candidate." It was obvious too, Hoover concluded, "that he had in mind that he would probably be nominated on the first ballot."[24]

The Dewey strategy for the nomination was to appear as a party leader and unifier and to secure enough delegate support, preferably from the big states, to create a bandwagon atmosphere.[25] This strategy rested upon three pillars. First, Dewey had to demonstrate political control over his own GOP organization in New York. In the summer of 1943, Dewey's lieutenant governor, Thomas Wallace, died, and a special election to replace him was set for November. Dewey's choice to replace Wallace was the president of the state senate, Joseph Hanley. Understanding that his own political ambitions for 1944 were linked to the outcome of this special election, Dewey exerted "superhuman efforts" to get out the farm vote in upstate New York and secure Hanley's victory. His work paid off, and Hanley won with more than 350,000 votes on Election Day. "This is a great victory," former president Hoover wrote to Dewey, "and the whole of it is due to you." "Your stock," another Dewey supporter wrote, "is at a new high. . . . Shall we start selling?"[26]

Second, Dewey had to exhibit conservative domestic policy credentials to an anti–New Deal Republican base that was predisposed to support Bricker for the nomination. The opportunity for Dewey to excite his base came on February 12, 1944, in a speech at the Republicans' Annual Lincoln Day Dinner in New York City. Entitled "Restoration of Constitutional Government," it was a scathing indictment of Roosevelt and the New Deal. Polished, articulate, and relentless—if sometimes loose with the facts—Dewey began his address by reflecting upon the wisdom and character of Abraham Lincoln and contrasting it with that of FDR. Unlike the current president, Dewey argued, Lincoln was a "plain man" with "integrity of character," who "knew that he was not perfect, not all wise, not given the ability to solve the problems he faced in easy strokes of brilliance. He would have been the last to call himself indispensable."

Dewey then charged that while the great menace of Lincoln's day was the violent secession of the states, the great threat to America in 1944 was the more subtle, but equally dangerous, "abdication of the states." Conveniently ignoring Lincoln's emphasis on national power over states' rights, Dewey declared that "free government must always work from the bottom up, and not from the top down. . . . It is in local units that men and women can most fully sense and practice the responsibilities of citizenship. Once we have ceased to do that, once we concern ourselves merely with a four-year choice between one or another ruler, then we will be a ruled people." This, he insisted, was what Roosevelt had aimed for as early as 1933. It was then—with a power-hungry president and a newly elected and inexperienced Democratic majority—that an "American autocracy" was established.

By the end of the decade, Dewey added, Americans had come to understand that the abandonment of local government under the New Deal was a surrender to autocracy. Even before the war, Dewey said, Americans "were moving to recapture their freedom and the basic right of local self-government. They sensed that the Democratic Party was no longer the party of the people . . . [but] the New Deal Party, irrevocably committed to absolutism at the seat of the National Government." Unfortunately, Dewey said—taking a jab at Willkie's presidential run in 1940—Americans "had no Lincoln to tell them in simple words what the trouble was." Then, in the 1942 midterm elections (of which Dewey himself was a product), the American people once again turned to the party of Lincoln to "preserve their Constitutional system of Freedom." Republicans, he noted, now had governors in 26 states (as opposed to 8 in 1933), and represented three-fifths of the nation.

He then talked about his own record as governor since 1943. "The spirit of the remedies applied by the Republican Administration of New York State was to bring the people back to the practice of self-government, of relying upon ourselves," he said. "The strength of a nation is the strength of the people. The strength of the people is where they live. . . . Without them, as some seem to have forgotten, there would be no Federal Government. By revitalizing the State of New York we have greatly strengthened the National Government for war and for the peace to come."

Although it was warmly received by the media in general, not all journalists were impressed with Dewey's address. Max Lerner of the New York paper *PM* called the speech—and its "twisting" of Lincoln's memory—"sickening." Furthermore, he wrote, Dewey was "too small a man for the big job of the Presidency" and was thus trying to cut the job down to his own size.[27] Republicans disagreed, and Dewey continued to lead in state and national polls. A United Press poll in February also revealed that he was the leading choice of most Republican senators.[28]

The third pillar of Dewey's pre-convention strategy was to demonstrate substance and internationalism in the area of foreign policy, and appeal to Willkie voters. On April 27, just days after Willkie's defeat in the Wisconsin primary, Dewey addressed the American Newspaper Publishers Association and announced—in a speech partially prepared by John Foster Dulles—his support for a postwar international organization. Unlike Bricker's lackluster performance a few weeks earlier, Dewey was articulate, substantive, and convincing. The nation, he said, must "organize in cooperation with other nations a structure of peace backed by adequate force to prevent future wars."[29] "Dewey Condemns Isolation" was the headline in London's morning paper, the *Daily Express*. The *New York Times*, meanwhile, described the speech as "the most explicit and detailed exposition of his views on foreign affairs since he became generally regarded as the most probable Republican nominee for the Presidency." Even former president Hoover, who had advised the governor against the speech, approved of it, later admitting that "your judgment was better as to the timing of the speech than mine."[30]

By April 1944, Dewey seemed close to achieving his goal. A Gallup poll indicated that he led the Republican presidential field with 45 percent support. Willkie, who had been openly campaigning for weeks, came in a distant second with 21 percent. "It looks as if Tom Dewey would be the Republican nominee," Robert Taft privately noted in a letter to his aunt in March. "I can get on with him," Taft added, "although I think he is much too bossy. He is the best speaker on the Republican side, particularly on radio."[31] Writing to Dewey that winter, historian James Truslow Adams spoke for many Republicans when he admitted a change of heart from 1940. "I did not want a President [then] with a DA's mind," Adams wrote, "but the governorship of New York is a different matter and as I look over the possible candidates. . . . I am beginning to feel that you might do the most to save the situation. I voted for Willkie last time."[32] As Adams's letter implied, a crucial part of Dewey's successful march to the 1944 presidential nomination was his public image as a moderate and experienced governor who could save the GOP from foreign policy extremists on both sides of the ideological spectrum.

CHAPTER 9

The Republican National Convention

The twenty-third Republican National Convention that convened in Chicago on June 26, 1944, was one of the most listless conventions in the party's history. Attendance was low, with a peak of only twenty thousand (or two-thirds of the capacity of Chicago Stadium) on closing night. In contrast to previous conventions, there were few marches, and "no leaping on seats, [and] no stampeding when the Presidential nominee stepped into the platform spotlight, only a swelling roar, the din of cowbells, [and] the shrill of ear-piercing chorus of whistling."[1] Several things contributed to this dullness. First, Republicans met for their convention just three weeks after D-Day. Not surprisingly, party leaders were concerned with projecting the right tone and striking a solemn note that reflected the gravity of the times. "The battle of Normandy subdued our conflicts at home," GOP House leader and convention chair Joseph Martin later recalled. "We took our cracks at New Deal 'collectivism' and Roosevelt's 'court-packing,' but they did not crackle the way they used to before the real guns were firing."[2] Deliberately, then, partisan celebrations were held to a minimum, and convention speakers "trimmed rabblerousing phrases . . . to make place for themes of war."[3] From beginning to end, solemnity—and not raucous partisanship—characterized the Republican convention.

This was especially evident in the keynote address delivered by California governor Earl Warren on the opening night of the convention. Overall,

Warren emphasized unity of national purpose and underscored Republican support for the war effort. The primary task facing the United States, he noted, was "To get our boys back home again—victorious and with all speed." This war could not be fought and won, then, as Democrats or Republicans. It was "an All-American War," he insisted, and "There is a place for every American in it." In addition, Warren promised that Republicans would put the public welfare above private self-interest, put the nation above the party, put the progress of the whole American community above special privilege for any part of it, and—with a slight jab at Roosevelt—"put indispensable principles, once and for all, above indispensable men."[4]

The weather also worked to squelch Republican enthusiasm at Chicago. A blistering heat wave engulfed the city, with the temperature on the street surpassing 90 degrees and breaking local records. The temperature inside the convention hall, meanwhile, registered at a sweltering 105 degrees. The *New York Times* described the heat and humidity in Chicago as "suffocating" and observed that "The heat quite evidently oppressed what would otherwise have been a more exciting show."[5]

Another reason for the lackluster mood in Chicago was the virtual pre-convention collapse of all candidacies except that of Governor Dewey. The outcome of the convention, then, seemed predictable and thus generated little excitement. By the end of the twentieth century, such coronations were commonplace. Prior to 1944, however, most conventions—especially those that did not involve an incumbent president seeking another term—were long and contentious affairs. For example, in 1924, it took the Democratic National Convention two weeks and a record 103 roll call ballots to settle upon a nominee. While this was not the first ballot nomination for Republicans, it did represent a clear move toward the tightly controlled and well-scripted modern conventions of the late twentieth and early twenty-first centuries.

In addition, there existed at the convention a general spirit of defeatism regarding the party's chances in November. Unlike Harry Truman, who also faced a deflated and unenthusiastic Democratic convention in 1948, Dewey failed to inject excitement into this gathering by promoting a bold and substantive policy initiative, such as a strong platform plank on civil rights. On this point in particular, Dewey and the Republicans missed a golden opportunity to reconnect with black voters. A reliable constituency for the GOP since Reconstruction, black voters shifted their party allegiance in 1936 and cast a majority of their ballots for Roosevelt and the Democrats. According to historian Nancy Weiss, this shift was grounded in the New Deal and not civil rights. Indeed, the Democratic Party, still largely dominated by white southerners, had not changed its views on race, but neither had it excluded blacks from the economic benefits of the New Deal.[6]

In a 2004 essay on Dewey and civil rights, Simon Topping observed that the New York governor was actually well positioned in 1944 to make significant inroads into the Democrats' recent black majority. Indeed, in his successful campaign for governor in 1942, Dewey was intentional about garnering support among black voters, endorsing the *Pittsburgh Courier*'s "Double V" campaign to combat tyranny abroad and discrimination at home and even campaigning in Harlem. He also delivered several speeches in which he denounced "the millstone of discrimination, prejudice and intolerance" and insisted that it was "absurd to talk about eradicating evils in other countries when we have not wiped out those evils at home."[7] On Election Day 1942, Dewey won a spectacular statewide victory, "counting Harlem among the wards in which he was victorious" and becoming the first Republican governor in New York in 20 years.[8]

In his first two years as governor, however, Dewey—despite some welcomed appointments—failed to live up to his campaign rhetoric. By early 1944, the governor had "two strikes against him in the minds of thinking Negro voters."[9] One strike was his support of a "states' rights" soldier vote bill. In 1943, the Roosevelt-backed Green-Lucas bill was introduced in Congress, providing for federal absentee ballots for all personnel in the military—some five million of whom were overseas. Specifically, it aimed to simplify absentee voting by giving a ballot to all servicemen in advance of federal elections and allowing them to mark it at the appropriate time—instead of requiring each soldier to apply for a ballot, wait to receive it, and execute it weeks later. A special bipartisan War Ballot Commission (WBC) was also proposed to oversee the entire process. Southern Democrats and most Republicans, including Dewey, opposed the bill, preferring states, and not the federal government, to allocate the soldier vote. The rationale behind this opposition was different, however.

Washington Post writer Mark Sullivan summed up the Republican position in mid-March 1944, noting that "If a soldier in the armed forces is moved to vote by his own initiative, if he takes the trouble to write his State capital and ask for an absentee ballot—such a soldier is likely to vote the same way he would have voted were he at home in time of peace." If, on the other hand, a soldier, otherwise disinterested, votes simply because "voting is made easy for him . . . [then he] might tend to vote for Mr. Roosevelt because he is the Commander in Chief."[10] Meanwhile, southern Democrats, such as Congressman John E. Rankin and Senator James O. Eastland, both from Mississippi, were motivated in their opposition by a desire to prevent black soldiers from voting and, as Eastland bluntly admitted, to maintain "white supremacy."[11]

Despite the racism associated with the states' rights position, Dewey, like most Republicans in Congress, continued to oppose Green-Lucas. "For the past eleven years," Dewey told his state legislature in March 1944, "the National Administration has assiduously cultivated the concept that state and local governments are trivial and of no consequence." The "soldier's ballot," he complained, was limited to federal elections and assumed "that the thirty-odd governors and all the state legislators to be elected this year are not important enough to affect the interest of the soldier at home or abroad." He proposed instead the New York Soldier Vote Law, which passed the legislature in July. Under this state law, every member of the armed forces from New York would be given a postcard. The soldier would then have to sign his name and his home and service address on that card and mail it to the War Ballot Commission at Albany. Should a soldier fail to receive a postcard, a simple letter or card to friends or family would serve the purpose if sent to the state capitol. The information would then be processed, and the soldier shortly thereafter would receive a full ballot with the name of every state, local, and federal candidate for office printed on it.[12] *Crisis* magazine, however, quickly noted that Dewey did not even "take the trouble to dissociate himself from Rankin" and insisted that "Anyone who joins Rankin cannot have the Negro vote."[13]

A second strike against Dewey was his refusal in the spring of 1944 to support an anti-discrimination measure drafted by his own Committee on Discrimination in Employment. Chaired by Dr. Alvin Johnson, president of the New School for Social Research, the committee of 25 drafted two bills. One set up a civil rights bureau in the State Attorney General's Office, while the other made it unlawful for labor unions and employers to discriminate against individuals because of "race, color, creed, national origin or ancestry."[14] On March 17, Dewey announced that while he was "thoroughly in accord" with the principles of the committee's "well intended proposals," the proposals themselves were poorly crafted and unworkable.[15] Specifically, he faulted the "Johnson bill" for being rushed and for failing to provide an appeal mechanism involving the courts.[16]

According to biographer Richard Norton Smith, Dewey did not want to push a bill considered woefully imperfect at a time in which "the whole idea of government as an enforcer of civil rights [was] still considered radical by many."[17] In other words, the governor did not feel the measures were substantive enough to merit the political fight. Thus, he recommended the formation of yet another committee to prepare an "integrated program" that "will give to our people an established basic policy aimed at eliminating discrimination in the social and economic structure of our State."[18]

While Dewey in fact courageously supported (and secured passage of) the Ives-Quinn Bill of 1945, which, among other things, "treated discrimination in the workplace as a misdemeanor, subject to a fine of $500 or a jail term of up to a year," he was roundly criticized in 1944 for his failure to support the Johnson measures. Eight members of the committee resigned in protest. The NAACP, meanwhile, declared that Dewey made the "wrong choice," noting that discrimination in the workplace was one of the most important issues among black voters and that "any prospective candidate for the Presidency who is unwilling to take a stand on this matter is certain to be viewed with suspicion by Negro voters."[19] *Crisis*, the official magazine of the NAACP, added that, "When the job issue came up in his own state, in his own legislature, Governor Dewey missed the ball."[20]

Dewey did little to strengthen his image on civil rights at Chicago that summer. At a press conference in late June, just one day after his speech accepting the presidential nomination, the governor was asked a question from a black reporter on the issue of race. Did he, the reporter asked, favor the policies of racial segregation of the armed forces? Instead of seizing this opportunity to criticize Roosevelt and the Democrats on civil rights (and to further drive a wedge within their already divided ranks), Dewey was evasive, simply replying it was "a very difficult question," and that while he favored ending segregation in the armed forces soon, "he did not feel qualified to pass judgment on the military problems involved." Furthermore, when asked if he would promise, as president, to enforce the 13th, 14th, and 15th Amendments in the South, the governor commented only that he would "observe my oath to enforce the Constitution in all respects."[21]

The Republican Party's civil rights platform plank in 1944 condemned racial and religious prejudice and pledged the establishment of a permanent Fair Employment Practice Commission. It also favored antilynching legislation and the submission of a Constitutional amendment for abolishing the poll tax. Writing in a series of articles that summer (which were later published as a small book entitled *An American Program*), Wendell Willkie, who was not invited to speak at the convention, described the platform as distinctly superior to the Democratic one but still "tragically inadequate." Millions of black Americans, he noted, "distrust the Democratic Party which for years has deprived the Negro of his right to vote. . . . But in view of the economic advances and social gains . . . during the past twelve years, they will not leave that party for vague assurances of future action expressed in pious platitudes, or for a 1944 version of states' rights doctrine, or even for procedures which, however legally correct, in practical effect indefinitely postpone correction of sore and desperate abuses."[22]

Addressing the Republican convention moments before the platform's adoption, D.H. Sims, bishop of the African Methodist Episcopal Church in Philadelphia, observed that the present moment provided the party of Lincoln with an opportunity to restore lost confidence and lost votes. "If the Party will castigate the poll tax, mob violence, discriminations in job opportunity, unfair employment practices in labor and industry, this," Sims declared, "will be a demonstration to the world in general and to the Negro in particular that we [Republicans] are placing the welfare of the whole American community above that of any special section of it."[23] Despite the platform's relative boldness and the impassioned plea from Bishop Sims, Dewey and the Republicans did not emphasize civil rights in the fall campaign. They were too aware of divisions within the Democratic Party, especially between northeastern liberals and southern conservatives, and hoped to exploit them. Specifically, then, the party—following the strategic lead of Hoover and Landon—avoided alienating white southerners disgruntled with Roosevelt and the New Deal. Thus, Dewey and the GOP once again "missed the ball."

Overall, the party platform elicited little convention controversy—although Willkie partisans complained that on foreign policy the mere following of the Mackinac Declaration of 1943 did not go far enough in committing the party to internationalism. On domestic concerns, meanwhile, the platform called for lower taxes, a Constitutional amendment "providing equal rights for men and women" in the workplace, and the creation of a Department of Agriculture. The ratification of the 22nd Amendment was foreshadowed with Republicans favoring a Constitutional amendment "providing that no person shall be President of the United States for more than two terms of four years each." The platform attacked the New Deal in only general terms, focusing mainly on the "selfish and partisan control over the functions of Government agencies where labor relationships are concerned" and a "bungled and inexcusable machinery program and confused, unreliable, impractical price and production administration."[24]

The most critical assessment of the New Deal, of course, fell under the platform's discussion of labor. Specifically, Republicans charged the Democratic administration with "the perversion" of the Wagner Act, which "menaces the purposes of the law and threatens to destroy collective bargaining completely and permanently," and the emasculation of the Department of Labor. In addition, the GOP condemned, first, "the conversion of administrative boards, ostensibly set up to settle industrial disputes, into instruments for putting into effect the financial and economic theories of the New Deal"; second, "the freezing of wage rates at arbitrary levels and the binding of men to their jobs as destructive to the advancement of a free people"; and third, "the repeal by Executive order of the laws secured by the Republican Party to abolish 'contract labor' and peonage." Another four years of New Deal policies, the platform concluded, "would centralize all power in the President, and would daily subject every act of every citizen to regulation by his henchmen; and this country could remain a Republic only in name."[25]

The convention was not completely void of spark, however. On the second night of the convention, for example, former president Hoover spoke on "Freedom, the Job of the Youth." Hoover definitely longed for a return to public favor, and for years since 1932 (and as late as 1940), he had harbored hopes for a return to the presidency. That was behind him in 1944. He focused now on a future for the party in which he would not be a part. Alluding to Dewey, he said, "In every generation youth presses forward toward achievement. Each generation has the right to build its own world out of the materials of the past, cemented by the hopes of the future.... This Convention is handing the leadership of the Republican Party to a new generation. And soon to support these younger men there will be an oncoming generation who will differ from all others.... I rejoice that this is to be."[26]

Hoover also interjected an issue that would come to be emphasized by Republicans in the fall campaign—that is, that "the Communists and their fellow travelers are spending vast sums to reelect this [New Deal] regime." According to the former president, the New Deal was—not unlike those violent "European revolutions" of recent years—destroying (through a "dictatorship of bureaucracy") every safeguard of personal liberty and justice. Could, he asked, an administration that forged "shackles on the liberties of the people" in peacetime be trusted to return freedom to the people from the shackles of war? No, he concluded, "Only by a change in administration will our returning soldiers find freedom preserved at home."

The night closed with the fiery reporter, correspondent, and playwright Congresswoman Clare Booth Luce of Connecticut. Luce, the wife of *Time* editor Henry Luce, was attractive, bold, and controversial. Her speech was intended to excite the delegates with old-fashioned partisan banter. She did not disappoint. After distinguishing G.I. Joe (the American serviceman) from G.I. Jim (the friend or brother of Joe who has already fallen in combat), she took direct aim at Roosevelt's foreign policy. Conveniently ignoring Republican anti-interventionist rhetoric prior to Pearl Harbor, Luce asked: "Do we here in this Convention dare ask if Jim's heroic death in battle was historically inevitable? If this war might not have been averted?

We know that this war was in the making everywhere in the world after 1918. . . . Might not skillful and determined American statesmanship have helped to unmake it all through the '30s? Or, when it was clear to our Government that it was too late to avert war, might not truthful and fearless leadership have prepared us better for it in material and in morale, in arms and in aims?"

Luce then unveiled her main criticism: "The last twelve years have not been Republican years," she said. "Maybe Republican Presidents during the '20s were overconfident that sanity would prevail abroad. But it was not a Republican President who dealt with the visibly rising menaces of Hitler and Mussolini and Hirohito. Ours was not the Administration that promised young Jim's mother and father and neighbors and friends economic security and peace. Yes, peace. No Republican President gave these promises which were kept to their ears, but broken to their hearts. For this terrible truth cannot be denied: these promises, which were given by a Government that was elected again and again and again because it made them, lie quite as dead as young Jim lies now. Jim was the heroic heir of the unheroic Roosevelt decade: a decade of confusion and conflict that ended in war."[27]

Despite all his strategizing for the nomination, Dewey had made very little plans for a running mate. His first choice was California governor Earl Warren, who refused, citing his pledge in 1942 not to seek national office. Dewey's advisors interpreted this explanation as a slap at the New York governor, who in 1942 had made a similar promise. However, Richard Norton Smith, in his 1982 biography of Dewey, observed that "Warren was a man of modest means and could hardly afford a $5,000 a year pay cut, or supporting his young and growing family in a faded Washington hotel. And Warren shared the widespread doubt that any Republican could put FDR out of the White House at the height of the war."[28]

In the end, Dewey focused on his only serious challenger at the convention, John W. Bricker of Ohio. Bricker continued to be a potential problem for Dewey as the convention opened in Chicago. Still a favorite among conservatives, the Ohio governor remained adamant that he was still a force to be reckoned with for the presidential nomination. Arriving in Chicago on June 22 (four days before the RNC officially convened), Bricker—greeted by supporters (calling themselves the "Bricker Battalion") and a band—told reporters that "I will not withdraw, and my name will be presented in the convention." When asked by a reporter if he would accept second place, Bricker replied: "That's something I will never have to pass upon because I am quite confident that the Vice Presidential nomination will never be offered to me."[29] The Ohio governor had not participated in the spring primaries but instead hoped for a deadlocked convention in which Dewey—pitted against numerous "favorite son" candidates—failed to get the necessary 529 votes to secure the Republican nomination. "If Governor Dewey is not nominated on the first or second ballot he will not be nominated at all. I know it, every newspaper man here knows it and the Dewey managers know it," Ohio representative Clarence J. Brown, a Bricker aide, told reporters in Chicago on June 23.[30]

Such hopes, however, were unrealistic. Dewey had been working hard for many weeks to squelch "favorite son" candidacies and was close to having the nomination secured by the time the convention officially opened on June 27. Indeed, the same day Bricker arrived in Chicago, one of Dewey's top advisors, J. Russell Sprague, presented to the press the names of Republican leaders from 29 states who had—as Sprague phrased it—joined the movement to "draft" Dewey. The following day the New York Times noted a "Dewey Majority Appears Certain by Convention Eve," and that "the convention seems likely to proceed according to schedule with adoption of the platform Tuesday night, the nomination of the candidate for President Wednesday night and with the nomination of the candidate for Vice President and adjournment on Thursday."[31]

Meanwhile, the Ohio delegation—in an obvious (and ultimately unsuccessful) attempt to outflank Dewey's forces—passed a resolution that requested the convention to invite "all persons whose names are to be presented in nomination" to address the convention. The rationale behind this scheme was that Dewey, an undeclared candidate, could not accept an invitation to appeal to the convention in person, while the more dynamic and personable Bricker could, and would use any such occasion to rally support. "If John Bricker appears before the convention," Ohio representative George Bender told a meeting of Republican delegates, "his nomination and election will be assured.... He would make a speech that would sweep the convention."[32]

Bricker's support was not very wide, but it was deep among conservatives. While Dewey was not despised by conservatives (as was Willkie), the New York governor was clearly not one of them. In fact, in mid-May, Dewey was given an unsolicited strategy memorandum from a small group of eastern Republicans (that included Prescott Bush of Connecticut) that called on Dewey to avoid "hackneyed Republican phrases. At no time let any utterance ... employ the clichés associated in the popular mind with the Old Guard Republicans: free enterprise, the American way, etc." The American people—although shaken in their belief in the New Deal—were, the memo concluded, "equally weary of the traditional 'Tory

Talk' of the Republican Old Guard" . . . and would "react unfavorably to the 'damn Roosevelt' technique."[33]

Conservatives could not have disagreed more. They were disappointed in the moderate nominees of 1936 and 1940 and wanted, in 1944, "a man of courage" to carry the Republican banner. "The American people," Senator Robert Taft, a Bricker supporter, told reporters on the eve of the RNC, "want a direct fight on the New Deal and on President Roosevelt. There is no one who will carry that fight so directly and so definitely as John Bricker."[34]

Ultimately, Dewey's hold on the convention was too tight for Bricker to break. Shortly after midnight on Wednesday, June 28 (the last day of the convention, and only hours before the nominations and roll call for president), Bricker was visited in his suite at the Stevens Hotel by Brownell and Sprague, who proposed that the Ohio governor withdraw from the presidential race in return for the vice presidential nomination. Bricker agreed to the arrangement, and the following morning, around 11:51 a.m., he appeared before the convention and delivered what his modern-day biographer has described as "the most effective speech of his career."[35]

Introduced by Congressman Joseph Martin of Massachusetts, Bricker, wearing a light-colored suit, strode on stage "amidst a tumult of applause." After an "unusually enthusiastic floor demonstration" that lasted nearly 20 minutes, Bricker—"lowering his arms to horizontal as evidence of an earnest appeal to be permitted to proceed"—began his address: "Mr. Chairman, members of the Convention, ladies and gentlemen: I am deeply grateful to the many friends who have expressed their loyalty to me, but far more important than that, to the cause for which I have tried to stand." Bricker then spoke of his recent travels around the country and of the importance of a Republican victory in November. He then quickly transitioned to the topic at hand: "A thousand times I have said to you that I am personally more interested . . . in defeating the New Deal philosophy of absolutism which has swept free government from the majority of countries throughout the world; I am more interested in defeating that than I am in personally being President of the United States."[36]

Over shouts of "No! No!" and "We Want Bricker," the governor then proceeded to his main point: "Appreciative as I am of the devotion to the cause which I have tried to represent . . . I understand it is the overwhelming desire of this convention to nominate a great, a vigorous, a fighting young American, the noble and dramatic and appealing Governor of the State of New York—Thomas E. Dewey. . . . I am now asking [my supporters] not to present my name to this convention, but to cast their votes . . . for Thomas E. Dewey for President of the United States."[37]

Bricker's speech was a sensation and set off another lengthy floor demonstration that the official reporter of the RNC, George L. Hart, described
as "an ovation such as few men in public life have ever received. . . . Wave
upon wave of applause greeted him as he bowed to the cheering delegates."[38]
Charles Eagan of the *New York Times* hailed Bricker's speech as "easily the
highlight of a convention . . . lacking in colorful events," while columnist
(and former New Dealer) Raymond Moley observed that "Mr. Average Delegate's mind and judgment is all for Dewey, but his heart belongs to Bricker."[39]
Robert Taft agreed, writing to Bricker in early July that "Your speech was
the highlight of the occasion and your willingness to accept the Vice-Pres-
idency was the only thing which prevented the convention from being a
very gloomy affair."[40]

Dewey's decision for Bricker was a popular one, and one that, in the end,
made much sense. After all, Bricker was the only Republican (besides Willkie)
who had actually openly sought the nomination. Thus, he had generated a
lot of enthusiasm, interest, and support—things the Republican ticket would
need in the fall. Bricker was also outgoing, colorful, and willing to go on the
attack—all things Dewey was not.[41] Furthermore, as a Midwest conservative, Bricker helped balance the ticket both ideologically and geographically.
Finally, he had the potential to bring the solidly Democratic South into play
in November. Under the advice of former president Hoover, who frequently
counseled the Buckeye governor, Bricker had begun in 1943 visiting with
southern business, party, and civic leaders. He had been generally well received and actually had some appeal in the South. Indeed, later in the campaign, Bricker traveled through Tennessee and Kentucky, writing to Dewey,
"The crowd [in Kentucky] was responsive and everywhere Democrats came
to me and said they are voting on our side this year." In Tennessee, meanwhile, Bricker did not express much hope in carrying the state in November,
but he added, "the benefit of going into Tennessee is the confidence it will
give to some of the other [southern] states and the hope that we might build
up a two party system in other states to the benefit of the party."[42]

While Bricker was not Dewey's first choice, he did enjoy Dewey's respect,
if not friendship and confidence. Indeed, in a conversation with journalist
Raymond Moley in 1943, Dewey inquired about Bricker. Moley, who ad-
mired Bricker, praised the Ohio governor in generalities only to be interrupted by Dewey with the crack, "You haven't said a word that makes him
any better than Harding." "This nettled me," Moley later recalled, "but . . . I
set out to work and for twenty minutes I expounded with ample detail about
Bricker the administrator, the politician and the man. Dewey seemed better

satisfied, and when I saw him next, he said, 'I have grown to think Bricker is pretty good.' Then, possibly without knowing that he was giving my speech back to me, he elaborated on Bricker the administrator, the politician and the man."[43]

CHAPTER 10

Dewey—"An American of This Century"

On the afternoon of June 28, following Bricker's withdrawal (and that of other, second tier candidates, including Harold Stassen of Minnesota), Dewey's name was officially placed into nomination by Nebraska governor Dwight Griswold, who described the New York governor as "the spokesman of the future." A Dewey demonstration immediately broke out. "Delegates marched through the aisles holding aloft pictures of Dewey and placards bearing such inscriptions as 'Dewey Will Win!' 'America Wants Dewey!' 'Dewey, the People's Choice!' 'Win With Dewey!'"[1] The roll was then read. It was a Dewey sweep, with only one dissenting vote. Grant Ritter, a 54-year-old dairy farmer from Wisconsin, protested, "I am a man, not a jellyfish," and then cast his one vote for General MacArthur. By 2:30 p.m. that Wednesday, it was all over, and Dewey was the nominee. Shortly thereafter, Bricker was chosen unanimously for second place. Listening to the radio in Albany, Governor and Mrs. Dewey prepared to leave the governor's mansion and fly to Chicago. By 9:00 p.m. they were in the Windy City.

At Chicago Stadium, some twenty thousand Republicans jammed into the hall to greet the presidential nominee. At approximately 9:10, with the closing strains of "America," the Governor and Mrs. Dewey walked into the hall and stepped out on the tongue extending from the platform to the podium, loudspeakers, and microphones. The room was adorned in American flags and ribbons of red, white, and blue. Positioned in front of the podium at the end of the platform was a giant golden eagle statue with wings spread. Dressed in a gray pin-striped suit with red tie, the governor appeared dapper, calm, and confident. His wife, young and smiling, was wearing a black dress and an orchid corsage. "They were received with enthusiastic and prolonged applause, both bowing acknowledgement, first to those in front, then to right, left, and all round the great hall. A chair was provided for Mrs. Dewey on the platform's tongue, and she took the seat while the Governor stood at her side and continued bowing appreciation of the great acclaim."[2] Finally, at 9:20 p.m.—as Dewey removed a handkerchief from his pants pocket and wiped the sweat from his face—the permanent chairman of the convention, Congressman Martin of Massachusetts, struck the gavel and declared: "I now have the honor to present to you the next President of the United States, Thomas E. Dewey."[3] Speaking over the cheering crowd, Dewey began his acceptance speech: "Mr. Chairman and fellow Americans: I am profoundly moved by the trust you have placed in me. I deeply feel the responsibility which goes with your nomination for President of the United States at this grave hour of our nation's history ... [and] I accept the nomination."[4]

Dewey's convention speech was relatively short and crisp and addressed to a national audience (and not party workers). Specifically, he aimed to express three main foreign policy themes: unity, continuity, and credibility. "To our Allies," he declared, "let us send from this Convention one message from our hearts: The American people are united with you to the limit of our resources and our manpower, devoted to the single task of victory and the establishment of a firm and lasting peace. To every member of the Axis powers let us send this message: By this political campaign, which you are unable to understand, our will to victory will be strengthened, and with every day you further delay surrender the consequences to you will be more severe." In addition, he insisted that "The military conduct of the war is outside this campaign. It is and must remain completely out of politics. ... Let me make it crystal-clear that a change of administration next January cannot and will not involve any change in the military conduct of the war." Dewey also sought to identify the GOP as a credible and constructive participant in postwar planning. "There are," he said, "only a few, a very few, who really believe that American should try to remain aloof from the world. There are only a relative few who believe it would be practical for America or her Allies to renounce all sovereignty and join a superstate. I certainly would not deny those two extremes the right to their opinions; but I stand firmly with the overwhelming majority of my fellow citizens in that great wide area of agreement. That agreement was clearly expressed by the Republican Mackinac

Declaration and was adopted in the foreign policy plank of this convention."[5]

Only a small part of the speech dealt with domestic policy. Overall, it included the usual criticisms of the New Deal—namely, that it had not solved the Depression, that it lacked faith in America, and that it was old and worn-out. Unveiling what would become a recurrent theme, Dewey pledged "that on January 20th next year our government will again have a cabinet of the ablest men and women to be found in America. Its members will expect and will receive full delegation of the powers of their offices. They will be capable of administering those powers. They will each be experienced in the task to be done and young enough to do it. This election will bring an end to one-man government in America." Then, answering Herbert Hoover's plea for new leadership, Dewey declared that the country was fighting its way through to new horizons and that "The future of America has no limit."[6]

As his speech came to a close, Dewey—sacrificing effect in the convention hall to effect over the radio—strove for eloquence.[7] "True," he said, "we now pass through dark and troubled times. Scarcely a home escapes the touch of dread anxiety and grief; yet in this hour the American spirit rises, faith returns—faith in our God, faith in our fellow man, faith in the land our fathers died to win, faith in the future, limitless and bright, of this, our country. In the name of that faith," he concluded, "we shall carry our cause in the coming months to the American people."[8] The convention hall then erupted into "thunderous applause," and Dewey was joined by Governor Bricker on the platform. The two shook hands, and "the great stadium resounded to the cheers of the multitude."[9] "Dewey Snaps GOP from Coma," declared *Newsweek*. The presidential campaign of 1944 had officially begun.[10]

Enthusiasm over Dewey's nomination was not universal, of course, particularly among members of the press. Dewey had a very poor relationship with the news media dating back to his early days as a racket buster. He had a reputation for secrecy, strict control of information, and rudeness. In his *Yankee Reporter*, published in late 1940, *World-Telegram* journalist S. Burton Heath—a reporter who actually liked Dewey—lamented that, while Dewey was one of the brightest and ablest men of his generation, he was without humor and patience and had unfortunately "let conceit and unrestrained independence ruin his future, by making it impossible for him to work with those who are, in the eyes of the world and in their own esteem, his equals."

On one occasion, Heath recalled, a reporter, with a background in business news and not crime news, was assigned to interview Dewey about the benefits racket busting was having on New York businesses. This particular reporter happened to be an admirer of Dewey's record, and his story was to have national distribution. However, when during the interview he asked a naïve question about Dewey's crime-fighting days, Dewey snapped sharply, "That's a stupid question." The reporter was embarrassed and insulted, the article was never written, and thereafter, Heath concluded, "nothing I could ever say would make him write a line about Dewey unless by direct orders from his editors."[11]

Heath also noted the Dewey treatment toward reporters at large after the Republican National Convention in 1940. During a post-convention press conference, Dewey—for the record—was "sweetness and party harmony and no hard feelings. Off the record, however, he told the assembled reporters that Willkie's nomination was forced upon the delegates by Wall Street banking interests, which threatened to embarrass them by calling loans and mortgages unless they voted for Willkie." That afternoon one newspaper led with Dewey's off-the-record remarks and attributed them directly to him. Dewey was furious and at his next press conference told reporters (off the record) that "[I]f anything that I say off the record is used again, I'll stop talking off the record." It was during this same meeting with reporters that Dewey was asked, "'Will you run again for district attorney next year?' 'No,' he said flatly, and then snapped: 'And if any of you prints that, I'll bar him from this building as long as I'm here.'" For all his intelligence, Heath concluded, Dewey had "an amazing ability to alienate that little group of men who have made him what he is today. . . . From time to time one of these [newspaper reporters] gets along with him temporarily, and then joins the great majority who are Dewey-haters."[12]

Not surprisingly, Dewey was often treated with disfavor by the media. Almost always he was mocked as short, inexperienced, humorless, and ambitious.

One of the earliest critics of candidate Dewey was Benjamin Stolberg. Writing in the *American Mercury* in the summer of 1940, Stolberg criticized the then-district attorney as ambitious, opportunistic, ignorant, immature, and arrogant. Dewey, he argued, suffered from an inferiority complex. He was a "little boy," Stolberg wrote, who acted the way he did because of his short stature and youth. From that generalization, Stolberg concluded that Dewey hated his father, who was slightly taller than the son, and sought the presidency only to make up for his inadequacies, particularly his height. "Nothing less than the presidency will make him feel as big and mature as papa." This ridiculous and rather bizarre analysis had two main problems. First, Stolberg, for all his psychobabble, was neither a psychiatrist nor a Dewey intimate. And second, Dewey—though of a small physical frame—was not *that* short. He was 5'8"—roughly the same height as the average American male at that time.

Another critical, if less fanciful, piece came in early 1944 with Richard H. Rovere's article in *Harper's Magazine* entitled "Dewey: The Man in the Blue Serge Suit." According to Rovere, Dewey—though alert and possessed of a highly disciplined mind—lacked boldness. He was a cautious man, who stood "four-square and flat-footed in the middle" and refused to ever "say anything that has not been double-checked for safety and propriety." Indeed, the governor—through the employing of professional pollsters—had streamlined the old political practices of "sniffing the breeze, playing it safe, tapping the grass roots, or keeping the ear to the ground" into an exact science. He lacked conviction and vision and had, Rovere insisted, refused—like a third-rate congressman—to "face up to the real issues of our time." Furthermore, he was, Rovere argued, a "platitude king," piling up familiar phrases "so neatly and with such roundness of phrase that the listener or reader is sometimes deluded into thinking that he is following a weighty argument." With his trained baritone voice and courtroom manner of presentation, Dewey made even such bromides as "We shall have our freedom so long as we are all free!" sound good. Finally, Rovere dismissed Dewey's reputation as an economic miracle-worker in New York as "poppycock." The real credit for the state's booming economy and sound fiscal situation belonged to the war and to Dewey's Democratic predecessor, Herbert Lehman, who left the state in 1943 with a $40,000,000 surplus.

Washington correspondent I.F. Stone, writing in *The Nation* that summer and fall, was no more kind to the Republican hopeful. According to Stone, Dewey—while competent, courageous, and hardworking—was "extraordinary only in his drive, his singleness of purpose, the intensity of his ambition." The governor was, he continued, "wholly self-seeking," choosing "the law as a profession because he thought it offered the prospect of greater and more secure financial rewards than singing." Furthermore, his sensational stint as prosecutor in New York was opportunistic, a quick stepping-stone to the governorship (and the presidency), and "not the beginning of a job that he felt had to be completed in the interest of civic duty or clean government." In addition, Stone argued that Dewey—rather than being wicked, sinister, dishonest, or fascist—was simply "uninteresting," presenting no complexities, and deviating no way from type. "I can see nothing but the commonplace in his mind," he wrote. "I sense no lift of idealism in his spirit; his motivations seem to me wholly self-seeking." Finally, Stone complained that the Republican nominee reeked of self-assurance and was completely void of human warmth. "He is not what we call a regular guy. There is nothing in him of Willkie's rich curiosity, human interest, or careless vitality. Dewey is small stuff and cold fish, handsomer and physically robust but really a good deal like Coolidge, frugal spiritually, a man who does not give himself freely."[13]

The Independent Voters Committee of the Arts and Sciences for Roosevelt, meanwhile, circulated a 1940 pamphlet on Dewey entitled "St. George and the Dragnet," written by author and theater critic Wolcott Gibbs. While presenting an overview of Dewey's career, Gibbs spent most of his essay mocking either Dewey's appearance or personality. As to the candidate's appearance, Gibbs wrote that he "has a jutting jaw, high cheekbones, a slightly bulbous nose, and thick eyebrows. His face, on the whole, has a compressed appearance, as though someone had squeezed his head in a vice. His suits are custom-made but uninteresting, and always seem a little too tight for him. . . . Altogether—smallish, neat, and dark—he looks like a Wall Street clerk on his way to work; unlike the late and magnificent Harding, he is a hard man to imagine in a toga." On Dewey's personality, Gibbs noted that he "is simply a man with no time for comedy or other irrelevancies. His life outside his work is a little like the interval between rounds in a prizefight—a period of rest, therapy, and reflection about what to do next."[14]

Finally, there was the *New Republic*'s "Dewey: The Man and His Record," printed in late September 1944. According to this 20-page "Special Section," Dewey was neither a despondent, indecisive Hoover nor an easygoing, humorous FDR. Instead, he was a Calvin Coolidge "made vocal, equipped with overweening ambition, and not caring very much on whom he tramples, or how hard, in fulfilling that ambition."[15] The piece went on to discredit Dewey's record as prosecutor and governor and concluded with a consideration of "Dewey as President." The real guide to determining what to expect from a Dewey administration, the editors argued, was a careful appraisal of those upon whom the governor relied heavily for advice. His "cronies," including Jaeckle (described as having "storm-trooper tactics"), Bell, and Brownell, were, in the main, "publicity men, political strategists, or ghost-writers rather than experts on economics, finance, or political science. . . . Their function seems to have been to aid Mr. Dewey in his climbing the ladder of public office rather than to lay out policies which they would like to see the nation follow." A President Dewey, the authors surmised with hyperbole, would never stand out against these and other men (including isolationists and anti-New Dealers) and would thus "be a prisoner in the White House of the worst elements in the Republican Party, so far as concerns the two great objectives of our time: prosperity and peace."[16]

The New Republic also included in its special section several disparaging jokes and quotes at the governor's expense. For example, one reporter, on seeing Dewey's Great Dane, "Canute," asked—in an obvious reference to the governor's height—"Does he ride it to work!" Another journalist, appropriating an old vaudeville joke, added that Dewey, "having drunk too much coffee, had spent the night pacing up and down under his bed." With great glee, the liberal weekly also quoted several Dewey associates, such as one woman who stated that "You have to know Mr. Dewey very well in order to dislike him" and another who asked, "How can you vote for a man who looks like a bridegroom on a wedding cake?"[17] Overall, these and other reports undermined Dewey's image and built an inaccurate perception—which still lingers among many academics today—of Dewey as a small, inexperienced young man, quite vain and pompous, self-seeking and ambitious, and oblivious or contemptuous of the feelings and desires of others.

Still, Dewey did get some favorable coverage, especially in the news-magazines, including *Time, Newsweek, Life, Look,* and *The Saturday Evening Post*.[18] On the eve of the Republican convention, *Collier's* published "My Friend, Tom Dewey," by longtime Dewey associate and ghostwriter Hickman Powell. According to Powell, a Democrat and "convinced New Dealer," Dewey was "a crystallizer of agreement, a catalytic agent in bringing people together for effective purpose." For that reason, Powell concluded, he was "going to work my heart out to help elect a Republican as President of the United States."

In addition, Dewey enjoyed the publication of two campaign biographies. One, Rupert Hughes's authorized *Attorney for the People: The Story of Thomas E. Dewey,* first published in 1939, was updated and re-released for the 1944 campaign. Hughes was very close to his subject, later declaring: "I believe with all my heart that if he is elected he will not only do more to carry us through the oncoming crisis of the peace than any other man could do, or would do; but that he will go down in history as one of the purest patriots and most noble statesmen our country has ever known."[19] Dewey's staff gathered most of the material for the book, and Dewey reportedly went over every page of the manuscript personally. The book, which compared Dewey to Alexander the Great and William Pitt, was not taken seriously. Commenting on the work in *The Nation,* I.F. Stone tersely observed that Hughes "seems to have confused him [Dewey] with George Washington and Lucky Luciano with a cherry tree."[20] Another critic sarcastically compared the book "favorably with some of Albert Payson Terhune's hymns to the collie."[21]

The other Dewey biography, Stanley Walker's *Dewey: An American of This Century,* which the liberal *Nation* described as "local-yokel," was typical campaign puffery. The book was folksy in nature and, in an attempt to humanize the governor, detailed not only his career but also his personal life, including his love of golf, cigarettes, and family. Walker even spent an entire paragraph tracing the development of Dewey's mustache, which evidently began as a "tentative, unpromising wisp" while Dewey was on a bicycling trip in France in 1925 but was "soon full-blown and bristly."[22] On the positive side, about a quarter of Walker's 350 pages consisted of the text of several Dewey speeches, dating back to 1937 and ending with the 1944 speech of acceptance. While not a best seller, the book sold well, leading the RNC to report in late September that "retail sales to date are about 50 percent more than any previously published biography of a Presidential Candidate, including Roosevelt's."[23]

In Dewey, Roosevelt faced a formidable opponent. He was, one contemporary observed, "relentless, able, dramatic, and full of guts and tricks."[24] Furthermore, he enjoyed "an inner core of advisors and friends, including some extremely distinguished people, [who] have a loyalty to him little short of idolatrous."[25] Despite many strengths—including honesty, intelligence, vigor, and efficiency in administration—Dewey possessed several serious flaws that undermined his presidential bids.

For one, he was young and relatively inexperienced, especially in foreign affairs, at a time when the nation was involved in a global crisis. Dewey was also undoubtedly shy and uncomfortable with popular politics, and was thus often resented by his political peers for "the 'metallic' and 'two-dimensional' nature of his efficiency."[26] Furthermore, he was viewed as vindictive, suspicious, opportunistic, and cocky. Journalist John Gunther described him in 1946 as "one of the least seductive personalities in public life"—"crammed with ego" and "as devoid of charm as a rivet or a lump of stone."[27] "Tom Dewey," one public official was overheard to say in the mid-1940s, "is the only man I ever met who can strut sitting down."[28]

In private correspondence, Senator Robert Taft repeatedly used the word "bossy" to describe Dewey. Indeed, in a letter to a friend on the eve of the Republican National Convention in 1944, Taft observed that "While Dewey may be nominated, it is very clear that most of the Republican politicians dislike him, not so much on account of his views as his inclination to boss everything and everybody."[29] Years later, Dewey's apprentice and admirer, Richard M. Nixon of California, recalled a Republican fund-raiser in 1952 during which

> a paying guest who had obviously had too much to drink came up . . . [and] slapped Dewey on the back, told him he was the greatest governor in New York's history, and said he hoped he would run for reelection. As the man walked away, Dewey very deliberately knocked the ashes off his cigarette, which like FDR he smoked through a holder, turned to me, and said, "Who was that fatuous ass?" In fact, the man happened to be the publisher of a string of weekly newspapers in New York State. Like many brilliant people, Dewey

found it very difficult to tolerate fools. In politics, that is a fatal mistake for three reasons. First, the man might not be a fool. Second, even fools vote. And third, a fool might still have something worthwhile to say to you.[30]

Herbert Brownell, in a 1990 interview at the Miller Center in Charlottesville, Virginia, echoed this sentiment. While observing that Dewey's main asset was his intellect—"He was a brilliant student of public affairs and had an analytical mind that was remarkable"—Brownell held that Dewey's primary weakness "was that often he was his own worst enemy by not being political or diplomatic in the conversations he had with people." "Dewey," Brownell noted, "was candid with everyone. He was open in his discussions and simply wouldn't disguise his feelings to someone who wasn't quite as smart as he was politically."[31]

Dewey was also an artist (in this case a trained vocalist) and a perfectionist, and was thus very intense and focused. In his campaigns, the governor had a very keen sense of production, was very performance-driven, and was fanatical about detail. For example, in early October 1944, Dewey wrote his national radio director, Henry Turnbell, complaining that "at the last two speeches it was almost impossible to read my manuscript. This is the most serious possible handicap in delivery of a speech and I hope whatever radical steps may be necessary will be taken forthwith to see that in the future I can at least read my speeches." Revealing his sensitivity to applause, Dewey added: "I have an exceedingly bad impression of the way the applause has been handled in all of the speeches except Louisville and Oklahoma City, on the radio. I am sure this can be done very much better."[32] In a memo to Brownell a few months earlier, one of Dewey's media consultants commented on the candidate's propensity for perfection:

> There is one thing I would say to the Governor about this question of pictures and that would be to quit worrying about it and just be himself. When there is something to smile about—smile, and when the occasion calls for being serious—be serious. He is much too good to spoil the splendid effects he is getting by being too concerned about it.[33]

Ultimately, Dewey as presidential candidate was handicapped by fear— fear of his own good instincts and fear of making spectacular mistakes. As journalist Raymond Moley observed in 1949, "In any analysis of the art of politics the significance of Thomas E. Dewey must be in the amazing fact that he went so far with so little natural political endowment."[34] He was, Moley claimed, like Samuel Johnson's dog that walked on two legs: "He doesn't do it very well but the amazing thing is that he can do it at all."[35]

CHAPTER 11

Franklin Roosevelt and the
Pursuit of Democratic Party Unity

Just as the 1920 election left a mark on Democrats, so too did 1940 on Republicans. The seeking of a third term (especially on the heels of the ill-fated Court-packing scheme of 1937) seemed to confirm to many Republicans that Roosevelt aimed at dictatorship. His cynical approach to the third-term nomination in 1940 only fueled those beliefs. Indeed, it was Wendell Willkie's 1940 bid against Roosevelt that first used the slogan "no indispensable man" against the president. Incidentally, Willkie's charge was a play on a phrase Roosevelt himself had spoken in 1932. In a campaign address before the Republicans-for-Roosevelt League in New York City on November 3, Roosevelt—speaking of the problems facing the country and his own agenda—said: "A great man left a watchword that we can well repeat: 'There is no indispensable man.'"[1] Yet Roosevelt's words and actions in 1940 seemed to betray that sentiment, and the slogan was repeated by Dewey in 1944. In fact, one Republican cartoon that year (1944) summed up nicely the Republican attitude on this issue. In the cartoon, Roosevelt was depicted in ancient Roman attire (with the words "4th TERM" written on his chest), and eating "INDISPENSABILITY BALONEY" at a table. The caption above him read: "On What Meat Doth This Our Great Caesar Feed—"

Yet from a purely political perspective Roosevelt was in fact the Democrats' "indispensable man." Despite his own problems in the polls in the early 1940s, it was clear the Democratic Party would be in trouble without the president at the head of the ticket in 1944. Indeed, a September 1943 Gallup poll revealed that if some other candidate—Vice President Henry Wallace, for example—were the Democratic nominee, New York's Governor Dewey would win the election 60 percent to 40 percent.[2] Eugene Casey, executive assistant to Roosevelt, bluntly expressed this Democratic alarm when, in August 1943, he told the *Minneapolis Tribune* that if FDR declined from seeking a fourth term "my party looks sunk."[3] By the end of 1943, however, Roosevelt once again believed he would need another term—a fourth one—to win the war and to succeed where Woodrow Wilson had failed. "God knows I don't want to [run]," Roosevelt told one advisor early in 1944, "but I may find it necessary." That spring he told Admiral Leahy, "I just hate to run again for election," and expressed the hope that progress in the war would make it unnecessary for him to be a candidate.[4]

Still, a Roosevelt victory was not a foregone conclusion as Democrats convened in Chicago that summer for their nominating convention. Roosevelt had always been a polarizing figure, and he remained so during the war, as a letter sent from Braintree, Massachusetts, to the White House shortly after D-Day made perfectly clear:

My dear President:

. . . What insanity this war is, to drag our country in to save the British Empire.

The American people will never forgive you for the deaths, maimed and insane boys you are directly responsible for.

What are our war aims and what are we fighting for? Our finish will come when we go bankrupt, total Chaos and Revolution all because a willful President planned it that way.

God help you on Nov. 7th [Election Day]. Hope you can take the humiliation without committing suicide.[5]

Although the only Gallup survey to measure presidential approval during the 1944 election cycle was a December 1943 one that found FDR's approval rating at 66 percent, other early polls indicated some problems for the president. Earlier that year, only 39 percent of voters surveyed by Gallup indicated that they would vote for FDR in 1944 if the war was over. Meanwhile, 50 percent indicated they would definitely vote against him.[6] In a similar survey that May, Roosevelt's situation was still bleak. When Gallup asked again "If the war is over and President Roosevelt runs for a fourth term next year, do you think you will vote for him or against him?" only 31 percent of those surveyed said "Yes"—an eight-point drop from earlier in the year. An overwhelming 69 percent said "No." When asked if the war was not entirely over but looked as though it might be over soon, 51 percent said they would vote to reelect the president, while 49 percent said they would not.[7] Glee-fully, the pro-Dewey *Saturday Evening Post* reported that July: "You're Right, Dewey Has a Good Chance!"[8]

Meanwhile, some, including journalist Drew Pearson, doubted the president would even seek a fourth term. "Whether he would be president of a League of United Nations, or an American representative on it," Pearson wrote in late 1943, "is a detail."[9] The most important thing, he concluded, was that FDR's next four years reached beyond the national scene. Montana senator Burton Wheeler, an anti-Roosevelt Democrat, also predicted that Roosevelt would not run in 1944. His reasoning, however, differed from Pearson's. According to Wheeler, Roosevelt would retire from politics because "a definite Republican trend has set in and the President will be able to sense this far more quickly than any of his advisors."[10] However, there was never any serious doubt about a Roosevelt run at Democratic national headquarters. Only "the Champ" could deliver Democrats another victory in November.

The reasons for dissatisfaction with the president at the midway point in his third term were varied. In November 1943, Gallup asked Democratic voters in New York, New Jersey, and Kentucky who had shifted to the GOP in 1942, what they liked "least about the way the Roosevelt administration is handling things?"[11] The most frequent responses were: "incompetent and dictatorial management of home affairs," "coddling of labor," "government extravagance," "failure to keep prices down," and "bad job of rationing."[12] Meanwhile, in the South, many Democratic politicians were displeased with the administration over civil rights. In late 1943, John U. Barr, a wealthy New Orleans manufacturer and vice president of the Southern States Industrial Council, formed the Harry "Byrd for President Committee," which aimed to coordinate southern efforts to cast off the yoke of the New Deal and place the Virginia senator in the White House. A serious southern revolt, however, never materialized.[13]

Several books were published in 1944 about Roosevelt and his administration. The first was *What Manner of Man?*, a small biography written by *Fortune* writer Noel Busch. The book was part reportorial gossip, part history, and part psychoanalysis. Overall, Busch effectively detailed the White

House life of the president and gave behind-the-scenes glimpses of the Cairo and Tehran conferences—Roosevelt, for example, took with him 50 detective novels picked by the Library of Congress. He also criticized Roosevelt's "casual, illogical ways, his petulances, his taste for crises (which sometimes leads him to arrange a few when they do not occur naturally), and his occasional indulgence in grandiose administrative mismanagement."[14]

The weakest section of the book was Busch's attempt at what *The Nation* called "parlor psychoanalysis." For example, according to Busch, Roosevelt, in his 1937 battle to reorganize the US Supreme Court, "was really just a 'spoiled brat' who feels thwarted by legal authority."[15] On the whole, however, Busch—whom historian Allan Nevins described as an excellent reporter, a mediocre historian, and a wretchedly unconvincing psychoanalyst—inclined the balance in favor of Roosevelt, concluding that the president "still seems to be on his game, if not quite at the top of it."

Another book favorable to FDR, published in early 1944, was *"That Man" in the White House,* by Frank Kingdon. According to Kingdon, a former Methodist minister and president of the University of Newark, Roosevelt was a man of "political oomph"—provocative, dramatic, and "a powerful stimulus to the national imagination." Thus, "no matter who runs against him this year he will dominate the election simply because there is no personality of like flair and color to compete with his." Roosevelt was a strong man—the only one strong enough to hold the office—and a wise one. He was, Kingdon continued, true and incorruptible, "wholly dedicated to the principles of democracy, and willing and able to fight for them against their enemies at home and in the councils of the nations."[16]

Kingdon defended the president against 27 of the "most frequently heard criticisms," including dictatorship and communism. Roosevelt, he insisted, was not a dictator. Americans still had their civil liberties, freely functioning political parties, regular elections, and police and courts operating under the authority of laws duly adopted by Constitutional processes.[17] "Those who charge the President with being a dictator are either mentally incapable of understanding what a dictator is, or else guilty of deliberate falsehood."[18]

The president, he added, was not a communist either. "A communist," Kingdon wrote, "is one who believes that all the instruments of production should be socially owned, and that the way to bring this about is through a people's revolution that liquidates the owners of private wealth and puts all power in the hands of the proletariat." Yet production in the United States, he noted, was still privately owned, and "the owners of them are making higher profits than any since the last war. Those who charge the President with communism either do not know what it is, or else think that the people of this country are so ignorant that they can fool them by a lie." FDR, he continued, was not destroying capitalism, and he had not neglected the farmer or coddled labor. Instead, Kingdon concluded, he was a centrist—swinging neither to the left nor the right—and a strong and selfless leader who would never sell out America to other nations.[19]

Although Roosevelt did not write any books himself in 1944—as he did for the 1932 and 1936 campaigns—two collections of the president's speeches were published: *Rendezvous with Destiny*, edited by J.B.S. Hardman, and *Our American Way*, edited by Dagobert D. Runes and printed by the New York Philosophical Society. Roosevelt, however, did endure his share of unfavorable press. One critic was Robert Moses, city park commissioner for New York City, who wrote a scathing indictment of the president and the New Deal in an article entitled "Why I Oppose the Fourth Term," published in *The Saturday Evening Post* in early October 1944.

According to Moses, Roosevelt had destroyed the idea of the union of states, increased the conflict between the executive and legislative branches of government, promoted factionalism, appealed to class prejudice, and nearly ruined the federal judicial system. Furthermore, he doubted FDR's "ability to convert war to peace production, to provide full employment and to guarantee a reasonably swift transition from prodigious Government spending to reduced budgets and taxes." Although Moses argued that, under a Republican administration, those Democratic ills would be corrected, he only "opposed" Roosevelt, revealing a major gap in the Republican campaign—that is, the failure to generate excitement and passion about a Dewey presidency. Moses typified most Dewey voters. He was seemingly motivated more by opposition to Roosevelt than by support for Dewey.[20]

A major political issue facing Roosevelt in the summer of 1944 was the vice presidential selection. While the incumbent, Henry A. Wallace, enjoyed widespread popularity among rank-and-file Democrats as well as a majority of ordinary Americans, he was extremely unpopular with the senior leadership in the party. One strike against Wallace was his association with radical liberalism. As historian Robert Ferrell observed in his 1994 study on Truman and the Democratic National Convention, the general "idea of liberalism still carried immense appeal," but as an ideology it "was losing its attraction, and by 1944 the good economic times of the war era made it seem almost unnecessary." Furthermore, Wallace supporters—such as labor unions and the small fringe of American radicals, including socialists and some communists—offended the "more moderate liberals," who liked neither "the militancy of wartime union leaders, nor the socialists-communists."[21]

Another strike against Wallace was that many party leaders feared Roosevelt would not live through a fourth term. "I always felt that the Vice President would become the President," Edwin Pauley, treasurer of the DNC, later recalled. "Many people who had not been as close to Roosevelt as I was, didn't realize his infirmities as much as I did at the time. . . . I realized . . . that he was failing and that he would not be, if reelected, the same sharp and admirable President that we had had before, and that, therefore, we would have to rely on a successor."[22] Believing Wallace "was making too many pro-Soviet statements," and that his actions disqualified him from becoming, "either by election or succession, a proper President of the United States," Pauley, in early 1944, began conspiring with Roosevelt's appointments secretary, Major General Edwin "Pa" Watson, to manipulate the president's schedule.[23] Throughout the spring of 1944, Pauley and Watson ensured that there was a steady parade of "convention delegates, national committeemen, state chairmen, and governors whose refrain was 'Mr. President, we are all for you, but we cannot stomach Wallace.'"[24] Wallace supporters, meanwhile, were denied similar access.

A third strike against Wallace was that he was not very popular in the Senate in his role as president of that body. The vice president often kept to himself, and he did not build any strong friendships on Capitol Hill. According to historian Robert L. Messer, this was the death nail of Wallace's doomed candidacy. "To avoid the problems of Woodrow Wilson after the first World War, Roosevelt wanted to do everything he could to assure Senate cooperation in the coming peacemaking."[25] Finally, Wallace was viewed as a poor fund-raiser. According to Pauley, the vice president "was seldom sought as a speaker; and, when he was, we discouraged it. He was no good at raising money, and beyond this, he usually provoked an argument within the party ranks."[26]

In a secret White House meeting with the president on July 11, Pauley, DNC chair Robert Hannegan, former party chair Frank Walker, Chicago mayor Ed Kelly, and Bronx leader Edward Flynn discussed a number of vice presidential possibilities. The consensus was that Wallace was out—and should be replaced by someone like Sam Rayburn of Texas, Alben Barkley of Kentucky, James Byrnes of South Carolina, or Harry Truman of Missouri. Rayburn, Speaker of the House of Representatives, was an attractive possibility, but the certification of an anti-Roosevelt slate of delegates from Texas to the DNC that summer demonstrated he could not control his own state. Meanwhile, Barkley in the US Senate was, at age 67, deemed too old—especially considering the Republican candidate was only 42. He had also broken with Roosevelt that February, refusing to support the president's veto of a tax relief bill that the White House insisted was "not for the needy but for the greedy."[27]

Roosevelt's "assistant President" and close friend James Byrnes was stricken from the short list due to his southern origins, racial attitudes, and poor relations with labor. Race was a key concern of Roosevelt. Democrats had enjoyed a black majority since 1936, and black voters arguably made the difference for the president in his unprecedented third-term bid in 1940. In a close election, as 1944 was expected to be, the black vote, Flynn believed, would be crucial. Selecting a southerner for vice president, Flynn told Roosevelt, would cost him between one and three million votes.[28] It did not help matters for the South Carolinian that he had been born a Roman Catholic but left the church upon his marriage to an Episcopalian. Roosevelt also feared a backlash from millions of Irish Catholics in key eastern cities.

The president himself advocated Supreme Court justice William O. Douglas. The associate justice was in his mid-40s, loved the western outdoors, and delighted, as did Roosevelt, in gossip and off-color stories. Roosevelt believed him to be a "wonderful fellow" who "looked and acted on occasions like a Boy Scout, and would have . . . appeal at the polls—and besides, played an interesting game of poker."[29] Furthermore, Douglas had been a classmate of Dewey at Columbia University and had been first in his class each year. Hannegan, however, insisted that Douglas was not a strong enough party man to have a following and would thus be unacceptable to state and local party leaders and their followers. Hannegan's own recommendation to the president was his old mentor, US senator Harry S. Truman.

Truman and Roosevelt did not have an especially close relationship. The two had only met and spoken a few times in the ten years that Truman had been in the Senate. In 1940, Roosevelt—despite Truman's loyalty to the administration—supported his challenger, Lloyd Stark, in the Democratic primary in Missouri. Still, Truman, age 60, offered a number of positive qualities to the Democratic ticket. He was from Missouri, a border state—and thus had appeal in the South—and was considered a moderate on most issues, including race. In addition, he was well known and well liked in the Senate. Whereas the ever-aloof Wallace spent much of his time on trips abroad, "representing" FDR and ignoring senators, Truman was a regular in Speaker Rayburn's private Capitol Hill hideaway, the so-called Board of Education. It was there (Room 9) that legislators—after all of the official business of the day had been completed—would meet for a "libation." According to Truman biographer David McCullough, to be invited to join Rayburn, even once or twice in a term, was considered a sign that one had arrived.[30] Meanwhile, as chairman of the Senate Special Committee to Investigate the National Defense Program (or the Truman Committee, as it was popularly known), Truman had become very visible around the country, and earned a reputation for hard work, honesty, efficiency, and common sense.

As the July 11 meeting between party leaders and the president drew to a close, Roosevelt declared: "Bob, I think you and everyone else want Truman! If that's the case, it's Truman."[31] As the group dispersed, Hannegan, fearing the president might change his mind, asked FDR to put his commitment to Truman in writing. Roosevelt agreed but, to the DNC chief's later astonishment, used noncommittal language, postdated it July 19 (the day before the vice presidential nomination at the convention), and included Douglas's name. Roosevelt, who could be cold, calculating, and shrewd, was also—as this episode demonstrated—in control. While older and in poor health, FDR was nevertheless—as he himself understood—"indispensable" to a Democratic victory in November, and he intended to keep his options for vice president open.[32]

Although Roosevelt remained noncommittal on Truman, it was clear that Wallace and Byrnes were out of the running, and the president, who disliked unpleasant tasks, instructed Walker and Hannegan to inform them as such. However, both men were fighters, and both understood themselves to be important to the president. It did not help matters that Roosevelt refused to confront people with information he knew to be disagreeable. "He always hopes to get things settled pleasantly," the First Lady once remarked, "and he won't realize that there are times when you have to do an unpleasant thing directly and perhaps unpleasantly."[33] This was certainly the case with Wallace and Byrnes in 1944.

Knowing that neither Wallace nor Byrnes was an acceptable vice presidential choice, Roosevelt nevertheless gave assurances to both men—on the same day, July 12, and only hours apart—that they had his support. In fact, on July 10, when Wallace asked about the nomination, Roosevelt, perhaps out of a sense of appreciation for Wallace's service, reassured the vice president that he was his choice and even agreed to write a letter to the convention chairman indicating that "If I were a delegate to the convention I would vote for Henry Wallace."[34]

Again, on July 13 the vice president indicated that he would "withdraw at once" if Roosevelt felt him to be harmful to the ticket. Incredibly, Roosevelt replied that it was a "mighty sweet offer" but that he "could not think of accepting it." As Wallace later recalled, the president then drew him close, "turned on his full smile," and with a "very hearty handclasp" said, "While I cannot put it just that way in public, I hope it will be the same old team."[35] Thus, as long as the president refused to tell him to drop out of the race, Wallace, with a 65 percent approval rating in the latest Gallup poll, planned to go to Chicago and fight for the nomination.

Byrnes, meanwhile, was an entirely different problem for Roosevelt. A former senator from South Carolina, Byrnes was a close personal friend and longtime political ally. Ever ambitious, he had been a vice presidential hopeful four years earlier. After the selection of Wallace in 1940, Roosevelt nominated a disappointed Byrnes to the US Supreme Court. To the surprise of many Washington insiders, Byrnes accepted the post and took to the bench in June 1941. Shortly thereafter, of course, the United States entered World War II, and the once influential senator began publicly complaining that the cloistered atmosphere of the Court gave him, as he described it, "ants in my pants."[36] In early 1942, he resigned from the Court and took up residence in a small office in the East Wing of the White House as director of the five-man Office of Economic Stabilization (OES) responsible for controlling inflation through regulation of wages and prices.

As head of OES, Byrnes was FDR's "professional 'no' man" to all groups seeking higher wages, prices, or profits.[37] In that position, it did not take him long to make enemies, especially within the leadership ranks of organized labor, and in 1943, he asked to be relieved. Roosevelt then named him director of the Office of War Mobilization, in which he was responsible for presiding over "all manner of procurement, production, and allocation of goods and services related to the war effort." He was, one historian recently observed, czar over all the other wartime economic czars, and he soon became known in the media as "Assistant President for the home front"[38]

In his role as "assistant president," Byrnes enjoyed a free hand when it came to domestic concerns. "He could 'lay down the law' to cabinet officers and make independent decisions on priorities, personnel, and jurisdictional disputes, knowing in advance that the president would back him. Byrnes wanted the vice presidency, and he announced through Hopkins that he planned to run if the president had no objections.

On July 12, Walker informed Byrnes that his "chances for the nomination were not as good as they had been . . . [and] that Douglas and Truman were now strong possibilities."[39] Shortly thereafter Byrnes telephoned the president and asked him if he had changed his mind about his being a candidate. "You are the best qualified man in the whole outfit and you must not get out of the race," Roosevelt assured Byrnes. "If you stay in, you are sure to win."[40] In a White House meeting with Byrnes the next day, the president again encouraged his friend, promising that he would not express a preference for anyone.

According to historian Robert Ferrell, who has written the most exhaustive account of the 1944 Democratic convention, Byrnes knew the president well enough to know that Roosevelt would never tell him he was out. Ambitious and a "slick conniver," Byrnes "preferred to hedge an issue he thought he could force at the convention."[41] Thus, when he was approached on July 14 by Hannegan and Walker, who again informed him that Roosevelt favored either Truman or Douglas for vice president, Byrnes refused to accept defeat and telephoned Roosevelt at Hyde Park. "[I]t would make it very difficult for me," he told Roosevelt, if the president had in fact instructed Hannegan and Walker "to say to their friends that . . . [you] prefer[red] Truman first and Douglas second, and that either would be preferable to me because they would cost the ticket fewer votes than I would."[42]

Resorting to what Ferrell described as "outrageous subterfuge," Roosevelt insisted that this was incorrect. "That is not what I told them. That is what they told me. . . . We have to be damned careful about language. They asked if I would object to Truman and Douglas and I said no. That is different from using the world 'prefer.' That is not expressing a preference because you know I told you I would have no preference."[43] Byrnes was not fooled, Ferrell argued, but the conversation "allowed him to continue the charade that the president really wanted him."[44] Still in the race (and now aware of a potential rival), Byrnes called an unknowing Truman in Independence, Missouri, that same day, July 14. "Harry," Byrnes said, "the President has given me the go sign for the Vice Presidency and I am calling up to ask if you will nominate me." Truman readily agreed.[45]

Despite his persistence and closeness to Roosevelt, Byrnes, who had clashed with labor over demands for increased pay in 1943, was simply unacceptable to labor. And labor—especially Sidney Hillman, who was unalterably opposed to Byrnes—was too vital for a Democratic victory in the fall for the president to ignore its wishes. At age 57, Hillman was a Lithuanian-born Jew and former head of the powerful American labor federation, the Congress of Industrial Organizations (CIO). An early supporter of Roosevelt and the New Deal, he was appointed by the president to an advisory board of the National Recovery Administration in 1933. Unwilling to join the ranks of the Democratic Party with its strong base of support in the South, Hillman helped forge the American Labor Party, which supported Roosevelt in both 1936 and 1940.

In 1943, Hillman formed the Political Action Committee (PAC) to circumvent the newly passed Smith-Connolly Act, which prohibited campaign contributions from labor organizations. According to Hillman, the PAC was not a political party but an organization "to educate the people on their political rights and how to use them to improve their own conditions and to help banish poverty and the fear of poverty from our land."[46] It stood against every reactionary force, he insisted, while standing for (1) a complete Allied victory over the Axis and the destruction of fascism, (2) all-out aid to returning servicemen, (3) full employment at fair wages, (4) good housing, medical care, and education for all, (5) equality of opportunity regardless of race or religion, (6) a just and adequate Social Security system, and (7) planning for a lasting peace.[47]

The CIO-PAC was one of the first attempts in the United States to organize labor for political purposes on a national scale. Ultimately, it spent $1,000,000 in support of Roosevelt in 1944. Although the law forbade PACs from drawing on union treasuries or donating money directly to candidates, Hillman could solicit "voluntary" contributions and put out his own material. In addition, he "undertook the huge task of reclassifying union membership lists, which were arranged by shop rather than by ward or precinct, so that registration drives could be conducted and tabs kept on voter turnout." Toward this end, the former labor leader joined efforts with Earl Browder's American Communist Party—which had dissolved as a political party and reformed itself as the Communist Political Association—to find the necessary skilled and committed organizers to staff national and regional PAC offices.

Byrnes was then out of the running, and he was informed as much on Monday, July 17, the opening day of the convention. The official reason— a convenient excuse that may have been planned by FDR all along—was that the president had stipulated that any vice presidential pick must first be cleared by CIO leaders, including Hillman, and that Byrnes had failed to secure clearance. Although deeply bitter, Byrnes did not resign his White House position, nor did he bolt the party. Instead, he graciously released Truman from his pledge to nominate him and then quietly left Chicago.

CHAPTER 12

The Democratic National Convention

On July 19, Democrats arrived in Chicago to hold their twenty-ninth national convention. Unlike Republicans, who had met in the same place a few weeks earlier, Democrats were in a festive mood. The war was being won, the economy was booming, and Franklin Roosevelt had consented, once again, to be a candidate for reelection. While sometimes fragmented along many different policy and ideological lines, Democrats rallied one last time behind their leader, a man they understood to be "indispensable" to both party unity and electoral victory. Delegates—equipped with red, white, and blue fluorescent victory "Vs"—were confident and enthusiastic. Often overshadowed by the vice presidential selection struggle, the 1944 Democratic National Convention was itself remarkable for its old-fashioned, peacetime, hardball, "politics as usual" tone. Two speeches, in particular, stood out as especially noteworthy—and harsh.

The first was the keynote address delivered by Oklahoma governor Robert S. Kerr, whom *The Washington Post* described as a "strapping and eloquent orator of the old school."[1] Republicans, Kerr declared, were hateful, blind, and obstructionist, and their young presidential nominee a vague, inexperienced, and reactionary disciple of Herbert Hoover. "Who," he asked, "will represent the United States of America? An untried leader who has not even told his own people what his views are? Or the man who has from the start declared his position in clear and certain words, and who has the respect and esteem of all the United Nations as no other living American?" In addition, the Oklahoman took Dewey to task for characterizing, in his speech before the RNC, the Roosevelt administration as a group of "tired old men." "Let us examine the record," Kerr exclaimed.

> Shall we discard as a "tired old man," the fifty-nine-year-old Admiral Nimitz?
>
> Shall we discard as a "tired old man," the Lion of the Pacific, sixty-two-year-old Admiral Halsey?
>
> Shall we stop his onward sweep to redeem the Philippine Islands and discard as a "tired old man," sixty-four-year-old General Douglas MacArthur?
>
> Shall we discard as a "tired old man" the Chief of all our Naval Forces, sixty-six-year-old Admiral King?
>
> Shall we discard as a "tired old man," the greatest military leader of our nation, sixty-four-year-old General George C. Marshall?
>
> No, Mr. Dewey, we know we are winning this war with these "tired old men," including the sixty-two-year-old Franklin D. Roosevelt as their Commander-in-Chief![2]

Convention delegates then broke out into a 39-minute demonstration.

Kerr was not finished, however. Dewey, he charged, was an isolationist in disguise—another Harding—who sought to crucify Roosevelt just as the Old Guard had done to the "great-hearted Woodrow Wilson" some 25 years previously. Then, in an obvious attempt to neutralize one of Dewey's more promising positions—that is, that the next administration would be a peacetime one—Kerr argued that Republicans could not be trusted at home once the war was over. Reminding Americans of Hoover's "stupid and brutal" crushing of the Bonus Army in 1932, he declared that, "When this war is won, a grateful nation will not forget, nor go back on its returning service men and women; nor will this nation go back to a Republican Administration that did go back on the returning servicemen of World War I."[3]

The most heated and controversial point in Kerr's speech, however, was a question he raised about midway through his text. Criticizing Republican isolationists in Congress prior to Pearl Harbor, he asked, "Shall we restore to power the party whose national leadership, under the domination of isolationists, *scrapped and sank more of our fleet than was destroyed by the Japanese at Pearl Harbor*? [italics added] Or can we fail to support the Democratic Administration under which America has become the greatest naval power on earth?"[4] Surprisingly, Kerr's speech motivated little public response. Among the nation's major newspapers, only the Republican-friendly

Chicago Daily Tribune chimed in, observing, "One thing we know: When we suffered the disgraceful defeat at Pearl Harbor the commander-in-chief was not a Republican."[5]

The following day, Indiana senator and permanent chairman of the convention Samuel Jackson described 1944 as a "fateful" election, and he warned that "in the fiercest, most devastating war mankind has ever known" a Democratic defeat would mean battleships for Hirohito and legions for Hitler. "Frankly," Jackson continued, "could Goebbels do better himself to bolster Axis morale than the word that the American people had upset this administration ... ? We must not allow the American ballot box to be made Hitler's secret weapon!"[6]

Jackson's speech was but one example of an aspect of the 1944 campaign often overlooked—Nazi-baiting by Democrats and other Roosevelt supporters. Throughout the fall, there were numerous references to Dewey's "Hitler mustache" in speeches and campaign literature. For example, one pro-Roosevelt leaflet, paid for by the Socialist Party of Oregon, read:

> Behind the mask of "Tom Thumb" "Double-Talk" Dewey and his "Hitler Mustache" stands Hog-Joweled, Heartless Hoover, every Labor Union Wrecker, Ku Kluxer, Jew-Baiter, Poll-Taxer, Negro-Hater, Press Prostitute, Radio Rat, Putrid Pulpiteer and ghoulish War Profiteer! IF YOU'RE SCREWY ... VOTE FOR DEWEY![7]

Supporters of Dewey, including John Foster Dulles and Senator Gerald Nye, were also charged with being pro-Hitler. "US Fascists Want ... [Dewey] in the White House," declared a publication of the New York County American Labor Party.

> They Like Dewey—and Our Enemies Too
>
> December 6, 1941 ... Pro-Axis
> November 7, 1944 ... Pro-Dewey
>
> They Have Not Changed![8]

Another pro-Roosevelt piece to compare Dewey with Hitler was a cartoon by Arthur Szyk of the *New York Post* that showed Hitler and Hirohito carrying election banners that read: "Don't Vote for Roosevelt!" The intended message was that the two Axis leaders would welcome a change in Washington, hoping that a Dewey presidency might not be as aggressive in prosecuting the war.[9] The animated short *Hell-Bent for Election* was released in July 1944. The film was sponsored by the United Auto Workers of America and depicted Roosevelt and Dewey as two trains. Roosevelt was a modern bullet train while Dewey was a slow, aged, 1929 "defeatist limited" steam engine hauling "hot air," a "business as usual sleeper," increased taxes, apples for insurance, and a park bench for social security. The conflict of the 13-minute film centered upon a switch operator who represented the American voter. The operator's duty was to ensure that the Roosevelt special stayed on course. Unfortunately, however, he was constantly being distracted (and lulled to sleep) by another character—a wealthy Dewey supporter— who looked like Hoover and, at one point, transformed into Adolf Hitler. Ultimately, the Dewey train of special interests and misery was derailed by the operator/voter while the Roosevelt "Win the War Special" proceeded confidently toward "a better world." The film ended with an exhortation to voters to "Oh! Get behind the President," reminding them that "[If] you want to have security. . . . You've got to get out and vote."[10]

The Democratic Party itself, as suggested by Jackson's speech, also focused on Hitler and morale. Late in the campaign, for example, the office of Roosevelt aide Harry Hopkins considered circulating an unconfirmed report that the German chief of staff had urged Hitler to seek an armistice. Hitler, however (the report claimed), "rejected the proposal on the ground that an election was coming up in the United States and if Roosevelt was defeated and Dewey elected the unity of the United Nations might be shattered, especially in view of Dewey's statements with reference to Russia."[11]

The first night of the convention was also decision time for Truman. That day the president's letter "endorsing" Wallace—written three days earlier— was released. "I have been associated with Henry Wallace during his past four years as Vice President, for eight years earlier while he was Secretary of Agriculture, and well before that," Roosevelt informed Chairman Jackson. "I like him and I respect him and he is my personal friend. For these reasons I personally would vote for his nomination if I were a delegate to the convention. At the same time, I do not wish to appear in any way as dictating to the Convention. Obviously the Convention must do the deciding."[12] It was hardly a ringing endorsement. Indeed, journalist Arthur Krock described it as the "'easiest-way-of-putting-it' letter, which in effect gave notice to the convention leaders that, if they could agree on someone else satisfactory to the President, Mr. Roosevelt would make no greater effort to assist Mr. Wallace."[13]

Unlike Wallace, Byrnes, and others, the Missouri senator did not want the nomination. On July 13, just six days before the convention was to convene, Truman wrote to his wife, Bess, from Kansas City about an exchange with a *Kansas City Star* reporter named Roy Roberts. "Just gave Mr. Roberts a tough interview saying I didn't want the Vice Presidency. Mr. Roberts says I have it in the bag if I don't say no—and I've said it as tough as I can."[14] Indeed, Truman had pledged his support to Byrnes. In another exchange with reporters in Chicago on July 19—the opening day of the convention—the senator, responding to a reporter's remark that as vice president he might "succeed to the throne," insisted, "Hell, I don't want to be president."[15] "I'm satisfied with where I am," he told another.[16] That night from Truman's room in Chicago's Stevens Hotel, Hannegan placed a call to Roosevelt on the West Coast. Roosevelt asked Hannegan, "Have you got that fellow lined up yet?" to which the chairman replied he had not. "Well, tell the Senator," Roosevelt shouted, "that if he wants to break up the Democratic party by staying out, he can; but he knows as well as I what that might mean at this dangerous time in the world. If he wants to do it, anyway, let him go ahead." The president then slammed down the phone. The senator was stunned. "Well, if that's the situation," he told Hannegan, "I'll have to say yes. But why the hell didn't he tell me in the first place?"[17]

The second day of the convention also witnessed the nominations for president. There was never any real doubt that Roosevelt would be granted a fourth campaign. On the evening of July 20, the roll call began, and Roosevelt's name was placed in official nomination by Senator Alben Barkley of Kentucky, a feisty Democrat who had, on occasion, broken with the president on domestic issues. Roosevelt, Barkley declared, was "endowed with the intellectual boldness of Thomas Jefferson, the indomitable courage of Andrew Jackson, the faith and patience of Abraham Lincoln, the rugged integrity of Grover Cleveland, and the scholarly vision of Woodrow Wilson."[18] A 30-minute floor demonstration followed Barkley's speech, and then Roosevelt's name was seconded by four others, including Vice President Wallace, who described the president as "the greatest liberal in the history of the US" and as "the most experienced military strategist" to ever occupy the presidency.[19]

Wallace's speech was preceded by one from Mrs. Fred T. Nooney, a delegate from Florida, who placed the name of Virginia senator Harry Byrd into nomination. He was, Nooney said, a man of integrity and courage who fully believed "in the principles of democracy as laid down by our forefathers, those great lawmakers of our nation, who firmly and unswervingly believed that a President of these United States should serve no more than two terms in office." "I think it is time," she concluded, "to go back to Virginia, the cradle of Democracy, for a true Democratic President to lead us out of the maze of red tape and centralized bureaucratic governmental control."[20] Byrd's nomination was shortly thereafter seconded by the Mississippi, Texas, and Virginia delegations. Byrd, however, had not consented to his name being placed in nomination and posed no serious challenge to the president. Roosevelt easily won the nomination on the first ballot, receiving 1,086 votes to Byrd's 89.[21]

That night, July 20, Roosevelt delivered his acceptance speech to the convention. Unlike previously, he did not accept from the convention hall. Instead, he addressed enthusiastic Democrats live and over the radio from an undisclosed location. Six days earlier, he had departed Hyde Park, making his way by rail to Marine Base, San Diego, where, in a small, specially equipped train car, he planned to officially accept his party's nomination before traveling, covertly, by cruiser to Pearl Harbor. Accompanying Roosevelt were Admiral Ross T. McIntire (White House physician), Samuel Rosenman (speechwriter), Elmer Davis (head of the Office of War Information), Dr. Howard Bruenn (heart specialist), and Grace Tully (the president's secretary), among a few others. As the president prepared to deliver his speech, moving-picture and still cameras and radio broadcasting equipment were brought into the tiny railcar to document the event.

Meanwhile, on the convention floor in Chicago, delegates listened to writer Quentin Reynolds introduce the president. Reynolds, who had just returned from visiting with troops, spoke of soldiers' hopes for the future. "Your sons know this," he said. "[T]hey know that all of America has contributed to making the victory possible. But they also know one other thing. They know that this mighty achievement . . . was accomplished under the leadership of their Commander-in-Chief and ours—Franklin D. Roosevelt." Then, amidst thunderous applause, Chairman Jackson announced: "Ladies and gentlemen of the Convention: the President of the United States!"[22]

"Mr. Chairman, Ladies and Gentlemen of the Convention, My Friends," the president began. "I have already indicated to you why I accept the nomination that you offered me—in spite of my desire to retire to the quiet of private life. You in this Convention are aware of what we have sought to gain for the Nation, and you have asked me to continue." Roosevelt then announced that he would not campaign "in the usual sense." "In these days of tragic sorrow, I do not consider it fitting. And besides, in these days of global warfare, I shall not be able to find the time." He did, however, qualify the statement, adding that he would "feel free to report to the people the facts about matters of concern to them and especially to correct any misrepresentations."[23]

Overall, Roosevelt's speech was nonpartisan in nature and aimed at highlighting his role as commander-in-chief. Elegant and above the fray, the president told his listeners that he was presently at a naval base performing his duty under the Constitution. "The war waits for no elections," he declared. "Decisions must be made—plans must be laid—strategy must be carried out. They do not concern merely a party or a group. They will affect the daily lives of Americans for generations to come." He then pledged himself to three goals: to win the war, to form an international organization with armed forces to prevent another war, and to provide returning veterans and all Americans with employment and decent standards of living.[24] In a long series of "They will decide" sentences, he then cited his administration's record in both foreign and domestic policy. "They will decide on the record—the record written on the seas, on the land, in the skies. They will decide on the record of our domestic accomplishments in recovery and reform since March 4, 1933, and they will decide on the record of our war production and food production—unparalleled in all history, in spite of the doubts and sneers of those in high places who said 'It can't be done.'"

Roosevelt then ended his speech by doing two things that were very uncharacteristic for him—he admitted mistakes and he read a quote. In an attempt to preempt Republican attacks that he was unprepared for war in December 1941, Roosevelt admitted, "We have made mistakes. Who has not? Things have not always been perfect. Are they ever perfect in human affairs?" No, but the objective, he insisted, remained clear, and that was to win the war and secure a lasting peace for generations to come. The quote he read was from Abraham Lincoln's Second Inaugural Address, delivered after the nation's last wartime election. Assuring voters that, like Lincoln, he too looked forward to the coming peace, he closed by reading:

> with firmness in the right, as God gives us to see the right, let us strive on to finish the work we are in; to bind up the Nation's wounds; to care for him who shall have borne the battle, and for his widow, and his orphan—to do all which may achieve and cherish a just and lasting peace among ourselves, and with all nations.[25]

The convention hall erupted in prolonged applause. Meanwhile, inside Roosevelt's special railcar, a photographer snapped what turned out to be a very unfortunate and unflattering picture of the president. With his mouth open—probably in mid-speech—Roosevelt's face looked, as *Time* observed, "gaunt and slack, [and] his eyes and cheeks hollow."[26] Not surprisingly, the photograph soon made itself into print, and as one White House intimate observed, "started tongues wagging . . . all through the United States."[27]

After the president's speech, party leaders in Chicago prepared for the vice presidential vote the following day, Friday, July 21. Their plan to put Truman over the top was twofold. One was to release Hannegan's note from

FDR (postdated July 19) that stated he would "be very glad to run with either" Truman or Douglas. The letter was printed in the Friday morning (July 21) newspapers and, of course, generated much excitement. The other was to spread the word, delegation to delegation, that Roosevelt was convinced Truman would cost him fewer votes than any other candidate. That evening—after the formal nominations of Wallace, Truman, and others—the roll call began. On the first ballot, Wallace received 429 1/2 votes, just 160 votes short of the necessary 589. Truman came in second with a strong 319 1/2 votes. On the second ballot, which occurred immediately after the first, Truman picked up support and secured the nomination, receiving 1,031 votes to Wallace's 105. Chairman Jackson then announced, "Will the next Vice President of the United States come to the rostrum? Will Senator Truman come?" Truman made his way to the stage and reading from a sheet of paper said: "Honor. I've never had a job I didn't do with all I have. I shall continue in the new capacity as I have in the US Senate, to help the commander-in-chief to win the war and save the peace. I have always been a supporter of Franklin D. Roosevelt in domestic and foreign policy and I shall continue to do just that with everything I have as V.P."[28]

Truman proved to be a good choice, but he too was not without some flaws. He was, for example, associated with the corrupt Kansas City boss Tom Pendergast and, as such, was viewed by some as small, petty, and not especially bright. The Republican nominee had made his career on fighting corruption, and some Democrats feared that Truman would play into Dewey's "campaign story." Also, the senator was a very dull formal speaker. He was at his best unscripted, but an unscripted Truman was an invitation to disaster. Listening to the Democratic convention from Albany, Thomas Dewey told a visitor that he was pleased with Roosevelt's selection of Truman. "Why, Herb [Brownell] ought to send him a check for that," Dewey joked. "Truman will help us more than he'll help Roosevelt."[29]

CHAPTER 13

Thomas Dewey and the Making
of a Wartime Campaign

Republicans had reason for cautious optimism in 1944. Although the president was certain to carry the labor vote, the Solid South, and "the millions of Federal officeholders" (a group *The Saturday Evening Post* compared to the "lice of Egypt"), the 1942 midterm had revealed that Republicans could begin with a base of support of about 20 million votes. If the GOP could add approximately 10 million independent votes to its column in 1944, a Republican victory, party leaders believed, was very possible. Specifically, Republicans sought to target the middle class, small businessmen, white-collar workers, housewives, and farmers. "If these groups are at last convinced that we need a national house-cleaning," *The Saturday Evening Post* observed in July 1944, "Governor Dewey will win."[1]

As political scientist Hadley Cantril observed in an essay for *Public Opinion Quarterly* that fall, Dewey did in fact have a chance of offsetting Roosevelt's wartime advantages and achieving a November upset. For one, many Americans might think (by Election Day) that the war was already won, and that it was time for a fresh start at home. Also, Cantril wrote, "for most people, international affairs are not nearly as important as domestic affairs—the immediate day-to-day, bread-and-butter problems of jobs, wages, and personal security." Indeed, within a postwar, domestic primacy framework, the playing field was more level. In an Office of Public Opinion Research (OPOR) poll in August, asking "After the war, which man do you think would do the best job of running our affairs here in this country," 46 percent of those surveyed said Roosevelt, and 43 percent said Dewey. In that same poll, when voters were asked which party they felt would bring the greatest postwar prosperity and the greatest number of jobs, 38 percent indicated the Republicans, and 34 percent the Democrats. Most promising for Dewey was a Gallup poll in July that indicated 50 percent of those surveyed would vote for him if the war in both Europe and the Pacific was over. Only 40 percent said they would vote for FDR in such a scenario.[2]

Following the Republican National Convention, Dewey worked quietly behind the scenes, laying the foundation for the fall campaign. A key to electoral success, he believed, was party unity—something conspicuously absent in 1940. Indeed, in what the *New York Times* called a "pep talk" before national committeemen in late June, Dewey stressed the necessity for intraparty harmony and cooperation in "the gigantic effort we will make . . . toward the saving of the Republic and the winning of the war." Democrats and the Roosevelt campaign, he warned, would undoubtedly seek to divide them. "You can be sure that they are experts at division," he said. "They have been creating the appearance of division among the American people for years. They will now try to create division in the party. They will not succeed."[3] Throughout July and August, Dewey developed the themes, organization, and strategies that he hoped would carry him to victory that November. His chief message, which he insisted should be "repeated and repeated," was that "It is time for a change."[4]

Several themes soon emerged to support that message. One was that a change of administrations—even during war—was both needed and okay. "We can risk an election," he told supporters in Albany on July 1, "because to us that means we are free men and women. We are going to keep the things we are fighting for and strengthen them by having an election in these times. . . . As a result of this campaign we will prove that in the process of fighting a total war this country can preserve its sacred free processes and become stronger as a result of an election."[5] Speaking to reporters shortly after Democrats left Chicago, Dewey—alluding to the dropping of Wallace a few days before—added that the argument that the country should not "trade horses in midstream . . . was demolished in Chicago when they changed one-half of the horse."[6]

The governor also highlighted community, the American spirit, and freedom. Speaking on July 7 before eight hundred of his neighbors in Pawling, New York, Dewey—relaxed and emotionally moved—insisted that "it is the basic tradition of our country that if our neighbors need something we turn out and help them." Americans, he added, lived in "mutual friendship, without intolerance, without distrust, without even a vestige of violence; without ever expressing ourselves in a nasty or derogatory way about opinions and beliefs of our neighbors." It was this essence of the country that America was fighting for in the war—"to keep our communities, the communities that we love, thus free, and always free, of dictation and overbearing dominance or any kind of oppression, either from business, labor, or government." Ultimately, he concluded, "We are fighting to keep this country of ours free and to keep our people just like our people here in Pawling."[7]

Another theme emphasized by Republicans was that the next administration would be a peacetime administration. "This should be said over and over again," Dewey instructed advisor Stanley High in early September.[8] The chief problem for a President Dewey, one RNC pamphlet advised campaign participants that fall, would not be what America requires to win the war "but what America will require after the war is won."[9] Similarly, Dewey wanted to dispel any notion that "changing horses in midstream" was incompatible with obtaining victory in the war. After all, he wrote High, Great Britain changed governments earlier in the war, and in many states across America since 1941, Republicans had replaced Democrats. In both cases, the war effort was strengthened "and thereby speeded victory."[10]

In addition, Dewey stressed "jobs—jobs—jobs" and the failure of Roosevelt and the New Deal. "Every speech should be an *attack* speech," RNC literature instructed supporters. "We have to have hardhitting, down-to-earth, chapter-and-verse material showing how flagrantly . . . the New Deal has failed."[11] Dewey, then, indicted the administration for bureaucratic inefficiency and a tax burden that was "unendurable" and harmful to small business. He also charged that the administration was determined to keep servicemen in the military after the war. "They have been saying for six months," Dewey wrote that summer, "that they intend to keep the young men in the Army because there will be no jobs. We propose to bring them home at the earliest practical moment and leave occupation of our defeated enemies to volunteers."[12]

The campaign also stressed the takeover of the Democratic Party by "the bosses of the corrupt big-city machines and the radical left wingers who are closer to communism than to any other political philosophy."[13] Specifically, Republicans highlighted the influence of Sidney Hillman and his CIO-PAC at the Democratic convention. On July 25, just four days after Democrats adjourned in Chicago, Arthur Krock of the *New York Times* wrote an article entitled "The Inflammatory Use of a National Chairman." In the piece, Krock examined what he called "one of the deepest controversies of the convention"—the selection of Truman over Wallace and Byrnes for the vice presidential nomination. According to Krock, the whole affair damaged the Democratic effort in 1944, producing internal party discord—especially with the followers of Wallace and Byrnes. Ultimately, he noted, blame rested solely with "the one man who controls the Democratic party—the President." Convinced he would live forever, Krock argued that Roosevelt met with party leaders, including DNC chair Robert Hannegan, that summer to discuss the vice presidency, and casually instructed them to "clear everything with Sidney [Hillman]."[14]

Although he had some of the facts wrong—apparently Roosevelt said "Clear *it* with Sidney"—and did not know the maneuvering that accompanied the preliminaries to and the course of the convention, Krock was right about the role labor (in the person of Hillman) played in the vice presidential pick, and what it did to Byrnes's candidacy. The Democratic National Committee immediately issued a denial, insisting that "No such thing was ever said by the President.... [I]t was never uttered."[15]

Republicans seized on the story immediately. Ford Bond, director of the Republican Radio Campaign, quickly released a one-minute radio announcement denouncing the CIO-PAC's "stranglehold on the New Deal party." Cartoons, jingles, and flyers were also prepared for publication. One cartoon, for example, was entitled "In His Side Pocket" and depicted a smiling Hillman placing a donkey in his front, dollar-sign-adorned suit pocket. An RNC flyer, meanwhile, described Hillman as so powerful that he could—from "a guarded hotel room in Chicago"—issue orders to Democratic leaders "and knock the assistant President [Byrnes] off his perch as Vice Presidential candidate of a party of which ... [he] is not even a member."[16] A Republican jingle set to the tune of "Good Night, Ladies" that declared:

Good night, Perkins,
Good night, Ickes,
Good night, Browder

You're leaving us at last.
Pack your grip and roll along,
Roll along, roll along,
Pack your grip and roll along,
And clearing with Sidney is past![17]

Finally, Dewey instructed his surrogates to emphasize his own vigor and administrative abilities over an administration that was tired, worn-out, and old. "It cannot be said too often," he wrote, "that what Thomas E. Dewey offers is a Get-up and Get-Going American Future . . . [and] that this year we can end our wanderings in the New Deal's Defeatist Wilderness."[18] This contrast with the Roosevelt administration was significant, he believed. Indeed, speaking before a hometown crowd in Owosso, Michigan, in early September, Dewey stressed "that by bringing a fresh, a new and courageous administration to this country which believes in the United States and in its future we can strengthen our opportunity for a great peace."[19]

In Tulsa that same month, he told supporters that he would go to Washington and give it "the largest and best house cleaning that anybody ever did." He would, he promised, "clean house on those political satellites which have fastened themselves on your pocketbooks and mine for twelve years. I should like to get rid of the wasters . . . [and all] the elegant collection of loafers."[20] Voters, an RNC study observed that summer, in fact desired "a return to character and integrity in government and in the men who govern. . . . This year the American people want a return to a leadership that has deep moral convictions and the faith of our forebears. There should be a great emphasis on those things which, on the deeper levels of life, really matter."[21]

A *Dewey-Bricker Song Sheet*, set to the tune of "The Battle Hymn of the Republic," synthesized and attempted to popularize the campaign's main themes:

> They say to change your horse while in the middle of the stream,
> Is not the smartest thing to do, but this can plain be seen,
> A horse that's run twelve years should be retired to pastures green,
> So vote Republican.
>
> Vote for Dewey and for Bricker,
> Win the war and do it quicker,
> Vote for Dewey and for Bricker,
> And keep our Country free.
>
> They both are honest, capable, and men of proven worth,
> Their heads are clear, their minds are strong, their feet are on the earth,
> They're trained to guide our destiny, they'll put our country first,
> So vote Republican.[22]

Dewey also used the post-convention, pre–Labor Day period to meet with his vice presidential running mate, John Bricker. The vice presidential campaign, like the presidential one, was a relatively new phenomenon in 1944. One of the first vice presidential candidates to wage a forceful campaign was President William McKinley's running mate in 1900, Theodore

Roosevelt, who delivered over 650 speeches to an estimated 3 million people.[23] Other early, active vice presidential candidates included Democrat Franklin Roosevelt in 1920 and Republican Charles Dawes in 1924. The two vice presidential candidates in 1944, Bricker and Truman, possessed feisty temperaments and waged energetic campaigns. Both too were used by their campaigns to attack the other and to energize their respective bases. Both seemed to relish their roles.

On July 26, Bricker met with Dewey at the governor's mansion in Albany, and afterward took questions from reporters. The meeting was an opportunity for the two men not only to discuss the campaign but to provide a photo opportunity for the press. While Dewey was relaxed and affable, Bricker—very humble anyway, and well aware that Dewey's staff held him in low regard and had preferred Earl Warren for vice president—seemed uncomfortable. He snapped irritably at the press, and in a response to a reporter's question, he stumbled, allowing that he would welcome the support of anyone interested in defeating Roosevelt. "'That's how elections are won,' he casually explained. Asked if that view extended to the extreme racist Gerald L.K. Smith of Shreveport, who was in the process of organizing his own presidential campaign, Bricker responded affirmatively, adding that Smith's vote would 'count like all the rest.'"[24]

A few days later, Smith announced that Bricker would be his vice presidential running mate. "I had paid little attention to Gerald L.K. Smith or his movement until last night, when he associated my name with him and his movement," Bricker told reporters in St. Louis. "I shall not have my name used in any such connection. I hate demagoguery, religious intolerance and racial prejudice. They can destroy our free government as they have around the world. I shall fight them as long as I am in public office and as long as I live."[25] Similarly, Dewey issued a statement characterizing Smith as "one of those rabble rousers who, like Adolf Hitler, makes racial prejudice his stock-in-trade. His contemptible attempt to associate himself with Governor Bricker is a sinister effort to smear the Republican candidate for Vice President."[26] Following the Smith debacle, Bricker began stumping throughout most of the 48 states.

In sharp contrast to Dewey, Bricker understood how to excite a crowd. In late summer, Brownell planned a grueling schedule for the Ohio governor, which, in the end, resulted in over 15,000 miles traveled and over 200 speeches delivered. Ultimately, Bricker was used for three things. First, he was the attack dog. Dewey felt uncomfortable in such a role. Thus, Bricker attacked New Dealers and Communists throughout the fall, in contrast to Dewey's more policy-oriented speeches. This enabled Dewey to appear above partisan politics and appeal to independents who had supported Roosevelt in the past. Second, Bricker, on the attack, generated energy among the party faithful—especially among conservatives, who possessed a strong dislike for Roosevelt and the New Deal. Dewey's low-key strategy risked boring these voters into apathy. Someone, then, was needed to motivate them to the polls. Bricker's campaign filled that need. A gifted speaker, he rallied the party faithful wherever he went. Indeed, after the election that November, Herbert Hoover told Bricker "that your speeches and your work in the campaign were magnificent. It saved a much worse defeat."[26] And third, Bricker actively sought to win the "middle" states of the "South": Kentucky, West Virginia, Tennessee, Oklahoma, and Missouri. These states, the Dewey team believed, had the potential to swing Republican. In a close election, winning one or more of these typically Democratic states could make the difference.

On September 9, Bricker delivered his "acceptance speech" for vice president before the Indiana Republican Editorial Association in French Lick, Indiana. It was—like all his speeches that fall—a scathing indictment of the New Deal. The issue of 1944, Bricker insisted, was "Shall the United States continue to be a republic?" Overall, he criticized the administration for abuse of power, confused lines of authority, duplication of effort, inadequate fiscal controls, loose personal practices, and bureaucratic arrogance. He also railed against the communists and the CIO-PAC. The Roosevelt administration, he charged, had—with the "sinister support of notoriously corrupt political machines," such as Sidney Hillman's CIO-PAC—committed "cold, calculated, and deliberate acts" to undermine the Constitution. "It is time," he concluded, "to elect a President who will clear everything, not with Sidney, but with Congress and the American people."[27]

Dewey also used this pre–Labor Day period to work the party organization and strengthen his ties to Republican governors. In early August, he convened a two-day GOP Governors Conference in St. Louis. These governors represented three-fourths of the American people, and 314 electoral votes—more than enough to win the presidency. As Herbert Brownell later remembered, "Each [governor] . . . was really the active head of the Republican campaign effort, and sometimes the state people disregard the national campaign and spend most of their time trying to elect the state ticket. . . . We also wanted them to see Governor Dewey in action. Many of them didn't know him very well personally. We thought if they could see him at close range, see his dynamic qualities, see how he was organizing the campaign, that they'd have more of a personal interest in seeing him succeed."[28] Furthermore, as a "Strictly Confidential" radio bulletin from the RNC to the state committees explained that August, "We believe a discussion of local issues by the candidate for the presidency will let the people of your state know that he is familiar with them and how he thinks on them."[29]

The specific purpose of the conference was to articulate a Republican vision for postwar domestic concerns. While the Roosevelt administration was criticized, the overall result was a detailed statement of policy on reconversion and postwar jobs, veterans, affairs, highways, public works, public lands, the National Guard, agriculture, unemployment compensation, and insurance. The governors announced support for the G.I. Bill of Rights, a federal highway program, public works projects in times of national economic crisis, state regulation and control over insurance businesses, and a state-led improvement and extension of unemployment compensation.[30] Although it was not published in book form, the GOP governors program did represent the Dewey-Bricker plan for America in 1944.

Another pre–Labor Day concern for Republicans that the Dewey campaign addressed was foreign policy. The war and postwar planning issues were obvious disadvantages to Dewey, who had no military experience. To offset this problem and even preempt Roosevelt's expected strategy of concentrating on the war, Dewey—with the help of his chief foreign policy advisor, John Foster Dulles—worked to create a "bipartisan" statement on postwar foreign policy (namely, debate on a postwar world organization) that would in essence remove the issue from the campaign.

The backdrop for the implementation of this strategy was the Dumbarton Oaks Conference, which was to meet in Washington that fall and make preliminary plans for a permanent postwar international organization (the future United Nations). On August 16, Dewey issued a statement from Albany, expressing deep disturbance over recent reports indicating that conference members—the United States, Great Britain, the Soviet Union, and China—planned to "dominate the world by force and through individual agreements as to spheres of influence." That the Allies had developed overwhelming power over their enemies did not, he argued, "give us the right to organize the world so that we four will always be free to do what we please while the rest of the world is made subject to our coercion. That would be the rankest form of imperialism. Such a proposal would be rejected by the American people."

In a departure from his controversial comment to reporters at Mackinac the previous year—in which he spoke of a permanent postwar alliance with Great Britain—Dewey hoped to bridge the gap between himself and the defeated Wendell Willkie, whose One World concept was grounded in the idea of self-determination, and who had yet to endorse the governor. He also hoped to garner support among American voters with ethnic ties to "smaller"

Eastern European nations like Poland. "The problem of future peace has two aspects," Dewey continued. One related to the defeat of Germany and Japan and the other to the promotion of postwar peace. As to Germany and Japan, Dewey insisted that they must be "wholly and conclusively defeated. More than that, they must be rendered permanently powerless to renew tyranny and attack." The achievement of those goals, he acknowledged, rested in the unity and power of the four Allies. However, as to the promotion of postwar peace, the Allies must not sink into the abyss of power politics but "rise to a new high level of cooperation and joint effort among respected and sovereign nations to work for and to preserve the peace of the world through all the years to come, based on freedom, equality, and justice."[31]

Secretary of State Cordell Hull was alarmed by Dewey's statement and the following morning issued a statement of his own, insisting that the governor had misconstrued what was planned for Dumbarton Oaks. "Governor Dewey can rest assured that the fears which he expressed in his statement are utterly and completely unfounded." The purpose of the conference, the secretary said, was to discuss the most feasible and desirable methods of establishing the kind of organization envisaged in the Moscow Declaration and US Senate resolution (the Connally Resolution). Furthermore, the conference was merely "preliminary to similar discussion and early conference among all the United Nations and other peace-loving nations, large and small." Responding to reporters' questions, Hull added that he would welcome a conference with the Republican nominee to "straighten out any points connected with the postwar organization and a nonpartisan approach to it."[32]

The following day, August 18, Dewey sent a telegram to Hull, informing the secretary that he was accepting the offer, and that he had designated John Foster Dulles as his representative. In addition, Dewey stated that he was "convinced that every effort to organize both temporarily and permanently for the establishment of lasting peace should be accelerated," and that he was happy to extend his fullest cooperation to the end that the result should be wholly *bi-partisan* and should have the united support of the American people.[33] Hull received Dewey's message while in a cabinet meeting at the White House. Roosevelt, the secretary later recalled, agreed that he should send a reply agreeing to meet with Dulles, but he expressed skepticism regarding any nonpartisan agreement with leading Republicans.[34]

After receiving Hull's reply on August 19, Dewey and Dulles met with reporters in Albany and elaborated on their views of world organization and postwar security. The looming question of the day, they said, was determining whether the problem of controlling Germany and Japan would be a world organization task or a regional one. If it was a world organization task, Dulles explained, then "you almost necessarily have to have a Four Power control of that world organization, because the four great powers who win this victory are not going to take any chances with the fruits of victory, of losing them through turning the control of Germany and Japan over to a world organization which is so diffuse and general in its organization that there cannot be assurance that the terms of the peace would be carried out." That scenario, they argued, was unacceptable because it would lead to the Four Powers controlling the world body, and thus the world. The positive alternative, they insisted, was for control of the defeated nations to be the task of the four big powers *and* certain regional and liberated nations. For example, in the case of Germany, liberated countries like France, Belgium, Poland, and the Netherlands, partnering with the United States, Great Britain, and the Soviet Union, would assume certain specific tasks in controlling the defeated Reich. Japan, meanwhile, would be controlled by China, the United States, and Great Britain. The Soviet Union might play a role there too should it join the war in the Pacific.[35]

The meeting between Dulles and Hull took place in Washington the following Wednesday, August 23. Dulles, suffering from a nerve ailment in his foot, was in excruciating pain and on crutches. He was in such discomfort that he could not travel by train or plane. Accordingly, Dewey arranged for him to travel to Washington in a state vehicle—an act that was roundly criticized in the press. Washington columnist Drew Pearson, for example, chastised the governor during a Sunday night broadcast for allowing Dulles, who literally had to be driven door to door wherever he went in Washington, to waste rationed gasoline. Pearson insisted that he had seen Dulles himself on the street and that he had looked quite fit. "The truth was," Dewey later recalled, "that Foster was in such bad shape that he was going on two crutches to every meeting, and when he got to the home of the friend he was staying with, he got into the house on his crutches and went upstairs on his knees. . . . He belonged in a hospital—where he was, before long."[36]

The Hull-Dulles discussions lasted for three days. In their first meeting Hull presented Dulles with the administration's latest draft of the proposed United Nations Charter and a four-page memorandum summarizing the charter's provisions. Overall, the organization was open to membership of all peace-loving countries, large and small, on the basis of their sovereign equality. All members were equally represented and voted as equals except in budgetary matters, where the vote would be proportioned to each nation's financial contributions. All members were likewise eligible to serve on the Four Powers–led Executive Council (a precursor to the Security Council) and to participate in elections to the body. In fact, as to the makeup of the Executive Council, there were more small states than large ones. Although the "Big Four" had veto power in the use of force, they could not undertake any coercive action by themselves. Finally, all member nations were to contribute armed forces and facilities in accordance with their respective capacities to undertake any kind of joint action.

In addition, both men were in agreement on the basic proposition that it was important to create a world organization that was supported by all Americans regardless of party. Also, they both agreed that such an effort would be unsuccessful if it had a partisan—in this case, Democratic—label attached to it. They disagreed, however, on which foreign policy matters—aside from the world organization—should be removed from partisan debate. Hull wanted an agreement broad enough to cover not only the creation of "the United Nations" but also all subjects relating to the future peace, including the controversial arrangements that might be made with the Soviet Union for the future of Poland. Dulles, of course, was adamantly opposed to any such broad agreement. For him and Dewey, the important issue was to forge a "bipartisan" approach solely to the creation of the United Nations. In the end, Hull and Dulles agreed to disagree (or at least be vague) on this point. Their public statement released on their last day of meetings, August 25, read:

> The Secretary maintained the position that the American people consider the subject of future peace as a nonpartisan subject which must be kept entirely out of politics.
>
> Mr. Dulles, on behalf of Governor Dewey, stated that the Governor shared this view on the understanding, however, that it did not preclude full public nonpartisan discussion of the means of attaining a lasting peace.[37]

The word "nonpartisan" in the above statement was also the subject of great debate between the two men. Dulles preferred the use of the word "bipartisan," implying that both parties would be involved on a political basis in policy making toward the UN organization. Hull, believing this to be an attempt at gaining political advantage, insisted instead upon the more general "nonpartisan," meaning that neither party would be involved in that policy making on a political basis. In addition, Hull maintained that "under our constitutional structure, we could not have both parties sharing the responsibility. The party in power had the responsibility for the execution of foreign policy. This responsibility could not be delegated. The opposition party ... had the moral responsibility not to base its opposition, if any, to our proposals for the United Nations organization on partisan grounds."[38] After several hours of discussion, Dulles finally agreed to the word "nonpartisan."

The result of these discussions, Dewey wrote the secretary of state on August 25, "constituted a new attitude toward the problem of peace."[39] Hull replied in agreement on September 4, adding that the discussions and Dewey's letter "constituted a heartening manifestation of national unity on the problem of establishing an international peace and security organization." He then suggested to Dewey that they might make their exchange of letters public "so that there might be fuller public understanding of our common ground on this important subject."[40]

Two days later, Dewey telephoned Hull and agreed to give the letters to the press. He also suggested a few changes in the proposed UN charter. One was that the right to bring a question to the attention of the General Assembly or the Security Council be extended to any state and not limited to member states. Another was that treaty conditions should be included in the subject matter that might be brought to the attention of the Assembly or the Council. Hull agreed to send them immediately to Under Secretary of State Edward Stettinius at Dumbarton Oaks with the request that they be incorporated into the final document then being formulated. None of the parties at the conference objected, and Dewey's suggestions were written into the final draft. Throughout the rest of the campaign Hull continued—through former German ambassador Hugh Wilson—to maintain contact with Dewey and Dulles. Although he had to remind Dewey on a few occasions that he too had played a role in initiating the nonpartisan agreement, Hull later acknowledged that the governor "uniformly rendered excellent service to the nonpartisan approach toward the United Nations."[41]

Hugh Gibson, a former diplomat and coauthor of several Herbert Hoover books and essays, was not so pleased with the arrangement. Writing to the former president in late August, Gibson lamented the Dewey outreach to Hull. Gibson believed the candidate should have avoided the issue at all costs, and he blamed the entire enterprise—which he described as "childish"—on Dulles. "I am told," Gibson continued, "all the opening speeches for the Dumbarton Oaks Conference were carefully rewritten in the light of Tom's first statement in order to stress the rights of small nations. If he had kept his lip buttoned they might well have stressed the role of the big fellows and given him a chance for a blast. In addition he would have been able to rip the hide off them for their hypocrisy in ignoring the rights of Poland and the Baltic States." Dewey's agreement with Hull, Gibson concluded, now "precluded [Dewey] from doing that and they will make a monkey of him."[42]

Gibson's and Hoover's complaints aside, the Hull-Dulles agreement to keep partisan politics out of the discussions on the creation of the United

Nations was remarkable in several ways. It prevented the topic of the United Nations from being engulfed—as it had at the end of the First World War—in furious Senate controversy and partisan attack. Hull did not want the Roosevelt administration to make the same mistakes as Woodrow Wilson had 25 years earlier. Wilson had been very partisan—especially during the wartime midterm elections of 1918—and had, as the war drew to a close, ignored Republicans and, to a most unfortunate end, excluded them from the peacemaking process. For his part, Dewey did not want his party to play once again the roles of vengeful antagonist, isolationist, and obstructionist. He genuinely believed—as his comments since 1941 had indicated—that the United States must have an internationalist foreign policy, and that post–World War II isolationism would spell the doom of the Republican Party.

From a campaign standpoint, the Hull-Dulles talks were remarkable in the political benefits they provided for the Dewey campaign. In one stroke Dewey was able to remove a subject divisive to his party from the political discourse while simultaneously centering the campaign on his perceived strength, domestic policy. Furthermore, as Senator Arthur Vandenberg shrewdly observed in late August, the meetings potentially robbed "the Administration of its campaign argument that it would 'break the continuity' of the peace negotiations if Roosevelt is defeated."[43]

As August gave way to September, Dewey was on the offensive and enjoying a small lead in the Labor Day polls. Writing to Hoover in mid-August, Herbert Brownell acknowledged that while "the months July and August are ... always the most difficult ones in these political campaigns," the Dewey campaign was nevertheless "confident that we have built up a good working team ... and have achieved considerable progress in uniting the party and arousing enthusiasm among the workers for our prospects of victory and the need for hard work."[44] Inside the White House, meanwhile, aides worried whether the president still had "that old campaign magic." He often seemed tired and depressed, and even disinterested. At the end of August, Roosevelt told Margaret Suckley, his archivist at Hyde Park, that he would not be surprised if Dewey won in November. Democrats, he said, seemed too confident of success and were thus "just not bothering to register for victory."[45]

CHAPTER 14

FDR—Commander-in-Chief

Democrats in 1944 interpreted the political landscape much differently than Republicans. For example, their studies of the party's 1942 decline revealed that Democratic setbacks were the result not of Republican popularity but of a falloff in voter participation. Only 28 million people voted in the 1942 elections, 8 million fewer than in 1938, and nearly 22 million fewer than in 1940.[1] This drop in participation, Democrats believed, reflected wartime social upheaval: "young men in the armed forces lacked the opportunity or incentive to cast absentee ballots, and war workers who had recently taken jobs in different states could not meet [one- and sometimes two-year] residency requirements."[2] Inconvenience and time away from work without pay were additional factors in the low participation levels of 1942. This decline in turnout hit Democrats, who relied heavily upon draft-age voters and the working classes, especially hard. "In district after district the Republican vote fell slightly or remained stable, but the Democratic vote dropped precipitously."[3] Victory in the 1944 presidential contest, Democrats concluded, depended primarily upon a high turnout of voters.

Several obstacles confronted Democrats in the area of voter turnout—obstacles they had been unable to overcome in the midterm elections two years earlier. One problem was that many young voters were serving overseas in the armed forces. In the midst of a global war, these young citizen-soldiers often lacked the opportunity or incentive to request and then cast absentee ballots. Another problem was that many wartime workers, as discussed earlier, were on the move in search of work in various war industries. If workers crossed state lines—and many did—they were confronted with residency requirements that hindered voting. For example, in 1944, five states demanded two years of residency to vote, while thirty-two others insisted on at least one year.[4]

Furthermore, workers who did meet residency requirements were often reluctant to forfeit wages by taking time off, and those working night shifts or overtime found voting an inconvenience. It did not help matters that many war plants were on the outskirts of towns, often requiring a timely and potentially costly commute. As the 1944 campaign season approached, Democrats, who relied heavily upon younger and working-class voters, were desperate to energize and activate eligible voters. DNC chairman Robert E. Hannegan, addressing the party's national convention that July, expressed this strategy publicly. "Our job," he said, "is to go to the people of America and lay the facts before them. It is to cite the record. It is to tell the simple truth. Our job is to see to it that our people are registered. It is to see to it that they vote. It is to work for as big a soldier vote as we can get. It is to go to the American people, person-to-person."[5] A key element of the president's reelection effort, then, was to motivate voters to go to the polls.

The Roosevelt campaign also sought to distance the president from partisan politics and stress instead his role as wartime commander-in-chief. Through the use of surrogates, pamphlets, and radio advertising, Roosevelt endeavored to win the election by presenting to the American people a platform of experience and accomplishment and the necessity of continuity in the war effort. Specifically, the Roosevelt campaign reminded voters of Herbert Hoover and the last time Republicans held power. Hoover and the Depression were always Democratic favorites in election years. In 1944, Democrats attempted to portray Dewey as a young Hoover. One Democratic poster entitled "Remember Me?" featured a large picture of Hoover flanked by two smaller ones of Dewey and Bricker. Its message was clear: "On With Roosevelt Or Back On The Rocks."[6]

Meanwhile, in a speech entitled "For What the Hell Should We Apologize?" (later published and distributed by the DNC), Mark Etheridge, publisher of the *Courier-Journal* and the *Louisville Times*, stressed the legislative accomplishments of the Roosevelt administration versus the promises of Dewey and the record of Hoover. Citing various pieces of alphabet legislation, Etheridge chided those Democrats, who occasionally spoke of the administration with a note of apology in their voices. "Is any Democrat," he asked, "ashamed that we took a banking structure which had had 5,770 failures in the four years of Hoover . . . and restored confidence, virtually eliminated failures and insured losses?" Were Democrats "not proud that through housing projects all over this country, we have taken people out of the squalor and filth of rat-infested slums and given them a chance to breathe good air and their children a chance to be something better than gutter rats? . . . Are we ashamed that we fed the poor and the unemployed? Are we ashamed that because of us, old people are drawing pensions all over the country?"[7]

A key figure in the Roosevelt campaign who was used to be a visible player for the administration on the campaign trail and to keep Dewey on the defensive was the Democratic nominee for vice president, Harry Truman. On August 18, Roosevelt met with Truman for the first time in the campaign. The two lunched on the lawn of the White House and discussed a long list of general topics, including the place and date of Truman's formal acceptance speech. In his memoirs, published in 1955, Truman recalled thinking a lot about the president's health in the fall of 1944 and wondered "whether President Roosevelt himself had had any inkling of his own condition." The only indication he had that the president might be aware of his failing health was in their White House meeting in August, when the president asked Truman how he was going to travel. "I told him I intended to cover the country by airplane," Truman remembered. "'Don't do that please,' he told me. 'Go by train. It is necessary that you take care of yourself.'"[8]

On the night of August 31, Truman delivered his first official speech of the campaign. Speaking in front of the old red brick courthouse in his birthplace of Lamar, Missouri, the senator declared—in an obvious reference to Dewey—that "Tomorrow's challenge is today's problem. The proven leadership of our successes must continue. The fortunes of the future for which our boys have fought, bled and died must not be endangered by entrusting them to inexperienced hands. There is no substitute for experience, which can be gained only through the years of application and service."[9] This issue of experience and trusted leadership was a recurring theme, and its irony was evidently lost on Truman—a man who was being groomed for the presidency and who had about as little foreign policy experience as the governor of New York.

Following his official "acceptance speech" at Lamar, "party leaders soon developed a grueling campaign schedule in which Truman would be the workhorse, crisscrossing the country to rouse the troops."[10] He traveled, as FDR wished, by rail, in an old combination sleeper and dining car called the *Henry Stanley*, and was accompanied by a small staff including Hugh Fulton as campaign manager and speechwriter; young Matt Connelly, an investigator for the Truman Committee, who was recruited to be "an all-around arrange-ments man"; and Paul A. Porter, a bright young liberal from Kentucky, who was the DNC's publicity director and was tapped to help with press rela-tions.[11] Beginning in early October and continuing through Election Day, Truman spoke in more than 15 states and 20 large cities, including New Or-leans, Los Angeles, Portland, Minneapolis, Milwaukee, Akron, Boston, New York, and Pittsburgh. Although an unexciting speaker, Truman hit at Dewey and the Republicans with great energy and zeal. "It was a very enthusiastic tour," he later remembered. "I stopped at every little stop where the train stopped. It was the first whistle stop tour, but it wasn't referred to as a whistle stop tour in those days."[12]

Like his Republican counterpart, Truman endured his own fair share of controversy and embarrassment. In late September—unwittingly conform-ing to the GOP's message that he was a machine crony—he told reporters, "I am a Jackson County organization Democrat and I'm proud of that. That's the way I got to be judge, a senator and the candidate for Vice President. A statesman is only a dead politician. I never want to be a statesman."[13] Then, in late October, while in Peoria—and shortly before his scheduled visit to Boston, where the Irish Catholic vote was at stake—the Truman campaign was rocked by Hearst news reports claiming: "Senator Took [Ku Klux Klan] Oath in 1922." The story, spread by an old enemy of the senator's from Mis-souri, was false. The charge, which Truman denounced as a lie, was easily put down, though the candidate and his staff did fail to disclose that he had once paid a $10 initiation fee.

Meanwhile, it was reported, correctly, that the candidate's wife, Bess, was on the Senate payroll. Truman was embarrassed and was roundly criticized. Republican Clare Booth Luce, whom the senator despised, began referring to Mrs. Truman as "Payroll Bess." The congresswoman also declared that "If, as Truman had said, his mother didn't bring him up to be a statesman, then she would not be disappointed."[14] Angry at the attack on his wife, Truman privately commented that Luce should spell her last name "L-O-O-S-E."[15]

The Roosevelt campaign also emphasized Dewey's reputation for oppor-tunism—something journalist John Gunther observed in 1946 to be a key cause of Dewey's lack of popularity in some political quarters. "Most Ameri-cans," Gunther noted, "like courage in politics; they admire occasional mag-nificent recklessness. Dewey seldom goes out on a limb by taking a personal position which may be unpopular on an issue not yet joined; every step is carefully calculated and prepared; he risks almost nothing; he will never try to steal second unless the pitcher breaks a leg."[16] Democrats hoped to exploit that perception by searching Dewey's public statements for errors and contraditions. One pro-Roosevelt pamphlet entitled "Cock-a-doodle Dewey" brought home this point:

Dewey or Don't He?

Lend Lease? "Don't like it. Let's ignore it."
Then "I'm against it!" Then "I'm for it!"
The Russians? "Horrid folk, don't touch 'em!"
A little later: "Love 'em, clutch 'em!"

The wind blows east. The wind blows west.
The Gallup Poll's the acid test.
What's his policy, what's his bent?
He wants to be our President.[17]

Another talking point pushed by the administration was the argument that the political and economic preparation for international peace and post-war security should be left to those who had been waging the war and had been in constant association with the Allies.[18] Democrats, then, implied that any fundamental change in the civilian government would imperil postwar security and give an opportunity, which the incumbents would not, to isolationists and economic "Tories" to turn back the clock of progress and invite World War III.[19] The safe—as well as deserved—course was to give a "vote of confidence" to the commander-in-chief, who had directed a successful war.[20]

In late July, Roosevelt traveled to Pearl Harbor and met with his top Pacific commanders, including General MacArthur and Admiral Chester Nimitz, to discuss strategy—something, critics charged, he could have done without leaving the White House. Indeed, from Albany, Dewey derisively referred to it as "Mr. Roosevelt's holiday."[21] Upon his return to the United States on August 12, Roosevelt—largely out of the public eye since July 20 and his acceptance speech from an undisclosed location—decided to address the nation from Bremerton Naval Yard in Washington state. Standing on the deck of a destroyer—and with Puget Sound as a backdrop—the president reported to the national radio audience on his just concluded Pacific trip "when nearly all the time I was within easy reach of enemy action."[22] The wartime backdrop of the speech was impressive. Roosevelt, the *New York Times* noted, stood "bareheaded and suntanned . . . under an upraised forward gun, surrounded by members of his military and naval staffs who had traveled with him."[23]

While Republicans viewed the speech as political and demanded equal radio time, reaction to the president's speech was generally positive. "[H] e seemed," *Time* observed, "healthier, more alert." While "his face still had the thin and careworn look it has worn for months, he was," the magazine added, "lightly tanned, and looked rested and fit."[24] The *New York Times*, meanwhile, described Roosevelt as "tanned and jovial."[25] In the 1946 *Nothing to Fear: The Selected Addresses of Franklin Delano Roosevelt*, editor B.D. Zevin referred to the speech itself—one that Roosevelt wrote himself—as a "vivid and detailed report of [the President's] voyage."[26] Speechwriter Samuel Rosenman, however, disagreed, describing the address in his own memoir as "a dismal failure"—"a rambling account" that was "ad-libbed . . . in a very ineffective manner."[27]

Listening to the speech over the radio, Rosenman "had a sinking sensation of concern that something must have happened to the President since I had left him in Hawaii. His voice and delivery seemed so different."[28] That speech, along with the unflattering photograph of Roosevelt in San Diego in late July, led many, Rosenman wrote, to conclude "that 'the old man is through, finished.' His friends and supporters of many years shook their heads sorrowfully and said, 'It looks like the old master has lost his touch. His campaigning days must be over. It's going to look mighty sad when he begins to trade punches with young Dewey.'"[29] Rosenman's concerns aside, the president's post-convention actions garnered approval from voters. Indeed, on August 17, just a few days after the speech at Bremerton, a *Fortune* poll found that Roosevelt enjoyed an eight-point lead over Dewey—up two points from the last poll taken four weeks earlier.[30]

The status of the president's health soon became a major issue in the presidential campaign—and one that certainly threatened to eclipse the commander-in-chief image that Democrats had been promoting. From late 1943 to early 1944, Roosevelt was plagued with colds and bronchial infections. He lost weight and came to look especially worn and tired. "I think all of us knew Franklin was far from well," the First Lady later recalled, "but none of us ever said anything about it—I suppose because we felt that if he believed it was his duty to continue in office, there was nothing for us to do but make it as easy as possible for him."[31] That spring, the president's physician, Ross T. McIntire, scheduled a thorough physical examination. On March 28, Howard G. Bruenn, a lieutenant commander in the Medical Corps and cardiology consultant to the Naval Hospital in Bethesda, Maryland, examined Roosevelt—the first cardiologist ever to do so. Bruenn diagnosed the president as having hypertensive heart disease—FDR's blood pressure at the time of exam was 188/105—cardiac failure (left ventricular), and acute bronchitis.[32]

Breunn advised McIntire that the president be placed on a regimen of bed rest, sedation, digitalization (treatment with digitalis to improve cardiac function), codeine for cough control, salt restriction, and weight loss. McIntire was shocked. "You can't do that," he said. "This is the President of the United States!"[33] Eventually, McIntire relented, and Bruenn's recommendations (with some modifications) were implemented. Roosevelt's blood pressure, however, continued to rise. On April 3 it was 210/108. The next day it was 226/118, and on April 5, 218/120.[34]

Roosevelt, perhaps unaware of the seriousness of his condition, announced his decision to seek a fourth term on July 10. No physician ever advised him not to seek reelection. In fact, McIntire reportedly even told the president that "With proper care and strict adherence to rules . . . [your] chances of winning through to 1948 . . . [are] good."[35] According to physician Hugh Evans, in a 2002 study on Roosevelt's health, the medical culture of the 1940s "generally promoted a lack of candor in discussing serious diseases. Illness or its progress was not customarily discussed with patients, unless they failed to comply with doctor's orders. Presidential health matters were assumed to be private, rarely reported frankly or with clinical detail."[36] Roosevelt never inquired, Evans noted, and neither Bruenn nor McIntire ever informed.

Ultimately, the American people were unaware of the true status of Roosevelt's health in 1944. The White House—wanting to portray the commander-in-chief as alert and fit—consciously conducted a misinformation campaign. In March, McIntire told reporters that Roosevelt "was in better health than at any time since he entered the White House."[37] In October, as speculation about the president's health intensified, McIntire added that "the President's health is perfectly O.K." and attributed Roosevelt's being underweight to dieting. The president, McIntire told reporters, was "proud of his flat—repeat f-l-a-t—tummy" and "doesn't want to get that bulge back."[38] DNC chair Robert Hannegan, meanwhile, insisted that Roosevelt—contrary to rumors—was "very vigorous, the picture of health."[39]

Even Truman, after meeting with Roosevelt in mid-August, told reporters that "The President looked fine and ate a bigger lunch than I did. He's still the leader he's always been and don't let anybody kid you about it. He's keen as a briar."[40] Privately, however, Truman was more candid, noting that "His hands were shaking and he talks with considerable difficulty. . . . It doesn't seem to be any mental lapse of any kind, but physically he's just going to pieces."[41] Truman wasn't the only concerned one close to Roosevelt. In mid-September, Secretary of War Henry Stimson confided to his diary that "I have been much troubled by the President's physical condition. He was distinctly not himself Saturday."[42]

In his 1993 memoir, *Advising Ike*, Herbert Brownell, RNC chair in 1944, recalled that "Although we did not fully know about the president's condition at the time ... we did know that the pictures of the president portrayed an ill and tired man." In light of Roosevelt's appearance and the rampant rumors about his health, the RNC's publicity director, Steve Hanigan, then "prepared an elaborate document for Governor Dewey's consideration, which made the president's failing health a major campaign issue and demanded full disclosure." Dewey considered it, Brownell remembered, but his advisors were divided on the issue. Congress was heavily Democratic, and so there would certainly be no congressional inquiry into the state of the president's health. Furthermore, the press seemed disinterested and did not do any investigative reporting on the subject. In the end, Dewey decided not to tackle the health issue directly, fearing a backlash in the wartime atmosphere. Hanigan resigned in protest.[43]

CHAPTER 15

"The Listening Campaign"

While Roosevelt emphasized his role as commander-in-chief, Dewey launched a month-long campaign swing around the country by rail. He would not whistle stop, however. That, he said, would be inappropriate under the wartime conditions. Indeed, swing voters, one Republican strategy paper noted that summer, were "looking for simple integrity . . . based not only on the impression of the nominee's record, but on the character of the nominee's message and the manner in which it is delivered." Specifically, they wanted someone "who will talk as a plain man, who will reveal calm competence, and a readiness to conduct the affairs of the United States in the constitutional way."[1] Dewey, then, planned to bypass many of the larger towns, as well as the large crowds and, in his major speeches—which he kept under 20 minutes—aim "at the radio audience, rather than those to whom he spoke directly."[2] While his main focus was listening (rather than talking) to business leaders and local machine Republicans, he also hoped to use his national addresses to establish the ruling issues for voters that fall.[3] On September 6, Dewey left Albany accompanied by his staff and about 70 journalists and embarked by train on what he called "the Listening Campaign."[4]

Several things characterized this "Listening Campaign." First, it coincided with what *Newsweek* called an "almost sullen silence . . . [and the] manifest avoidance of political discussion" across the country. Voters, the magazine added, were weary, cynical, and apathetic, betraying a "marked absence of enthusiasm for either [Dewey or Roosevelt]."[5]

Second, it was executed with "almost metronomic precision."[6] At every important stop, *Time* noted, the routine was the same: a short speech to the station crowd, a 25-car motorcade to the leading hotel, a half-hour press conference, followed by closed conferences with local party leaders, farmers, businessmen and later, as Dewey moved further west, ranchers and lumbermen. He met for 30 minutes—"no more, no less"—with each of these groups and followed the same procedure—briskly shaking hands all around and telling his guests, "Well, I'm here to learn what your problems are." He usually answered a few questions, "but mainly he just listened."[7]

And third, "the Listening Campaign" lacked warmth and traditional "backslapping informality." Indeed, *Time* called it a "strange kind of campaign," where the candidate's "deportment was precise and correct, at times even chill."[8] Years later, Herbert Brownell, RNC chair and a longtime Dewey friend and ally, recalled that at a rodeo in Nebraska, Dewey chose to bypass the opening ceremony in favor of going to a hotel and putting the finishing touches on his scheduled speech. "Instead of the big cheer that we had expected [when he finally arrived], he was booed, and the crowd completely overlooked the splendid speech he made on farm issues."[9]

While focusing greatly on small towns and local party organization, Dewey also visited large cities, including Philadelphia, Seattle, Portland, San Francisco, and Los Angeles, and delivered seven major policy addresses. His first was in Philadelphia on September 7, where, addressing a crowd of about 13,000 at Convention Hall, he laid the foundations for his case for election. With "total, smashing victory in sight," the next four years, Dewey insisted, would be largely peacetime years. Thus, the prospects of success as a nation at peace depended on whether or not the American people replaced an old, tired, and bickering administration with one that was fresh, young, vigorous, and competent. Specifically, he charged that the New Deal had failed to achieve economic recovery and had made a three-year depression last eleven years. Never, he added, was there "a worse job done in running our government. When one agency fails, the New Deal just piles another on and we pay for both. . . . Meanwhile, the people's business goes to pot and the people are the victims."[10]

Dewey also seized upon a remark by General Lewis Hersey, the director of the Selective Service System, about demobilization. Speaking to reporters in Denver on August 21, Hershey speculated on the "gradual release" of American soldiers following the war and declared that "It is cheaper to keep men in the Army than it is to set up an agency to take care of them when they are released."[11] Hershey's statement, which "did not represent Administration policy," initially generated little controversy.[12] The *New York Times* even interpreted it as "Hinting at a possible work relief program after the war."[13]

Dewey, however, translated the remark differently, telling supporters in Philadelphia that Hershey exposed the "defeatism" of the Roosevelt administration. Ultimately, he insisted, the 1944 campaign was one against an administration that had "lost faith in itself and in the American people"—one that was afraid of the peace (and a continuation of its own failed economic policies) and afraid of America. "I do not share that fear," Dewey declared. "There can be—there must be—jobs and opportunity for all, without discrimination on account of race, creed, color or national origin."[14]

According to *Chicago Sun* reporter Tom Reynolds, who was traveling with the campaign, the word for this stop was "apathy":

> The crowds on our arrival were hardly normal shopping crowds. Their chief salute was "where'd you get the gas?" The crowds that did gather were notable for being about 70 per cent women. The men are away at war or working on war jobs. The city GOP machine didn't fill the Convention hall—I counted 15 empty tiers of seats in the back. Dewey, himself, didn't think he did so well—his voice was so complicated acoustically by the bounce off those empty tiers.[15]

The intended audience, however, was the larger national radio audience, where on the whole Dewey's remarks were met with approval. "The Democrats," the *Elmira Star Gazette* concluded, "have found out that their perpetual candidate, Mr. Roosevelt, is not running against Hoover this time. Governor Dewey . . . made plain, blunt charges and accusations against the New Deal Party that will have to be answered; or the voters will be wondering why."[16] Alf Landon, meanwhile, called the Philadelphia speech "great," adding that "I think Mr. Roosevelt is going to get very tired of you before the campaign is over."[17]

The following day, September 8, Dewey delivered his first major address of the fall campaign on foreign policy in Louisville, Kentucky. While he repeated the charge that "The New Deal proposes to keep men in the Army after this war is over" (something the *Jamaica Press* called an "unfortunate indulgence in partisanship" in an otherwise "high level exposition"), the bulk of the speech dealt with "the immediate problems of victory" and "the long-term, world-wide problems of organized peace."[18] Overall, Dewey argued that "the military defeat of Germany and Japan must be complete and crushing," their leaders dealt with "promptly, justly and relentlessly," and their nations disarmed.[19] He also forthrightly rejected isolationism as a basic policy for the United States and encouraged a bipartisan approach to postwar peace efforts.

Furthermore, he expressed agreement on the basic contours of any postwar world organization, including the creation of both "a general assembly comprising all peace-loving nations of the world" and a small council made up of larger nations. This world organization, he noted, would repel military aggression through the use of collective action, the mobilization of international opinion, moral pressure, and economic sanctions. The mere repression of conflict, however, was not enough. A key to lasting peace, he insisted, was being "fair and upright in our dealings with the smaller nations." Indeed, "The people of Poland, of France, of the Low Countries, the people of Norway ... and all other peoples of good will," he said, "are entitled to full partnership" in the postwar world. "[M]ight," he added, "can never make right. The United States and "a few strong friends must not assume the right to rule the world. It is the common obligation of the mighty to make common cause with the less powerful in the interests of justice and peace for all."[20]

While the Louisville speech was generally well received, the New York Post complained that "Governor Dewey has a way of marching bravely toward a full declaration on a great public question and then stopping just short of it." Perhaps, the editorial speculated, it was because of "his passion for public opinion polls." Or, "Perhaps that is what he really wants—to be a common denominator, easy to fit into the calculations of men of many shades of opinion." Regardless, the Post was disappointed that he failed to address "the basic questions" of how to convince Germany that it was in its future interest to follow a peace instead of a war policy and how to neutralize for all of Europe the pressures that create wars. Dewey, the paper concluded, was "a friendly, vague wave of the hand toward the future."[21]

From Louisville, Dewey traveled to his hometown of Owosso, Michigan, where he received "a rootin'-tootin' old-time political reception" from 25,000 "howling supporters."[22] Accompanied by his wife and mother, Dewey spoke extemporaneously from the steps of City Hall, telling the throng that with the election of "a new and courageous administration"—one that "understands what real democracy is"—America "can release once again the mainsprings which come from the Main Streets of our towns."[23] The stakes in November were high. "In this election," he concluded, "lies the hope of continuance of our free system of government. In this election lies the hope of a peace that will not be the property of any one person or any one party. It is bigger than any of us."[24]

The Dewey campaign spent the next ten days traveling across the American Midwest, cultivating local leaders responsible for delivering the votes in their areas. These private talks with professionals, and "not the flat and routine public speeches," greatly enhanced Dewey's election prospects, making him, as one modern historian observed, "the most dangerous opponent Roosevelt had yet faced."[25] Constantly competing with war news, and with no major speech scheduled until September 18, Dewey made headlines during this phase of "the Listening Campaign" through skillful use of his press conferences. He also relaxed his ban on extemporaneous, rear platform speeches and became more aggressive. For example, during a press conference in Valentine, Nebraska, on September 13, he created great controversy when in response to a reporter's question he declared that General Douglas MacArthur's "talents [in the Pacific] should be given greater scope and recognition"—especially since he was "no longer a political threat to Mr. Roosevelt."[26] Generating controversy, however, was riddled with risks. Indeed, one general, writing in the *New York Tribune*, publicly rebuked the governor, calling his remarks a "disservice to the country" and "neither wise nor helpful."[27]

The next day, in Sheridan, Wyoming, Dewey described the Roosevelt administration's efforts to transform the rugged nearby Jackson Hole region into a national park as "characteristic of the deviousness of the New Deal and its lack of respect for the rights and opinions of the people affected."[28] The remark elicited a strong response from Secretary of the Interior Harold Ickes, "a master of polished invective," who accused Dewey of "beagle-like snuffing about for votes," charging that the Republican nominee was "willing to enter judgment on any compliant against the administration, even without hearing the evidence."[29] According to Ickes, the 221,610-acre monument was actually the result of an initiative by Dewey's "political godfather," Herbert Hoover, and not Roosevelt. "One trouble with Mr. Dewey," Ickes added, "is that he apparently knows so little about the West."[30] At a press conference in Coeur d'Alene, Idaho, on September 16, Dewey countered that in all his meetings with various Western representatives, he was impressed by the "universal opinion" that no one in Washington "knew or understood their problems." Asked specifically about Ickes, Dewey playfully responded that, if he were elected, "get[ting] rid" [of Ickes] would be an act very high on any list, and ... would be a high patriotic service."[31]

On September 18, Dewey delivered a major address in Seattle, making what *Time* called "a smashing attack" on Roosevelt's labor policy.[32] The president, Dewey insisted, had—through "delay, bungling, and incompetence"—left labor adrift. "There is," he declared, "no course, no chart, not even a compass. We move, when we move at all, to the shifting winds of the caprice of one man." Furthermore, labor relations were "smothered under a welter of

agencies, boards, commissions, and bureaus." Hoping to appeal to blue- col-
lar workers, Dewey reminded his audience that it had been a Republican
president, William Howard Taft, who created the Department of Labor. He
then outlined his own program for change, promising retention of the Wagner
Act, calling for the abolition of unnecessary bureaus and agencies, and pledg-
ing to appoint an active and able secretary of labor "from the ranks of labor."[33]

The next day, September 19, the Dewey campaign crashed—literally. At
11:50 a.m. (PWT), Dewey's train—en route to Portland—ploughed into the
rear of a Great Northern passenger express near the small town of Castle
Rock, Washington. Several passengers on both trains suffered minor inju-
ries. The governor and Mrs. Dewey were badly shaken but otherwise fine.
"The wreck was damned unpleasant," Tom Reynolds wrote Steve Early a few
days later. "I've traveled a quarter of a million miles with your boss [FDR]
and the worst I ever got was a hangover."[34] Dewey, meanwhile, pressed on
to Portland, where that night he spoke to a crowd of seven thousand in the
city's Ice Arena.

Oregon, like Washington and the other states Dewey had visited during
his "Listening Campaign," was "in a state of flux" and thus very much "on
the fence."[35] In the speech, which was both well delivered and well received,
Dewey—countering Democratic arguments that the team fighting the war
should also end it—hit hard at "the indispensable man" theme, declaring:
"Let's have no more of this pretense about indispensable men. There are no
indispensable men. If our Republic after 150 years of self-government is dependent upon the endless continuance of one man in office, then the hopes
which animated the men who fought for the Declaration of Independence
and the Constitution have indeed come to nothing. The peace and prosperity of America and of the world can never depend on one man."[36]

From Portland the Dewey Special traveled to San Francisco, where on
September 21, at Municipal Hall, Dewey addressed the issues of political
freedom and economic security. In doing so, he attempted to chart a middle way between the "false alternatives" of complete government control on
the one hand and "the reactionary philosophy of dog-eat-dog" on the other.
Overall, he promised to continue the best parts of the New Deal while in-
corporating old-fashioned Republican values such as economic opportunity
and honest and efficient government. "Whether we like it or not, and regardless of the party in power, government," he declared, "is committed to some
degree of economic direction."[37] Indeed, certain government measures to
influence broad economic conditions were both desirable and inevitable.
The postwar years, for example, would require the federal government to
stabilize interest rates, ensure widespread job opportunities in private enterprise, and support farm prices against the menace of collapse.

The old, pre–New Deal days, then, were gone and would "never come back again." What America needed, he insisted, was "a new point of view toward the relationship between government and the people. The role of government cannot be the purely negative one of correcting abuse, of telling people what they may or may not do. Government must be the means by which our people, working together, seek to meet the problems that are too big for any one of us or any group of us to solve individually."[38]

The crowd, caught totally unprepared for such a declaration, offered only minimal applause. Conservatives immediately charged that Dewey had "climbed into bed with the president" and endorsed the New Deal. In his report to the White House, journalist Tom Reynolds noted that "Hal Faust of the Chicago *Tribune*, Dick Lee of the New York *News*, Warren Francis of the Los Angeles *Times*, and a dozen others gagged when we got the text of the speech. I got a service message from my office the next night that said that the *Tribune* had played the Dewey speech on page 10—'apparently under the impression it was Roosevelt talking.'"[39] Howard Brubaker of the *New Yorker*, meanwhile, mused that "Governor Dewey's visit to the Pacific Coast was fraught with peril. He was in a train wreck in Washington, and in California, he accidentally swallowed the New Deal."[40]

Then in Los Angeles the next day, September 22, Dewey tackled the issue of social security. Standing under a 52-foot American flag and accompanied by Hollywood personalities such as Ginger Rogers, Randolph Scott, Edward Arnold, and Cecil B. DeMille, Dewey addressed a crowd of over 90,000—in what one journalist described as an "out of this world" show that "took your breath away."[41] He began his remarks reflecting on his two-week trip across America. "I have done some talking," he said, "but a lot more listening," and the thing that impacted him the most was that "Men and women from all parts of our country have been fighting and working side by side in this war. They want to work together with the same unity when peace comes." Next, he reminded his audience of the three main priorities of a Dewey administration: winning the war, securing a lasting peace, and obtaining postwar economic security without sacrificing personal freedoms. He then moved toward his main topic, showing that social progress in America neither began with the New Deal in 1933 nor resided solely in the Democratic Party.[42]

Overall, Dewey unveiled a five-point program to broaden and strengthen social progress in the United States. First, he called for the Social Security Act of 1935 to be amended to provide old age and survivors' insurance to those, such as farmers, domestic workers, and the self-employed, who were not presently covered by a pension or retirement system. Second, he advocated widening the provisions of unemployment insurance to include those groups that were unprotected. Third, he promoted a return of the employment service, taken over by the federal government during the war, to the states. "After all," he said, "jobs are in the states, not in Washington—we hope." Fourth, he advanced—in only general terms—the development of "a means for assurance of medical service to those of our citizens who need it, and who cannot otherwise obtain it." And fifth, he called for the establishment of state and local information services for each veteran that provided "prompt and expert counsel as to his rights and opportunities."[43]

Meanwhile, concern grew inside the Roosevelt campaign. Dewey was "an active, spirited and able campaigner," Samuel Rosenman later recalled, and "as the stories continued to spread about the President's bad health, his weariness of mind and body, and his general disinterest in the political campaign," Republicans' prospects for victory brightened.[44] Furthermore, Dewey's repeated charge that Roosevelt wanted to keep servicemen in the Army after the war to prevent unemployment "began to take hold—especially among many American fathers and mothers who were anxious to get their boys home as soon as possible."[45] Indeed, in mid-September, Newsweek reported that Dewey had "scored marked gains in recent weeks and [that] the re-election of President Roosevelt is now in doubt."[46] According to the newsmagazine's "Election Trends panel," Dewey led in 19 states, holding 230 electoral votes, while Roosevelt enjoyed a lead in 26 states and a total electoral vote of 267—just one vote more than required for victory in November. Not surprisingly, Roosevelt "soon began to realize that it was necessary for him to get out again and fight hard."[47]

As Dewey made his swing around the nation, the White House, then, announced that the President would deliver an address to the Teamsters Union on September 23. Those close to Roosevelt believed him to be too preoccupied by the war to fully appreciate Dewey's challenge. Several factors were at play for Democrats on the eve of the Teamsters Speech. First was the issue of the president's health. He needed to appear robust. The fact that he would be seated worried some. Second was the need to defend the administration's record and to respond to Dewey's charges. And third, many Democrats wrongly believed Dewey was purposefully trying to bore the nation and thus drive turnout on Election Day to record lows. The president, his aides believed, needed to shake things up, energize his base, and electrify the nation. He did not disappoint. Although he remained seated during the speech, he was energetic, conversational, witty, and extremely partisan. It was arguably the best political speech of his entire career.

Roosevelt joked about his age (and by implication, his health), noting that he was actually four years older since the last election—a fact, he said, that seemed to annoy some people. He then masterfully incorporated mention of the Great Depression, adding that "in the mathematical field there are millions of Americans who are more than eleven years older than when we started to clear up the mess that was dumped in our laps in 1933." Still, FDR wryly noted, Republicans seemed intent on criticizing *him* for prewar economic turmoil. "Now, there is an old and somewhat lugubrious adage which says: 'Never speak of a rope in the house of a man who has been hanged.' In the same way, if I were a Republican leader speaking to a mixed audience, the last word in the whole dictionary that I think I would use is that word 'depression.'"

He also denied several "fantastic" charges made by Republicans, including one that the administration was planning to keep men in the armed services after the war was over for fear that there might be no jobs available for them at home. It was, he declared, a "callous and brazen falsehood" aimed at stimulating fear among American mothers, wives, and sweethearts. Furthermore, "it was hardly calculated to bolster the morale of our soldiers and sailors and airmen fighting our battles all over the world." Republicans, the president insisted, were attempting to distort his record and deceive the American voter. In fact, they had, he charged, already imported into the campaign the propaganda techniques of dictators. One technique "was all set out in Hitler's book—and it was copied by the aggressors of Italy and Japan. According to that technique, you should never use a small falsehood; always a big one, for its very fantastic nature will make it more credible—if only you keep repeating it over and over again."

The highlight of the speech, however, was the president's mention of his dog, Fala. Republican leaders, he said, had not been content with attacks on him, on his wife, or on his sons. "No, not content with that, they now include my little dog Fala. Well, of course, I don't resent attacks, and my family doesn't resent attacks, but Fala does resent them." Earlier, Republicans in Congress had charged that, while Roosevelt was in the Pacific in August, Fala had been left behind on an Aleutian island, and that the president had sent a destroyer back to find him at a cost to the taxpayers of "two or three, or eight or twenty million dollars."

"You know," Roosevelt added, "Fala's Scotch, and being a Scottie, as soon as he learned that the Republican fiction writers in Congress had out and concocted [that] story . . . his Scotch soul was furious. He has not been the same dog since." Roosevelt insisted that he was accustomed to hearing malicious falsehoods about himself—"such as that old, worm-eaten chestnut that I have represented myself as indispensable. But I think I have a right to resent, to object to libelous statements about my dog."[48]

The audience reaction was wildly enthusiastic. One member of the audience beat a silver bread tray with a soup ladle, while another smashed glasses with wine bottles every time the president ridiculed Dewey.[49] "The applause and cheers when he finished were startling to those of us who had seen him out campaigning in 1932, 1936, and 1940," speechwriter Samuel Rosenman observed. "Never had there been a demonstration equal to this in sincerity, admiration and affection. In the mind of every friend and supporter who stood and cheered and applauded in that large dining hall was the same thought: 'The old maestro is back again—the champ is now out on the road. The old boy has the same old fighting stuff and he just can't be licked.'"[50] "It was at this dinner," Eleanor Roosevelt remembered, "that Franklin really laid the foundation for Mr. Dewey's defeat. . . . By ridicule, Franklin turned this silly charge [about Fala] to his advantage."[51] Historian James MacGregor Burns later described the defense of Fala as a "dagger thrust . . . the blade lovingly fashioned and honed."[52]

Dewey, who listened to the speech over the state-of-the-art RCA radio system in his private rail car, thought the president's remarks to be "sneering and snide."[53] His rage "smoldering," Dewey now decided to cease being "constructive" and "give Roosevelt a little bit of his own medicine."[54] According to journalist Warren Moscow, Dewey's strategy all along was to "goad the President into replying to attacks on domestic policies. Then, when the President replied and was brought out into the open as a political candidate, the real personal attacks, with the heavy artillery rushed up, were to begin." However, the Dewey campaign was caught off guard by Roosevelt coming out so soon, and so strongly. Thus, Moscow concluded, the research material Dewey had been gathering for months now had to be sorted and prepared for response speeches hastily.[55]

Determined to implement his final, "attacking, attacking, attacking" phase of the campaign early, Dewey began planning for a major public response and even signed banknotes to help raise the necessary $27,496.46 to expand network coverage from 164 to 288 radio stations nationwide.[56] According to journalist Tom Reynolds, in a "confidential" report to White House press secretary Steve Early, the Dewey campaign was thrown into disarray and panic. In Belen, New Mexico, Reynolds noted, Brownell, who for hours had been desperately trying to communicate with Dewey by phone, finally made contact. "[T]he little governor," an unsympathetic Reynolds added, had to take Brownell's call "in a public booth before the eyes of all around." Even more humiliating, Henry Turnbull, Dewey's radio director, was also cramped in the telephone booth.[57]

The effect of Roosevelt's speech among the correspondents, Reynolds wrote, was "almost incredible. The Chicago Tribune and New York News crowd already were sour on Dewey, and when the President lifted him out of the water, they went even more sour. There wasn't a dissenting vote among the correspondents—Dewey was left in a position behind that he occupied when he left Pawling on Sept. 6. He must have felt it, too."[58] Similarly, Rosenman observed that the campaign was "jolted out of its rut. . . . Democratic forces were electrified, [and] Dewey was made fighting mad."[59] The Republican nominee, he added, "was too smart a campaigner not to realize how much he had been hurt by the Fala speech. But it was the kind of political speech which was so hard to answer that he should simply have ignored it."[60]

In Oklahoma City on September 25, Dewey rebutted Roosevelt's Fala speech before a crowd of over 15,000. His address was broadcast live over national radio and was interrupted 38 times by applause. "For two and a half weeks," Dewey began, "I have been laying before our people the program I believe we must adopt if we are to win here at home the things for which our American men are fighting abroad." In doing this, he explained, he had carefully considered the wartime circumstances of the campaign and had consciously avoided inserting politics into the war effort. The president, despite a pledge to the contrary, was now engaging in mudslinging, ridicule, and wisecracks. He had, Dewey continued, plumbed to the depths of demagogy by dragging into the campaign the names of Hitler and Goebbels. "Let me make one thing perfectly clear. I shall not join my opponent in his descent to mud-slinging. If he continues . . . he will be alone."[61]

Showcasing his skills as a prosecutor, Dewey then proceeded to indict the administration on the prewar economy, noting that ten million Americans were still unemployed in 1940 after seven years of the New Deal. "By waging relentless warfare against our job-making machinery, my opponent succeeded in keeping a depression going eleven long years—twice as long as any previous depression in our history, and the somber, tragic thing is that today he still has no better programs to offer. That is why the New Deal is afraid of peace, that's why it resorts to wisecracks and vilification—when our people want victory followed by lasting peace in the world—and jobs and opportunity here at home. That's why it's time for a change."[62]

Using the words of high-profile Democrats, including Truman, to make his case, Dewey also charged the administration with being ill prepared for war when it finally came in 1941. On the floor of the Senate in May 1943, he noted, "these words were uttered: 'After Pearl Harbor we found ourselves woefully unprepared for war.'" Was that Goebbels on the Senate floor? Dewey asked. No. "The very words my opponent calls a falsification came from the mouth of his running mate, Harry Truman. . . . Now listen to this: 'When the treachery of Pearl Harbor came we were not ready.' Mr. Roosevelt, was that from Dr. Goebbels? The man who said that was Alben Barkley, your Majority Leader of the United States Senate."[63]

Dewey concluded by employing another one of his campaign themes—that Roosevelt was not the candidate of the average Democratic voter but of special interests. "My opponent," he railed, "now announces his desire to be President for sixteen years. Yet in his speech . . . he called it a 'malicious falsehood' that he had ever represented himself to be 'indispensable'"—despite the fact that Truman recently told supporters that "'The very future of the peace and prosperity of the world depends upon his re-election.'" Truman had yet to be repudiated by Roosevelt, but the president, he added with a bite, "usually waits to shed his Vice-Presidents until they have served at least one term." In a sense, Dewey admitted, Roosevelt was indispensable. "He is indispensable to Harry Hopkins, to Mme. Perkins, to Harold Ickes . . . to America's leading enemy of civil liberties—the mayor of Jersey City. He's indispensable to those infamous machines in Chicago, in the Bronx, and all the others. He's indispensable to Sidney Hillman and the Political Action Committee, he's indispensable to Earl Browder, the ex-convict and pardoned Communist leader. Shall we, the American people, perpetuate one man in office for sixteen years? Shall we do that to accommodate this motley crew?"[64]

"FDR Asked for It" ran the headline of the *New York Telegram* the next morning. Traveling through Minnesota a few days later, Governor Bricker wrote that "Everywhere I have heard nothing but words of praise for your Oklahoma speech. It has given greater impetus to Republicans than anything that has happened. They are ready to go to town—raise money and get out the votes." From California, Dewey's campaign biographer, Rupert Hughes, wired that the speech was more than oratory—"it was an earthquake." Advisor John Burton, meanwhile, called it "positively the best political speech I ever heard. I went to bed happy for the first time in twelve years. Very big league!"[65] *U.S. News* added that the country "was going to have an old-fashioned, free-swinging campaign after all."[66]

According to historian Gil Troy, the Fala speech, contrary to popular opinion, was a rare political miscalculation by Roosevelt. Examining White House mail and editorials and "Letters to the Editor" from newspapers around the country, Troy noted that "regular" or "mainstream" Democrats—the very type Dewey wanted to attract—were three to one against the speech. Most complained about either the distasteful attempt to compare Dewey's tactics with Hitler's or the frivolous injection of a dog into the political discourse. "One citizen," for example, "reported to the Detroit *News* that 'Candidate Roosevelt's political speech filled me with a feeling of deep disgust and loathing.' When mothers are mourning and sons are dying, how can 'this man' think it 'fit to regale their ears with such insulting trash and triviality as the qualities and feelings of his dog!"[67] Many Americans still expected their president to remain above politics, and Roosevelt had disappointed.

Dewey initially felt good about his Oklahoma City response, writing Robert McCormick on September 29 that "It had seemed to me that I should maintain a constructive note until Roosevelt gave me my opening. When he did, I was glad to walk in."[68] In the end, however, Dewey may have missed an important opportunity to attract more independent-minded voters. By playing on Roosevelt's terms, he nullified any possible benefits from Roosevelt's error. Indeed, a Republican strategy memo written that summer by Harold Seymour, Lindsay Bradford, and Prescott Bush, advised, "Don't get involved in the opposition's campaign, or ever be put on the defensive." Furthermore, the memo warned that audiences "will react unfavorably to the 'damn Roosevelt' technique."[69] Dewey quickly realized his mistake. It was, he later recalled, "the worst damned speech I ever made."[70]

CHAPTER 16

"Such a Slimy Campaign"

As "the Listening Campaign" came to a close and September gave way to October, the Dewey camp faced several challenges. Roosevelt's recent Fala speech clearly thwarted Dewey's momentum, charged the Democratic base, and put Republicans on the defensive. Meanwhile, positive news from the war front reinforced the Roosevelt campaign's image of the president as a competent and successful commander-in-chief. At the end of September, American forces pushed into Germany, and on October 20, MacArthur launched the invasion of Leyte Gulf and began his dramatic recapture of the Philippines. Euphoria over this positive news from the war front translated into a "rallying effect" for Roosevelt. If the war had ended in August or September, there might have been—according to some late summer polls—enough of a time lapse between excitement and election to have given Dewey victory.[1] Instead, the *anticipation* of victory, which coincided with the election, generated short-term elation that aided Roosevelt. Ultimately, as Roosevelt biographer James MacGregor Burns observed in the early 1970s, Dewey, like his three Republican predecessors, "found it impossible to come to grips with his adversary. He had plenty of hard evidence for his charges of mismanagement and red tape and expediency—but words meant little in the face of MacArthur's and Eisenhower's triumphs abroad."[2]

Not surprisingly, the month of October witnessed a significant change in the tone of the race—into what Democrats described as "such a slimy campaign, conducted by sinister forces, while the world was in conflagration."[3] Sensing voter movement toward the president, Rupert Hughes advised Dewey that "The closing rounds of the contest demand the body punches and head-rocking that nobody can put over better than you."[4] "The only way to beat Roosevelt is to hit him right between the eyes," Colonel McCormick advised Dewey on October 9. Quoting a former Democratic congressman, he added, "I mean make the most of every scandal. Keep Pearl Harbor in the paper every day. . . . The only way to fight him is on his ground. He'll lie to your face. When you catch him in a misstatement, you can't get anywhere telling him he is mistaken. You have to call him a liar to his face."[5] Dewey responded a few days later, admitting that he now too leaned "much more heavily to the slugging type of campaign than I did earlier."[6]

A consistent problem for the Dewey campaign was finding a major issue on which to attack Roosevelt and thus neutralize his advantage as commander-in-chief. Pearl Harbor promised to be such an issue. The Japanese attack, and the administration's handling of military preparation in the weeks before, had been the subject of furious controversy in Washington for two years. Although the administration's official explanation for the attack was "slugged without warning," many critics of the president were less sure.[7] According to Dewey biographer Richard Norton Smith, Washington cocktail parties were enlivened with talk that—as two service boards of inquiry were privately beginning to reveal in the summer of 1944—US code breakers had broken Japanese war codes in the spring of 1941, and that the State, War, and Navy Departments, as early as that November, "had a reasonably complete knowledge of the Japanese plans and intentions and were in a position to know their potential moves against the United States."[8]

Sensing an opportunity, Republicans went on the attack. "The primary responsibility for the Pearl Harbor catastrophe," Congressman Ralph Church of Illinois declared in early September, "was in Washington and not in the Pacific."[9] A few days later, Congressman Forest Harness of Indiana introduced a resolution in the House of Representatives calling for a committee to conduct a special study of the attack and report back within 30 days.[10] "If the President of the United States is not responsible for this disaster," Harness declared, "he should be cleared promptly." However, "if, as Commander-in-Chief of the armed forces, he has been culpable in directing our military activities in Hawaii, the American people should have the true facts before they are called upon to pass judgment on his fitness for re-election to a fourth term as President."[11] Clare Booth Luce, meanwhile, charged that Roosevelt was "the only American President who ever lied us into a war because he did not have the courage to lead us into it."[12]

Then, in a speech before ten thousand supporters in Willkes-Barre, Pennsylvania, Bricker accused the administration of withholding facts about the "disgraceful Pearl Harbor episode" because of the harm that the revealing of the full story might do to the president's fourth-term bid. Overall, he called for a prompt court-martial of the Army and Navy commandants at Pearl Harbor and insisted that "the people were entitled to know the facts and that the war effort would not be injured, but helped by a complete revelation." There was no place in a republic, Bricker concluded, "for secret commitments, for closed-door conferences."[13] Believing the tragedy to have "reached the proportions of a national scandal," the Dewey campaign, Herbert Brownell recalled, decided early on to disclose "the truth about Pearl Harbor."[14]

Then, while campaigning in Tulsa, on September 26, just one day after his Oklahoma City speech, Dewey was approached by Colonel Carter Clarke of the Army Special Branch, who handed the governor a top-secret letter from the Army chief of staff himself, General George C. Marshall. The letter read:

> My Dear Governor:
>
> I am writing to you without the knowledge of any other person except Admiral King (who concurs) because we are approaching a grave dilemma in the political reactions of Congress regarding Pearl Harbor. What I have to tell you below is of such a highly secret nature that I feel compelled to ask you either to accept it on the basis of your not communicating its contents to any other person and returning this letter or not reading any further and returning the letter to the bearer.[15]

Dewey stopped reading, telling Clarke, "Marshall does not do things like that. I am confident that Franklin Roosevelt is behind this whole thing. Now if this letter merely tells me that we were reading Japanese codes before Pearl Harbor and that at least two of them are still in current use, there is no point in my reading the letter because I already know that . . . and Franklin Roosevelt knows about it too. He knew what was happening before Pearl Harbor, and instead of being reelected he ought to be impeached."[16] Dewey then returned the letter but consented to meet secretly with Clarke once he returned to Albany.

When later asked by a congressional panel why he decided to write Dewey, Marshall replied that he was worried about Pearl Harbor references from Republicans that were "growing more pointed as the campaign became more violent." While some, he testified, had suggested he go to Roosevelt "for help," the Army chief of staff believed that would be inappropriate. "I felt it absolutely necessary," Marshall recalled, "that Mr. Dewey feel sure that the President had no knowledge whatever of my action and that he feel sure that it was entirely non-political. That is the way, I understand, Governor Dewey accepted it."[17]

In Albany, on September 28, Dewey, along with trusted advisor Elliott Bell, met again with Clarke about Pearl Harbor and the Japanese codes. The governor, Clarke insisted, must not raise Pearl Harbor as a campaign issue. According to Clarke, the United States had in fact broken Japanese codes prior to Pearl Harbor, and they were still being used by the Japanese. If Dewey exposed this secret, the colonel continued, the Japanese would change their codes, and the American war effort in the Pacific would be undermined. Shaken and angry, Dewey "fumed that Roosevelt was 'a traitor' who had willingly or accidentally condemned more than a thousand men, and most of the Pacific fleet, to a watery grave." After repeated assurances from Clarke that Roosevelt had no knowledge of their meeting, Dewey, following a sense of patriotic duty and not wanting to "imperil 'untold American lives,'" instructed his aides to gather all the information thus far collected and "put it away securely and forget it."[18] Clarke then asked him if he wished to convey a message to Marshall, to which Dewey replied, "No message." Dewey's secretary, Lillian Rosse, later recalled the governor "looked like a ghost."[19]

This information, Brownell later argued, indicated "a shocking lack of co-ordination between the president, the state department, and the armed forces leading up to the tragedy of Pearl Harbor." Dewey's decision not to go public with it during the campaign, added Elliott Bell, another Dewey intimate, "was one of the most extraordinary examples of patriotism and self-restraint that has ever been exhibited, because it was tantamount to giving up his greatest chance to become president of the United States."[20] According to historian Robert Divine, "Marshall did the President a great favor. Pearl Harbor was a major political liability which the Republicans could have exploited to much greater advantage than they did. . . . A dramatic revelation that Roosevelt was reading secret Japanese messages and still was unprepared for the attack on Pearl Harbor might have had a devastating impact on the election."[21]

As Dewey frantically searched for an issue to drive voters away from the president, the Roosevelt campaign worked to keep their candidate above the fray. Indeed, a memo to the president in early October noted that "the net effect of Dewey's speeches is there is nothing gained or lost. . . . [H]e is inviting criticism and answers to his speeches from you in order to build himself up." Roosevelt's advisors, then, suggested that Dewey "be ignored by you personally, and that your future speeches be of a constructive type, telling what you plan to do in the post war era both internationally and domestically."[22] Prior to the launching of his final campaign tour on October 27, Roosevelt largely followed this advice, speaking out only twice that month—once in a national radio address on the importance of voting and again before a New York City foreign policy forum.

On October 5, Roosevelt addressed the nation from the White House and encouraged Americans to go to the polls on Election Day. "Nobody," he said, "will ever deprive the American people of the right to vote except the American people themselves—and the only way they could do that is by not voting at all." "The continuing health and vigor of our democratic system," he said, "depends on the public spirit and devotion of its citizens which find expression in the ballot box." He also addressed the issue of Communist support—refuting a charge made by Bricker in his acceptance speech. "I have never sought," the president insisted, "and I do not welcome the support of any person or group committed to Communism, or Fascism, or any other foreign ideology which would undermine the American system of government or the American system of free enterprise and private property." However, that would not, he added, "interfere with the firm and friendly relationship which this nation has in the war, and will, I hope, continue to have with the Soviet Union. The kind of economy that suits the Russian people is their own affair."

Roosevelt also warned of low voter turnout. He then rather boldly added that "The right to vote must be open to our citizens irrespective of race, color, or creed—without tax or artificial restriction of any kind. The sooner we get to that basis of political equality, the better it will be for the country as a whole." The most controversial part of the speech, however, involved soldier voting. After decrying the fact that "many millions" of American servicemen would find it "difficult in many cases—and impossible in some cases—to register and vote," Roosevelt—in a subtle barb at Dewey and the Republicans—prophesied that the American people would know whom to blame, "for they know that during this past year there were politicians who quite openly worked to restrict the use of the ballot in this election, hoping selfishly for a small vote."[23]

Speaking in Charleston, West Virginia, on October 7, Dewey—in his first major campaign appearance since Oklahoma City—launched a scathing attack against Roosevelt and incompetence in Washington. He began by countering Roosevelt's latest statements—in this case, about voter turnout and the spurning of support from the Communists—and reminding voters that in his home state of New York, 77 percent of all eligible servicemen had already been mailed ballots. "Despite my opponent's attempt to play politics with the soldier vote," Dewey argued, "every evidence indicates that we will have an ever larger percentage of soldier votes than we will of civilians. Let's have no more of this political pretense on a matter so important to us all." Dewey then counterattacked, boldly pointing out that Roosevelt was "relying for his main support upon a solid block of votes in [southern] states where millions of American citizens are deprived of their right to vote by the poll tax and by intimidation. Not once in twelve years has my opponent lifted a finger to correct this and his platform is cynically silent on the subject."[24]

On Roosevelt's denial of welcoming the support of Communists, Dewey feigned surprise. "Now, that is news," he said mockingly. "But doesn't this soft disclaimer come a little late?" Just the week before, he noted, Earl Browder, head of the Communist Party of America, had told 15,000 cheering supporters in Madison Square Garden that the reelection of Roosevelt was essential to his aims; that is, a continuation of the New Deal. Dewey did not suggest that Roosevelt was a socialist or communist. Instead, he explained that Browder and his ilk "love to fish in troubled waters. Their aims can best be served by unemployment and discontent. They remember that the New Deal in all its seven peacetime years never cured unemployment . . . [and that] we had to have a war to get jobs. That's why they want a fourth term and sixteen years of the New Deal."[25]

Dewey also loosely quoted New Dealer Adolph Berle from 1939. A part of Roosevelt's original brain trust, Berle, he noted, submitted a memorandum to the Temporary National Economic Committee, a New Deal agency established "to decide upon our future for us," in which he wrote: "Over a period of years, the government will gradually come to own most of the productive plants in the United States." The meaning of that, he insisted, was the development of a system where the government told "each of us where we could work, at what and for how much. Now, I don't know whether my opponent calls that system Communism or National Socialism or Fascism. He can take it any way he likes it. It's his program, not mine. But I do know it is not an American system and it's not a free system."[26]

A few days later, on October 16, before a crowd in St. Louis, Missouri, Dewey once again spoke on the need for competent leadership in postwar America. Government, he said, should meet three simple tests: Was it honest? Were the people who operated it competent to do their jobs? Did it have faith in the future of America, and "a wholehearted determination to make our system work"? By such standards, he charged, the Roosevelt administration— "the most spectacular collection of incompetent people who ever held public office"—was a miserable failure. He then went on to describe the "constant bickering, quarreling, and back-biting" within the White House, including squabbles between Harold Ickes and Harry Hopkins over money for their respective New Deal agencies, between Harold Ickes and Leon Henderson over the title "gasoline czar," and between Henry Wallace and Secretary of Commerce Jesse Jones over the vice president's "disgraceful" accusation that Jones had "done much to harass the . . . effort to help shorten this war." Central to all this quarrelling and confusion, he declared, was the president's own "consistent practice of evading responsibility" and passing the buck to his assistants. "What kind of government is this," Dewey demanded, "that even a war cannot make it sober down and go to work?" The Roosevelt administration, he concluded, had degenerated into "little men rattling around in big jobs. Our country cannot afford the wasteful luxury of incompetent people in high places who spend their time fighting each other."[27]

Another problem facing the Dewey campaign in early October was Wendell Willkie, who had provided Dewey with a "Hearty congratulations on your nomination" back in June but not an endorsement.[28] In August, Arthur Krock of the New York Times reported that Willkie was not satisfied with either candidate and would thus withhold his support until he was confident the foreign policy pursued conformed to the cause to which he was committed.[29] A few days later, Willkie publicly snubbed Dewey, when after the announcement of the Dulles-Hull meeting in Washington the governor requested (by telegram) a meeting with Willkie "to have the benefit of your views." Dewey, who had actually tried unsuccessfully to reach Willkie by phone, also asked the Republican maverick to telephone him "when convenient in the morning so that we could discuss the possibility of such an exchange of views."[30] Willkie in fact replied the following morning, August 20, but by telegram, and he was very curt. "I shall be very glad to meet *Mr. Dulles* on his way to the conference," Willkie wrote [italics added]. "I wish," he bitterly continued, "I had known of your desire for my views prior to your original statement. For several years I have been deeply concerned about the ill fate of the small nations inherent in military alliances between any or all of the great powers. But I have been equally concerned that there should not arise among our allies the notion that our party would in any way obstruct or endanger the success of an international conference."[31]

Dewey, who had campaigned for Willkie in 1940, was disappointed and frustrated. "I am sorry that you could not accept my invitation to join Mr. Dulles and *me*," Dewey replied later that same day [italics added]. "However, I am delighted that you will confer with Mr. Dulles in New York on his way to Washington, and I am confident that this will promote the constructive results which I am sure we all want." Willkie and Dulles, in fact, met on August 21 for an hour and a half (without reporters and photographers), and, at the conclusion of their discussion, issued a joint statement that, as the *New York Times* observed, still left "in doubt [Willkie's] stand on [the] party." "We have," the statement read, "conferred extensively about various international problems bearing on world organization to assure lasting peace. There was a full exchange of views not animated by partisan considerations nor having to do with any candidacy, but by the desire of both of us that the United States should play a constructive and responsible part in assuring world order."[32]

In October, Russell Davenport, a Willkie advisor, published an essay in the *American Mercury* entitled "Why I Cannot Vote for Dewey." According to Davenport, Dewey was not a man of conviction but of party. A political pragmatist, Dewey, Davenport complained, sought not to lead his party toward the achievement of ideological goals but toward "that most treacherous of political goals called 'party unity.'" Thus, to understand Dewey, one had to consider him in relation to his party. For when all compromises have been added up, Davenport argued, "it will be found that Mr. Dewey represents the Republican party far more than he represents Mr. Dewey." Specifically, Davenport was disturbed by the party's foreign policy platform, which he believed to be too vague and too open to manipulation by "nationalistic jingoes," who apparently, in Davenport's thinking, now controlled the Republican Party. Furthermore, there was no evidence that Dewey, who had a long record of vacillation, would stand up to conservatives. "He has," Davenport argued, "been isolationist and internationalist. He has been for alliances and against them. He was against lend-lease and then for it. He has been anti-Russian and pro-Russian. *He has never once provided leadership on a major issue in foreign policy. And on no major issue in foreign policy has he taken a consistent position.*" Thus, the election of Thomas Dewey to the presidency in 1944 would be to repeat the mistake of electing Warren Harding in 1920. The New York governor, he concluded, was nothing more than "'a disaster looking for a place to happen.'"[33]

Then, on October 8, Wendell Willkie suddenly died of a heart attack, having failed to endorse any candidate. Years later, FDR aide Samuel Rosenman wrote of a secret meeting with Willkie in July 1944, in which, he (Willkie) proposed joining with Roosevelt to forge a liberal and internationalist party in America. However, in his 1994 memoir, *Advising Ike*, Herbert Brownell insisted that Rosenman was wrong. According to Brownell, he and Henry Luce, editor of *Time* and a Willkie supporter in 1940, met with Willkie in a suite at New York's Waldorf Astoria Hotel late that summer. "Over cocktails and at dinner," Brownell recalled, "Willkie criticized Dewey and his policies; the attack was vehement. Suddenly he said, 'And I want you to know,

Brownell, that your man is going to be defeated and I am going to run for president in 1948 and will be elected.' After a pause he added, 'But I like you, Brownell, and want you to be my campaign manager in '48.'"

Recognizing an opening, Brownell replied that Willkie could not win the Republican nomination in 1948 if he did not endorse Dewey in 1944. Around midnight, Willkie "got up and lumbered off," with Brownell and Luce agreeing "that maybe the important job had been done." Shortly thereafter Brownell learned that Willkie had telephoned Eugene Pulliam, an influential Indiana newspaper publisher (and grandfather of future vice president Dan Quayle), asking him to set up time on a leading radio network so he could announce his support for Dewey. "Unfortunately," Brownell wrote, "a few days later, instead of listening to the planned speech, I was attending Willkie's funeral services."[34]

Still, Dewey felt slighted by his "fat little friend"—as he privately called Willkie. His refusal to support Dewey hurt the Republican campaign, especially with internationalist-minded independents who were otherwise tired of the New Deal. Reflecting upon his troubled relationship with Willkie, Dewey, years later, recalled: "[He] didn't [support me] when I was nominated for President in 1944, after he had been so badly beaten in Wisconsin by delegates I didn't recognize and had asked to withdraw. I was finally nominated. He never supported me, and he never did anything but snipe, and finally he went to a hospital and died of bitterness."[35]

A few days after Willkie's death, Dewey suffered another setback. On October 9, the Roosevelt administration released the content of the postwar security proposals made by the United States, Great Britain, the Soviet Union, and China at the Dumbarton Oaks Conference. Overall, the conference called for the creation of an international organization similar to the League of Nations, with a general assembly of all member states, an 11-seat security council (on which the founders would have permanent representation), and a world court of justice.[36] The proposals, however, made no mention of voting procedures on the Security Council, and avoided designating an authority responsible for committing troops against an aggressor.

A few days later, on October 12, Republican senator Joseph Ball of Minnesota—an internationalist and a sponsor of a 1943 Senate resolution calling for the creation of a United Nations Organization—released a public statement challenging the presidential candidates to address the question of "Should the vote of the United States' representative on the United Nations security council commit an agreed upon quota of our military forces to action ordered by the council to maintain peace without requiring further congressional approval?"[37] For Ball, the answer was "yes." In fact, the previous year he had published a book entitled *Collective Security*, arguing that "the right to wage aggressive warfare is the only sovereign right which must be renounced. The only sovereign obligation to be assumed is to join in collective action against aggression, whether actual or threatened."[38] Ball was regarded as a spokesman for those who had followed Willkie, and his support was deemed very important by both parties.[39] Like many other Willkie Republicans, he was lukewarm at best on Dewey and remained "on the fence." He indicated, however, that he would endorse whichever candidate answered the question to his satisfaction.

On October 18, Dewey delivered a major foreign policy speech before the *New York Herald-Tribune* Forum at the Waldorf-Astoria Hotel in New York City. In his speech, the Republican nominee spoke thoughtfully about America's new internationalist mission. "Japanese planes launched from a few aircraft on December 7, 1941, struck us a devastating blow at Pearl Harbor," he said. "If we fail to make secure the peace of the world, the next war will not begin by a surprise attack upon an outlying base. It will begin when robot bombs [intercontinental missiles] launched thousands of miles away suddenly rain death and destruction on our major cities." That threat, he explained, had greatly reduced the size of the earth. "If there should ever be a third World War, America would be in the front lines in the very first hour. That is not argument. It is a fact." Thus, the inescapable conclusion was that the United States must never again run the risk of permitting war to break out in the world. To this end, it must take the lead in establishing an international body to prevent future wars.[40]

Dewey also highlighted the "great achievements" of past Republican secretaries of state, such as Charles Evans Hughes, Frank Kellogg, and Henry Stimson. He was "a little tired," then, he said, of the attitude "that the United States had never shown any competence in foreign relations. At least, not until the last few years."[41] Next, he took the Roosevelt administration to task on the issue of Poland, "the first nation to resist the oppression of Hitler." The restoration of a free Poland, he declared, was "the outstanding symbol of what we are fighting for." Yet, its postwar future remained unclear. At the Tehran Conference with Stalin in late 1943, Roosevelt—assisted not by his secretary of state, but by Harry Hopkins, former head of the Works Progress Administration—"undertook to handle this matter personally and secretly." The result was that "Russian recognition of those whom we consider to be the true Government of Poland" had not yet been secured.[42]

Furthermore, the president's penchant for "handling foreign affairs on the basis of personal, secret diplomacy," Dewey insisted, was prolonging the war. Specifically, he attacked Hans Morgenthau's "scheme" at the recent Quebec

Conference. Once again, he noted, neither the secretary of state nor the secretary of war accompanied the president. Instead, Roosevelt took his secretary of the treasury, Morgenthau, "whose qualifications as an expert on military and international affairs are still unknown." A cabinet crisis erupted in Quebec, Dewey explained, when the work of the State and War Departments was supplanted by "ill-conceived proposals" from Treasury that essentially told the German people "that a program of destruction was in store for them if they surrender." While this plan was ultimately scrapped, Dewey noted that "Germany's propaganda Minister Goebbels has seized upon the episode to terrify the Germans into fanatical resistance. . . . Almost overnight, the morale of the German people seemed changed. They are fighting with the frenzy of despair. We are paying in blood for our failure to have ready an intelligent program for dealing with invaded Germany."[43]

Unfortunately for Dewey, most of the speech was eventually overshadowed by the Ball question, which he—in what turned out to be a major mistake—avoided. Believing the Hull-Dulles agreement of August disqualified him from making any specific statement on the United Nations, Dewey commented only blandly that "The world organization must be enabled, through the use of force, when necessary, to prevent or repel military aggression. It must be supplemented by a world court to deal with international disputes."[44] In its editorial two days later, the New York Times—while not mentioning the Ball issue—questioned Dewey's control over his party on foreign affairs and concluded that the speech did "nothing to change our view that the foreign policy of the United States during the next critical four years will be safer in the hands of the Democrats and Mr. Roosevelt than in the hands of the deeply divided Republicans and Mr. Dewey."[45]

Inside the White House, the Roosevelt campaign considered Dewey's oversight "a lucky break" and decided to take full advantage of it in the president's speech before the same forum three days later.[46] In fact, Roosevelt planned to use the New York event as an excuse to campaign in his highly competitive home state and to allow "the people to see him as he looks . . . and judge his physical fitness with their own eyes."[47] On October 21, he toured 51 miles of New York City in an open car, receiving "a remarkable tribute" from over 3 million people in "the biting cold and whipping rain."[48] At Ebbets Field, the president—discarding his hat and navy cape—briefly addressed ten thousand well-wishers at a rally for Democratic senator Robert F. Wagner. "You know," he told the rain-soaked crowd, "I come from the State of New York, and I have made a series of inspection tours here . . . but I have never been to Ebbets Field before. I have rooted for the Dodgers. And I hope to come back here some day and see them play."[49] According to the New York

Times, "The power of his voice as it filled the ball park was reminiscent . . . of an announcement of a change in Dodgers' batteries."[50] White House aide William Hassett, meanwhile, called his appearance "dynamic" and "radiant," making "plain everyday liars out of this species of vermin" who relentlessly carried on "a whispering campaign, a vendetta, against his health."[51]

From Brooklyn, Roosevelt traveled to Queens, the Bronx, Harlem, and mid-Manhattan. "I was really worried about him that day," Mrs. Roosevelt later recalled, "but instead of being completely exhausted he was exhilarated. . . . The crowds had been warm and welcoming and the contact with them was good for him."[52] He was clearly "moved" and "impressed" by the demonstration of support, Mayor Fiorello LaGuardia told reporters. "You could see it; he was touched by it."[53] According to Rosenman, Roosevelt "showed no ill effects from the drive; and after a hot bath and a few drinks, he was ready to proceed to the banquet room and his foreign policy speech."[54] Mrs. Roosevelt, however, recalled hearing "afterwards that some people thought he looked very ill that night, but I was not surprised because of course he was extremely tired."[55]

That evening, October 21, the president spoke to the Foreign Policy Association and attacked congressional Republicans for their pre–Pearl Harbor isolationist voting, extolled liberal and internationalist Republicans such as Secretary of War Henry Stimson, who appeared on the dais with Roosevelt, and warned that the conservative "likes of Joe Martin and Hamilton Fish would have controlling power in Congress if the Republicans won."[56] According to Hassert, the audience was largely Republican but keenly aware of the menace of isolationism. "Not in my observation," he wrote in his diary, "has the President had more thoughtful or appreciative listeners. Never before have I heard so serious a speech interrupted by such spontaneous and genuine applause."[57]

Unlike Dewey, Roosevelt addressed Ball's concerns squarely. "Peace, like war," the president explained, "can succeed only where there is a will to enforce it, and where there is available power to enforce it. The Council of the United Nations must have the power to act quickly and decisively to keep the peace by force, if necessary. A policeman would not be a very effective policeman if, when he saw a felon break into a house, he had to go to the Town Hall and call a town meeting to issue a warrant before the felon could be arrested."[58]

Once again Dewey was shocked. Roosevelt's statements were, he believed, inappropriate and a violation of the nonpartisan agreement of August 25. In route to Minneapolis, where he was scheduled to deliver a policy speech on farm issues, Dewey faltered when asked by a reporter if he now had a "feeling" on the issue. He replied awkwardly and slowly, saying, "I think that the answer to that is that I doubt that I will go into any details on that subject."[59] Shelving his farm speech, Dewey tried to rebound the next night, announcing that the US representative to the United Nations "must not be subject to a reservation that would require . . . [him] to return to Congress for authority every time he had to make a decision. Obviously Congress, and only Congress, has Constitutional power to determine what quota of force it will make available and what discretion it will give our representative to use that force."[60]

It was too late. That same day, while speaking in Baltimore, Ball formally endorsed Roosevelt for president. Dewey, he said, had failed to clarify his position. If Congress retained the right to decide on each occasion whether to supply troops for collective security, the United Nations would be nothing more than a debating society, lacking power to act, and "future aggressors will sneer at it just as Hitler sneered at the League of Nations."[61]

Although the Dewey campaign dismissed Ball as an "insignificant voice," his defection hurt. The Minnesota senator immediately became the new Willkie, appealing to both liberal Republicans and independents. In addition, Ball undermined Dewey in Minnesota where on Election Day he narrowly lost the state (and its eleven electoral votes) by 60,000 votes. Furthermore, it revived foreign policy as an issue—a weak point for Dewey anyway—and raised questions, if unfounded, about the sincerity of his commitment to internationalism. Announcing his own support for Roosevelt on October 21, journalist Walter Lippmann, who had supported Willkie in 1940, wrote, "I cannot feel that Governor Dewey can be trusted now with responsibility in foreign affairs . . . He has so much to learn."[62]

More importantly, the Ball episode as a whole resulted in the very thing Dewey wanted to avoid—it generated controversy and thus helped mobilize previously ambivalent Democrats to turn out on Election Day and vote for Roosevelt. For example, both the *Nation* and the *New Republic*, skeptical over Roosevelt's apparent abandonment of the New Deal, found the president's answer to Ball's question sufficient ground for endorsing a fourth term. Years later, Dewey himself acknowledged the impact of the affair, recalling:

> In the last week of the campaign Roosevelt broke his commitment and said in a very deft way that the town hall didn't have any power unless it had a policeman, thereby satisfying a great many people who felt that there should be a United Nations army, about which I had a good many reservations. I have been proved right, and he won the election. Not that that [alone] was responsible for his winning the election, but I'm sure it contributed.[63]

CHAPTER 17

Roosevelt and Victory

A momentum shift clearly occurred in October, and Dewey entered the final stretch of the 1944 presidential campaign in a weakened position. "The breaks were all in Dewey's favor until a few days ago," Hoover wrote Landon on October 23. "How much effect Roosevelt's demonstration of 'sound body and mind' by six hours in the rain, the opposition of Walter Lippmann, Ball and the *New York Times* and the increased city registration will have is difficult to see. Dewey may be able to demolish these efforts."[1] Ultimately, of course, he was unable to rebound. The Roosevelt campaign, aided by unfolding events in the war and Dewey's own verbal mistakes, was successful in maneuvering Dewey into a defensive position—a losing stance for any challenger.

Indeed, Dewey's election to the presidency, a Republican strategy memorandum from May argued, "is not so much a question of politics as it is a problem of public relations."[2] To be successful, he needed to employ a rhetoric strategy that avoided "the hackneyed Republican phrases" and attacked "the opposition by implication only"—advancing a reasoned demand for representative government instead.[3]

Dewey largely followed this advice for the Listening Campaign," his "constructive" policy-oriented phase of the campaign. In addition to unveiling policy programs, he often spoke in optimistic terms about unity in the country. For example, in Tulsa in late September, he promised to bring to

Washington an administration that "will never speak to one group for the purpose of inciting them to dislike, hatred or distrust of another group of fellow Americans."[4] "We want a government," he declared in Monett, Missouri, "which is a great unifier."[5] Desperate to regain momentum after Fala, and especially after the Marshall letter and Ball's endorsement of Roosevelt, he abandoned it. Ultimately, then, the election was a referendum not on the incumbent but on the campaign utterances of the challenger.

While Roosevelt did not want the White House directly engaged in a war of words with Dewey over the accuracy of his statements, Democrats spent most of October seeking to expose any misstatements and exaggerations from the Republican nominee and thus undermine his credibility. Speechwriter Rosenman even prepared a lengthy memorandum for the press pointing out "distortions of the truth" contained in Dewey's speeches. Many in the press, Rosenman later recalled, "used it; and later, in his own speeches, the President with effective sarcasm made veiled but telling references to this practice of Dewey's."[6] The goal, then, was to portray Dewey as a "slick prosecutor who knows that it doesn't always pay in a campaign to tell the whole truth."[7]

Throughout American history, candidates for office have emphasized their own particular side of a campaign issue and not necessarily the whole, and often more complicated, story. It is merely the nature of campaigns, which are, in fact, rivaling stories about the past, present, and future. This was certainly the case with both Dewey *and* Roosevelt in 1944. Each candidate exaggerated and distorted the other's positions, while conveniently neglecting any mention of those things that contradicted their own messages. The problem for Dewey was that he entered the campaign with a reputation, rightly or wrongly, for being opportunistic, dramatic, and full of tricks—someone who was not forthright, but who had "slipped," "slithered," and done "some fancy side-stepping" on a number of issues.[8] As Dewey stepped up his verbal attacks against the administration and made verbal gaffes—most notably the charge in September that MacArthur had not been adequately supplied in the Pacific because he posed a political threat to the president—Democrats countered with the message that "The mud-slinging continues" and that Dewey, "a master of the elastic rhetoric of the politician," could not be trusted.[9]

For example, on October 9, Sidney Hillman, speaking before the Ohio State CIO convention, called Dewey "a shallow, ambitious and inexperienced man who either dodged important issues or vacillated in his opinion." Unlike Bricker, who made no pretense of ever being anything other than "an old-fashioned Hoover reactionary and whole-hearted isolationist,"

Dewey, Hillman insisted, "has developed his own peculiar form of deliberate double-talk to the extent that the only way to judge him is to cancel out everything he says and judge him solely on what he has done or failed to do." Contradicting himself "five or six times" in his recent campaign swing across the country the Republican candidate, Hillman concluded, "forgets things that did happen" while remembering "things that never happened."[10]

A few days later, on October 14, Adolph Berle, assistant secretary of state, accused the Republican presidential nominee of "dishonesty" and attempting "to play fast and loose with the American public." In an open letter to the president, Berle complained of being misquoted—and having a single sentence taken out of context—in Dewey's Charleston, West Virginia, speech the previous week. Berle insisted that his 1939 statement about the government gradually coming to own most of the production plants in the United States was a fear—something "we wanted to avoid"—and not a policy direction. Indeed, the report from which the quote was "ripped" later emphasized that "It is the definite function of the financial system to make [private initiative] possible at all times." The New York governor "knows me quite well," Berle concluded. The two had served for two years together in New York City, and Berle even helped him secure the independent nomination for district attorney. "He knows, as does everybody else, that, while I want a finance system that takes care of little people as well as big, I have never been a Communist."[11]

In his own "whistle stop" tour across the nation in October, Harry Truman railed against Dewey and Bricker as "a couple of fakirs who just want to get into power."[12] Speaking from the platform of his railcar at El Paso, Texas, on October 14, Truman turned up the heat and referred to the New York governor as "another Harding" that the nation could not afford. Harding, the senator charged, "made no stand on peace" and as a result "we are now paying for that mistake in blood and treasure."[13] In California, he called Dewey a "straddler" on foreign policy, telling reporters that "Mr. Dewey either is not familiar with the facts [of military preparedness before the war] or he's covering them up for political purposes."[14] In an address at San Francisco's Commonwealth Club on October 17, he accused Dewey of "political chicanery" and insisted that his "greatest weakness" as a presidential candidate was his "inability to state facts."[15]

In Philadelphia, on October 30, DNC chair Robert Hannegan gave "full credit" to Dewey for doing his part "to cinch the outcome of this election in [Roosevelt's] favor." His campaign, Hannegan insisted, "has been a revelation to the American people, and the man who stands revealed, by his resort to the wildest untruths, by his callous disregard of the possible consequences of some of those falsehoods on this nation at war and the men defending it, and their families at home . . . that man is Thomas E. Dewey." Still, while Dewey had "started out, from the first gong, with wild swings," Roosevelt "has shown up with a terrific punch that is far too much for the little fellow in the Hoover corner."[16]

That same day, James Byrnes, speaking in Washington, asserted that the election of Dewey would delay victory in the war and put peace in jeopardy. A change in administrations, he argued, would cost precious time for the Allies to learn to what extent a new administration would carry out the policies of its predecessor. "Will it not take time," Byrnes asked, "to convince Stalin that he can work with a man who, as late as 1940, denounced the recognition of Russia by our Government and who is now criticizing the efforts of our Government to bring about a friendly accord between Russia and Poland, on which depend the peace of Europe and the existence of a free and strong Poland?" If America changed presidents, he continued, our Allies will believe America has changed. Also, if defeated, FDR would remain in office until January 20, during which time "Allied statesmen would pay little attention to the man who had been rejected as our spokesman." This, Byrnes concluded, was exactly what Hitler and Hirohito desired—something to disturb the existing unity and harmony of the Grand Alliance: "[Y] ou and I know the defeat of Roosevelt would revive their fading hopes, stiffen their opposition and delay the end of the war."[17]

Meanwhile, Roosevelt launched his last campaign swing, beginning in Delaware on October 27 and taking him through Pennsylvania, Indiana, Illinois, West Virginia, Connecticut, and Massachusetts, before ending on November 6 in Hyde Park, New York.

In Wilmington, he mentioned "some of the Republican political oratory that has lately been agitating the air waves." Paraphrasing Lincoln—who once remarked that his opponent in 1860, Stephen Douglas, tried in every possible way "to prove that a horse chestnut is a chestnut horse"—Roosevelt was sure that "you all [in 1944] know the difference."[18]

At Shibe Park, in Philadelphia, the president addressed an enthusiastic crowd of 35,000 to 45,000, and evoked the memory of his late cousin Theodore Roosevelt, who would have been 86 that day. "I think that Theodore Roosevelt would be happy and proud to know that our American fleet today is greater than all the other navies of the world put together," he declared. "And when I say all the navies I am including what was—until three days ago—the Japanese fleet."[19] Roosevelt then spoke briefly on the "glorious operations" in the Philippines that had resulted in a successful American landing in Leyte a week earlier. Taking a swing at Dewey—and amidst yells of "pour it on" from the bleachers—he asked "whatever became of the suggestion made a few weeks ago, that I had failed for political reasons to send enough forces or supplies to General MacArthur?" He also noted that "a prominent Republican orator" had recently described his administration as "'the most spectacular collection of incompetent people who ever held public office.'" That was a serious charge, Roosevelt mockingly insisted, "because the only conclusion to be drawn from that is that we are losing this war. If so, that will be news to most of us—and it will certainly be news to the Nazis and the Japs."[20]

Roosevelt also answered—"once and for all"—the Republican charge that his administration had made "'absolutely no military preparation for the events that it now claims it foresaw.'" The record, he argued, told a different story. His administration had rebuilt a Navy that "suffered conspicuously during three Republican administrations ... which not only scrapped ships but even prevented adequate target practice, adequate maneuvers, enough oil, or adequate supplies." Indeed, the battleships of Admiral William Halsey's powerful Third Fleet, which "helped to give the Japanese Navy the worst licking in its history," were all authorized between 1933 and 1938, and "construction had begun on all of those ... by September, 1940—well over a year before Pearl Harbor." Thus, "The record will show," he insisted, "that when we were attacked in December, 1941, we had already made tremendous progress toward building the greatest war machine the world has ever known." Some scoffed, however. "Less than three months before Hitler launched his murderous assault [in 1939], the Republicans in the House of Representatives voted 144–8 in favor of cutting the appropriations for the Army Air Corps. I often think how Hitler and Hirohito must have laughed in those days. But they are not laughing now."[21]

In brief informal remarks at Fort Wayne, Indiana, on October 28, Roosevelt again referred to Dewey's practice of taking his words out of context.[22] He had heard "some rather irritated comment by Republican campaign orators about taking a campaign trip," he said. "They don't like it ... [and] seem to believe that I promised them ... that I was not going to campaign under any circumstances, and therefore that they could say anything they wanted about my policies and my Administration." However, Roosevelt reminded the crowd that was not what he said in his acceptance speech. "I am going to quote from that speech very briefly—and I am sure you will pardon me if I quote it correctly—because, you know, a long time ago, when I was Governor of New York, I formed the habit of quoting correctly."[23]

Next, the president traveled to Chicago, where he addressed a crowd of 110,000 supporters packed into Soldier Field and another 150,000 in an outside overflow.[24] As was the case with his visits at Ebbets Field and Shibe Park, Roosevelt's car drove onto a specially built platform on the center of the field that enabled him to deliver his speech from his seat in the open automobile.[25] While the speaking conditions were difficult—a "cool, stiff wind was blowing in from the lake"—speechwriter Rosenman believed the speech at Soldier Field to be "the most dramatic example of the range and power of the President's speaking ability." His greatest asset as a public speaker, Rosenman recalled, "was his ability to associate himself closely with his listeners. He could give them the impression that they were all sitting down together discussing common problems, common successes, and common failures."[26]

Overall, he mostly avoided the campaign and cast instead a vision for "the future of America"—a vision that included "well built homes, with electricity and plumbing, air and sunlight," new highways, parks, hospitals, planes, and "cheap automobiles with new low maintenance and operational costs." Most importantly, he argued that foreign trade would be "trebled after the war," providing millions of new peacetime jobs.[27] "I believe in our democratic faith," he concluded. "I believe in the future of our country which has given eternal strength and vitality to that faith. . . . We are not going to turn the clock back!"[28]

Dewey spent the last two weeks of the campaign frantically searching for some new issue with which to attack Roosevelt. At Chicago Stadium on October 25, he revealed information concerning a Democratic fund-raising organization called the One Thousand Club. "I have here a letter written . . . last Monday," Dewey dramatically announced. "It is written on the letter-head of the National Democratic Campaign Headquarters, Little Rock, Arkansas, and signed by H.L. McAlister and Sam J. Watkins, State Finance Directors." The letter he then read was an invitation to Democratic donors to join the "One Thousand Club." It revealed that the idea for such a club originated with FDR, who said, "I think it would be a good idea to have a list of one thousand persons banded together from all over the United States to act as a liaison to see that facts relating to the public interest are presented factually to the President and members of Congress."

Donations and rewards were linked to this concept, with members "granted special privilege and prestige by party leaders." Furthermore, members would be called into conference on occasion to "discuss matters of national importance and to assist in the formulation of administration policies." Most importantly, to be a member, one had to donate $1,000 to the Democratic National Campaign Fund. "There, in crude unblushing words," Dewey declared, "is the ultimate expression of New Deal politics by the theory of

'Who gets what, when, and why.'" To his great disappointment, the story failed to generate any excitement.[29]

Then, in Boston on November 1, Dewey delivered the harshest speech of his career. The subject was "Factions and Power-Seeking Groups Which Support the New Deal," and it included a biting attack on Hillman and the CIO-PAC. The Dewey and Bricker campaigns and the RNC had been emphasizing "Clear everything with Sidney" since August. It was a staple topic for Bricker. For example, speaking in Parkersburg, West Virginia, in mid-September, Bricker departed from his prepared remarks and tore into Hillman and the PAC, declaring, "I condemn the President of the United States for selling out his party of great history and service to such a gang."[30]

In Detroit, Michigan, in late October, Bricker again attacked "foreign influence" within the Roosevelt administration, insisting that "Today, as never before, a foreign influence of the most subversive kind is trying to take over our American government by boring from within." Specifically, he recited "facts" submitted to a House committee (the Dies Committee) investigating un-American activities, which, he said, "conclusively prove that FDR and the New Deal are in the hands of the radicals and the Communists." Evidence presented to the Dies Committee, he declared, "showed that at least 82 leaders of PAC have been affiliated with organizations listed by Attorney General Biddle as Communist Front Organizations." For the first time in the history of the nation, Bricker concluded, "A foreign fifth column [alluding to Communist Russia] . . . is trying to swing a Presidential election. The all-out Communist support for the fourth term admits of no other interpretation. There has never been anything like this before because no American party or group has been willing to live as the obedient instrument of the policies of a foreign power."[31]

By mid-October, the RNC had stepped up its own efforts. Indeed, one RNC radio ad from October 19 asserted:

> During Roosevelt's administration we have seen Communism, like a snake crawl into control of many labor unions and many once-respected educational organizations. We find fellow-travelers in high posts in government bureaus. Notorious fellow-travelers have been guests in the White House! Today we see the well-known Sidney Hillman trying to gain control of the Democratic party through the Political Action Committee, which he organized and heads. To finance it, he demanded that labor unions collect a dollar from every member and turn the money over to him to use as he pleased, regardless of how the union members felt. At the Chicago Democratic Convention, President Roosevelt gave

orders to his workers to, "Clear everything with Sidney" before they made any decisions!

Why are the Communists and Fellow-travelers so anxious to keep Roosevelt in the White House?

Vote for Dewey on November 7.[32]

Dewey echoed these sentiments in his Boston speech, charging that to perpetuate himself in office for 16 years, Roosevelt had put the Democratic Party on the auction block, for sale to the highest bidder, and the highest bidders were the PAC and the Communist Party. "In this campaign," he declared, "the New Dealers attempt to smother discussion of their Communist alliance.... They insinuate that Americans must love Communism or offend our fighting ally, Russia. But not even the gullible believe that. In Russia, a Communist is a man who supports his government. In America, a Communist is a man who supports the Fourth Term so our form of government may more easily be changed."

The question of Communism in the United States had nothing to do with where a man was born, he insisted. "Every American—every one of us—traces his ancestry to some foreign land." The proof that Communism was not related to national origin was the "fact that Earl Browder, the avowed leader of Communism in America, was born in Kansas." Dewey's main target was Hillman—a New Dealer, he noted, who, with the help of the Communists, had taken over the American Labor Party in New York and was now endorsing Roosevelt's fourth term bid. The CIO leader, he continued, was the biggest political boss in America and a "Front for the Communists."

As chairman of the CIO-PAC, Dewey declared, "he stalks the country squeezing dollars" for FDR out of the hardworking men and women of America, "under threat that if they do not give the dollar, they will lose their jobs." Hillman and the Communists, he warned, were attempting to seize control of the New Deal, through which they aimed to control the whole of American government. "Nazism and Fascism are dying in the world," Dewey soberly concluded. "But the totalitarian idea is very much alive and we must not slip to its other form—Communism. All of these concepts are enemies of freedom and we must equally reject all of them. They would make the State supreme, give political power only to those who deny the supremacy of God and use that power to force all men to become cogs in a great materialistic machine."[33]

While the CIO-PAC and the Communists were, in fact, working closely together in states like New York, Michigan, and Pennsylvania to raise money, educate voters, and get out the vote, Dewey's Boston speech was a mistake in both timing and tone. As one Dewey advisor noted at the time, "You're speaking in Boston and everybody will know you're trying to get the Irish Catholic vote. It's going to look like a cheap play at a time when the Jews in this country are terribly sensitive, when they feel terribly threatened, they don't even know if they'll survive this war . . . and to a group they believe is largely unsympathetic, if not anti-Semitic, you've got this stuff."[34]

Addressing a large "Everybody for Roosevelt" crowd at Madison Square Garden the following night, Harold Ickes called Dewey an "intolerance chief" and charged that "this Dewey smear campaign of hate and prejudice follows the pattern contrived by Adolf Hitler and the unspeakable Goebbels." In a national radio broadcast, Robert Hannegan accused Dewey of building his campaign on "hate, lies, disunity, division, and bigotry," while Roosevelt had focused on "three simple issues: victory, peace, and jobs."[35] Meanwhile, in the White House, Roosevelt "fumed that this was the meanest campaign he'd ever been in, and promised retribution for some of the below-the-belt punches after Election Day."[36] Still, "The Boss is not worried," William Hassett recorded in his diary. "Vilification and falsification are being overdone."[37]

Having successfully drawn Dewey into extreme rhetoric, Roosevelt, in his remarks at Bridgeport, Connecticut, on November 2, appeared—in an obvious appeal to independents—serious and above partisan politics. Alluding to Dewey's angry speech of the previous day, the president told his audience that, "In this campaign, of course, all things taken together, I can't talk about my opponent the way I would like to sometimes, because I try to think that I am a Christian. I try to think that some day I will go to Heaven, and I don't believe there is anything to be gained in saying dreadful things about other people in any campaign."[38]

Two days later, in a speech at Fenway Park in Boston, Roosevelt stepped up his criticism of Dewey's Boston speech. "Speaking here in Boston," Roosevelt began, "a Republican candidate said—and pardon me if I quote him correctly—that happens to be an old habit of mine—he said, that quote, 'the Communists are seizing control of the New Deal, through which they aim to control the Government of the United States.' Unquote." Yet, on that same day, in a speech in Worcester, he promised that a Republican victory in November would end one-man government and forever remove the threat of monarchy in the United States. "Now, really—which is it—Communism or monarchy?" Roosevelt asked. "I don't think that we could have both in this country, even if we wanted either, which we do not. No, we want neither Communism nor monarchy. We want to live under our Constitution which has served pretty well for one hundred and fifty-five years."[39]

The president then reminded his audience that he had been reluctant to run again for the presidency, but that since the campaign had developed, he was "most anxious to win—and I say that for the reason that never before in my lifetime has a campaign been filled with such misrepresentation, distortion, and falsehood. Never since 1928 have there been so many attempts to stimulate in America racial or religious intolerance." When any politician, he concluded, says that the US government could be sold out to the Communists, "then I say that that candidate reveals—and I'll be polite—a shocking lack of trust in America. He reveals a shocking lack of faith in democracy— in the spiritual strength of our people."[40]

Dewey's last major attack on Roosevelt came on November 4 during an address at Madison Square Garden, where he again—this time more directly and forcefully—criticized the administration for the Morgenthau Plan—"a plan that was so clumsy that Mr. Roosevelt himself, finally dropped it." Yet, the publishing of the plan "was just what the Nazi propagandists needed." It was, he declared, "as good as ten fresh German divisions," putting fight back into the German army and stiffening the will of Germans to resist. "Almost overnight," he added, "the headlong retreat of the Germans stopped. They stood and fought fanatically." He then quoted a "military expert" in Newsweek and a United Press report, concluding that "the blood of our fighting men is paying for this improvised meddling which is so much a part and parcel of the Roosevelt Administration."[41] Roosevelt shrewdly ignored both him and the issue.

On election eve, November 6, the candidates made one last appeal to voters. The final Gallup poll reported a race too close to call, with Roosevelt enjoying a slight lead, 51 percent, to Dewey's 49 percent. In a radio address from Hyde Park, Roosevelt again distanced himself from partisan politics, speaking instead on "Our Task Now Is to Face the Future as a Militant and a United People." According to broadcast executive J. Leonard Reinsch, Roosevelt purposefully failed to use all of his allotted radio time so as to leave a 13-minute gap between the end of his speech and the beginning of Dewey's 11:00 p.m. broadcast. The networks, unable to preempt paid time, played slow organ music to fill the gap. Many voters, the White House believed, might turn off their radios and go to bed. They may have been right. The Republican program that began at 11:00 was "monotonous and deadly." Roosevelt listened from his home in Dutchess County and, noticing Fala asleep at his feet, remarked, "They even put my dog to sleep."[42]

At the very end of the 11:00 p.m. program, Dewey, live and from the Executive Mansion in Albany, delivered his last speech of the 1944 presidential campaign. The election, he said, might be the most fateful in American history. "These years 1945 to 1949 will be important, difficult years. They will require vigorous, hard-working, harmonious leadership, with abiding faith in America. But there has arisen in this campaign an argument that the people dare not change administrations because our country is in the midst of a great ordeal. Of course, there is nothing new in that argument. It was used four years ago, when we were at peace. In other countries, this same argument has been the pretext upon which men, originally voted into power by the people, have suspended popular government and maintained themselves indefinitely in power." Dewey then concluded with "three simple tests that must govern the decision of every American tomorrow." In the secrecy of the polling booth, he said, ask yourself these questions:

How can I help shorten the war?
How can I help secure lasting peace?
How can I help give us jobs and opportunity in the years that lie beyond our victory?

He was confident that if the American people soberly reflected upon those questions a Dewey victory was certain.[43]

Election Day 1944, clear and mild throughout the country, witnessed a near record turnout at the polls (over 47 million people in total). Roosevelt received 53 percent of the popular vote (and 432 electoral votes) to Dewey's 47 percent (and 99 electoral votes). Dewey carried only three of the states—Wyoming, Maine, and Bricker's Ohio—that Gallup had defined as "pivotal" on election eve (see Chart 3). Meanwhile, he narrowly lost his home state of Michigan (by just 1.02 percent), which Gallup had listed as safely in the Dewey column. In the end, the election was close, and a shift of just over 800,000 in the states Roosevelt won by less than 4 percent (and totaling 203 electoral votes) would have given Dewey an electoral majority of 302 (see Chart 4).

According to the National Opinion Research Center, which conducted a national election study in conjunction with the Psychology Department of Harvard University, the leading causes for voting for FDR included "Because of the war—we should not change during the war, best man at this time," "Because of his past-record—better man for the job, more experienced," and "Because he is for the common man." Those who supported Dewey, meanwhile, emphasized: "We need a change—four terms is too much—we are heading toward a dictatorship, tired of the New Deal, Anti-Roosevelt, Roosevelt won't live 4 years, hate to see Truman take over," and "To get rid of wasteful spending ... balance the budget ... efficiency in government, house-clean Washington, states' rights."

Chart 3: Gallup Poll vs. Results in 20 Pivotal States, November 1944

STATE	GALLUP %		ELECTION DAY %		
	FDR	DEWEY	FDR	DEWEY	MARGIN
California	53	47	56	43	475,599
Maryland	53	47	52	48	22,541
Connecticut	52	48	52	47	44,619
Pennsylvania	51	49	51	48	105,425
Massachusetts	51	49	53	47	113,946
New Hampshire	51	49	52	48	9,747
Oklahoma	51	49	56	44	82,125
Oregon	51	49	52	47	23,270
Idaho	51	49	52	48	7,262
West Virginia	51	49	55	45	69,958
Delaware	51	49	54	45	11,419
New York	50	50	52	47	316,591
Missouri	49	51	51	48	46,280
New Mexico	49	51	53	46	10,701
Illinois	49	51	52	48	140,165
Maine	48	52	47	52	14,803
Ohio	48	52	49	50	11,530
New Jersey	48	52	50	49	26,539
Wyoming	47	53	49	51	2,502
Minnesota	47	53	52	47	62,448

SOURCE: George Gallup, "Roosevelt Given Slight Advantage over Dewey in Final Gallup Report," *The Washington Post*, November 6, 1944, 1; Gil Troy, Arthur M. Schlesinger, and Fred L. Israel, eds., *History of American Presidential Elections, 1789–2008, Volume 3: 1944–2008* (New York: Facts on File, 2012), 1154–55.

Interestingly, only 4 percent of NORC's postelection survey indicated that Roosevelt's health was a factor in their voting decision, while 45 percent of those questioned expressed the belief that Communists would not have more influence under Roosevelt (only 24 percent said they would). Meanwhile, 64 percent of those surveyed believed that FDR waged the better campaign, while nearly 80 percent maintained that Dewey had waged the most negative one. Most voters received their news from the radio (59 percent). Newspapers came in second with 27 percent, and magazines last with 7 percent. Sixty-five percent indicated that they decided their presidential choice after the conventions. Of that number, 31 percent decided in the last four to six weeks of the campaign.

Chart 4: States Won by Roosevelt by Less Than 4%

STATE	ELECTORAL VOTE	MARGIN OF FDR'S VICTORY
Illinois	28	140,165
Maine	16	14,803
Massachusetts	16	113,946
Michigan	19	22,476
Minnesota	11	62,448
Missouri	15	46,280
New Jersey	16	26,539
New York	47	316,591
Pennsylvania	35	105,425
TOTAL	**203**	**848,673**

SOURCE: Gil Troy, Arthur M. Schlesinger, and Fred L. Israel, eds., *History of American Presidential Elections, 1789–2008, Volume 3: 1944–2008* (New York: Facts on File, 2012), 1154–55.

One of the most interesting questions asked by the NORC was "If the war had been over, do you (Roosevelt voter) think you would have voted for Dewey?" While only 28 percent of those who voted for FDR answered this question, of that percentage 21 percent indicated that they would have changed their vote, while 79 percent said no. Translated into real votes, it would have meant a swing of about 1.6 million votes to Dewey, and in the popular vote, at least, created a virtual tie.[44]

Shortly after 3 a.m., Dewey appeared in the ballroom of the Roosevelt Hotel in Manhattan and conceded defeat. "It is clear," he said, "that Mr. Roosevelt has been reelected for a fourth term, and every good American will wholeheartedly accept the will of the people." He then extended to the president his "hearty congratulations" and "earnest hope" that this next term would "see speedy victory in the war, the establishment of lasting peace, and the restoration of tranquility among our people." The election, he added, had revitalized the Republican Party and made it "a great force for the good of the country and for the preservation of free government in America."[45]

Despite the graceful concession, Dewey failed to send a traditional telegram of congratulations, and at Hyde Park, the president was not amused. "Always meticulous about the amenities," aide William Hassett noted in his diary, Roosevelt telegraphed the governor, "I thank you for your statement, which I have heard over the air a few minutes ago." Forgetting the Christian restraint he had talked about at Fenway Park a few days earlier, Roosevelt told Hassett, "I still think he is a son of a bitch."[46]

Conclusion
"Not a Word, Not a Comma"

Postmortems on the Dewey campaign quickly abounded. According to journalist Arthur Krock, Dewey's September speeches on labor and social security in California played a critical role in his defeat. As soon as Dewey finished his California speeches, Krock told Herbert Hoover, "the campaign was lost." Many conservative Democrats, he insisted, were deeply concerned about the collectivist tendencies of the New Deal and would have declared for Dewey if the Republican candidate "had established a fundamental difference on philosophical grounds between the New Deal and the Conservatives."[1] Author Benjamin Stolberg, meanwhile, blamed defeat on the failure of the GOP to "sufficiently understand ... [that] Twelve years of Communist and other Left wing propaganda in alliance with the Wallaces and Hopkinses, had created a phony but powerful intellectual front—reaching from academic and editor chairs to Hollywood and Broadway nightclubs—which cannot be overrun except by an intellectual and moral counter-organization."[2]

A few days after the election, Dewey aides were asked by reporters if the campaign had any regrets or wished to go back and do something differently. "Not a word, not a comma," was the reply. "The war," aides insisted, was the chief reason for the governor's defeat. Many voters, they added, were simply "reluctant to change leadership with the war being successfully prosecuted and nearing a climax."[3] While the war was definitely a leading factor in the

Republican loss, there were—team Dewey's confidence aside—several costly mistakes made by the campaign. One was Dewey's inability (or unwillingness) to narrow his focus to one or two issues. Indeed, his message, Arthur Krock observed shortly after the election, was "too much bird shot, too little concentrated fire."[4] Thus, he talked about everything from Roosevelt's age to ending one-man rule and saving America from the Communists. Similarly, Dewey's misstatements—particularly on MacArthur, Jackson Hole, and Willkie—hurt his credibility. Like other challengers in wartime presidential elections, Dewey faced the charge, which he unwittingly seemed to encourage, that he was indecisive, inexperienced, and contradictory.

Indeed, after Roosevelt's Fala speech before the Teamsters that September, Dewey, as Rosenman observed in his 1952 memoir, began "swinging wildly in a way that damaged himself rather than the champ."[5] The damage was manifested in three ways. First, the negative tone of his campaign pushed independent and undecided voters into the Roosevelt column. Second, his harsh rhetoric against the president drew greater attention to the campaign and helped mobilize an otherwise lethargic Democratic base to the polls. And third, his lack of focus fueled Democratic charges that he lacked conviction and a "clear stand" on the issues. "If a majority of the American people were willing to accept the hazardous precedent of a fourth [Roosevelt] term," the *New York Times* concluded, "it seems clearly because they were convinced that in this extraordinary crisis the Republican party offered them no satisfactory substitute for Mr. Roosevelt's experience in military affairs and foreign policy, and no equally good assurance that under Republican leadership the country could achieve a lasting peace."[6]

Another mistake was the Dewey campaign's missed opportunity with black voters. African Americans were especially bitter about segregation, discrimination, and humiliation in the armed services. As Willkie noted that summer, "from the battlefields of Italy to the gold-star homes here in America . . . [blacks] have learned that there is nothing more democratic than a bullet or a splinter of steel. They want now to see some political democracy as well."[7] To make matters worse for the administration, Roosevelt dropped Wallace from the ticket in 1944. The vice president was recognized as a champion for the rights of the common man of whatever race, color, and creed. It had been Wallace who had declared at the Democratic National Convention: "The future belongs to those who go down the line unswervingly for the liberal principles of both political and economic democracy regardless of race, color, or religion . . . there must be no inferior races. The poll tax must go."[8] Black dissatisfaction grew, then, with Roosevelt and the Democrats by 1944 and gave room for Republicans to strike.

Yet, neither Dewey nor his party forcefully addressed civil rights on the campaign trail. Much of the black press—especially following the soldier vote bill fight and the failure of New York's Fair Employment Act—was hostile to the governor, and he lacked a strong bridge to the black community and black leaders. There was no significant organization or effort to get out black voters. According to Henry Lee Moon in a postelection analysis, "The masses of the race were unconvinced of the ills of which they complained would be corrected by a Republican victory. They realized that all the discriminations which irked them had persisted under Republican administrations. Roosevelt, they knew, had not created their difficulties; he simply inherited them."[9]

Indeed, shortly after the election, Herbert Brownell, chairman of the RNC, noted that "a shift of 303,414 votes in 15 states outside the South would have enabled Governor Thomas E. Dewey to capture 175 additional Electoral College votes and to win the presidency with an 8 electoral-vote margin." In 8 of those 15 states, the black vote exceeded the number needed to shift the balance toward Dewey. For example, in Maryland, the 50,000 black votes cast in Baltimore alone for Roosevelt were more than double the president's 22,500 state plurality.[10]

Ultimately, Franklin Roosevelt won the 1944 race because he *campaigned* and because he was a master at putting his opponents on the defensive. This was especially damaging for Dewey, who excelled at prosecutions. Throughout the late summer and early fall, Dewey the Prosecutor had been methodically making his case against Roosevelt. The president, waging a Rose Garden strategy that was meant to emphasize his importance as the incumbent, seemed tired, disinterested, and vulnerable. After polls in early September showed Dewey with a slight lead, Roosevelt abandoned his Rose Garden strategy and began campaigning, beginning with the Fala speech in late September. In fact, FDR was the first president to use the neutral White House in partisan politics and to deliver radio addresses. Furthermore, he not only campaigned, but he campaigned effectively. Roosevelt seized the high ground on the UN armed forces issue when Dewey bungled it. He played the role of the dutiful president. And he successfully identified Dewey with isolationists and thus wooed independents and Willkie Republicans into his campaign. Simultaneously, Roosevelt's backers, including Sidney Hillman's CIO-PAC, were able—due to the excitement of the campaign—to interest more people and increase turnout. In those key states, big CIO-PAC cities like New York, Philadelphia, Chicago, Detroit, St. Louis, and Boston made the difference, giving him his fourth and final White House victory. Also, Roosevelt was impacted positively by what Dewey did not do—to share with the American people what he knew about Pearl Harbor and the administration's lack of preparedness.

Although the Democrats won the 1944 election, Dewey's low-key, reformist style helped modernize the GOP without upheaval—something Willkie could not have achieved. Shortly after the election, Ford Bond, Dewey's radio director, wrote that the objective of the governor had been to rebuild the party so as to be worthy of national trust. According to Bond, the Saturday before the election, Dewey took him aside, put his hands on his shoulders, looked him in the eyes, and said, "Ford, I don't want you to be too disappointed—I want to tell you now: We may not win this election. But win or lose, it will not be until sometime after November 7th that a great many of the voters will be with us, in what we are telling them now. Even though we might lose now, it's worth all the fight we're putting into it. So don't be too disappointed if the vote is against us on the seventh of November." Encouraged, Bond noted that "the 1944 campaign was only the beginning—the take-off—the 'D' day of a mighty effort. An arduous campaign to get on the road once again to better things—to the things for which America seems to have been designed. To a reawakening and sharpening of the [Republican] effort to drive ever onward and upward toward the American ideal."[11]

From the ashes of defeat—including his own—Dewey rebuilt the party of Hoover, to fit into (and to be a relevant alternative within) the post–World War II, New Deal order. He kept the party unified, while stirring it away from the midwestern isolationist influences of Senators Robert Taft and Joseph McCarthy and guiding it toward the more internationalist, "pragmatic" conservatism of Dwight Eisenhower and Richard Nixon. He did this in at least two ways. First, Dewey, through his "nonpartisan" foreign policy arrangement with Secretary of State Cordell Hull in August 1944, moved beyond Republican orthodoxy and set foreign policy outside the political arena. In doing this, he not only helped establish the precedent of a bipartisan approach to foreign policy in Cold War elections but also eliminated—at least from headlines—the constant bickering within the GOP on foreign policy. The general internationalist contour of that policy was no longer subject to political debate. Politics had now stopped "at the water's edge"—and that was good for the future of the Republican Party.

And second, he was an important agent of party modernization. As Dewey's only modern biographer, Richard Norton Smith, observed in the late 1970s, the electoral viability of a party is grounded in its "willingness to discard something of its ideological past and advocate new policies that improve upon those of the dominant party. This willingness to expand the existing framework of political consensus is accompanied, at the same time, by fealty to basic party traditions." Dewey employed this theory of party modernization, for example, at the Mackinac Conference of September 1943 when, three months *before* Tehran and Roosevelt's "Four Policemen" pronouncement, he fully embraced internationalism and called for a postwar organization including Great Britain, China, *and* the Soviet Union. According to Smith, Dewey, by 1942, had already dropped the "fuzzy isolationism" of his 1940 primary campaign and had philosophically "caught up with and passed Willkie"—*all the while holding to traditional Republican values in his rhetoric.* For instance, his call for international participation at Mackinac was coupled with reminders of the potential for economic benefits abroad. Speaking with a Republican voice, Dewey repeatedly told audiences that economic prosperity could be rescued from the artificial wartime levels through international trade and investments, and he thus justified internationalism to GOP skeptics as financially healthy. Few other, if any, Republicans could have done that and kept the party together in 1944—not Taft and certainly not Willkie.

In recent years, Willkie has become the internationalist favorite of many historians. Journalist Charles Peters, in *Five Days in Philadelphia: The Amazing "We Want Willkie!" Convention of 1940 and How It Freed FDR to Save the Western World* (2005), argued (as his lengthy subtitle suggests) that Willkie, by supporting a military draft and breaking opposition to it in Congress and within the Republican Party, helped forge an American army of 1.6 million on the eve of Pearl Harbor (as opposed to the previous 270,000). The 1940 Republican National Convention in Philadelphia was, Peters argued, equally important as the Battle of Britain in defeating Germany. Those were five days that saved the Western world, Peters states with great hyperbole, and Willkie was the "necessary man."

Although Willkie was bold and visionary and does indeed deserve credit for these stands in 1940 and 1941, he was not as effective as Dewey in transforming the GOP into a more internationalist party. Willkie—favorably described by historian John Morton Blum in the 1970s as a "Republican heretic"—was not a true party man. He had very shallow roots in the GOP and was thus suspected by a majority of the party faithful. In fact, he had been a lifelong Democrat until just shortly before the 1940 campaign. Furthermore, at the time of his death in the fall of 1944, he was flirting with the possibility of creating, with Roosevelt no less, a third party made up only of "progressives." A party "heretic," he could not persuade the party "faithful."

It was the "faithful" Dewey who made the Republican Party safe for internationalism (and thus transformed the party permanently) by his two campaigns for the presidency in 1944 and 1948 and in engineering the nomination of Dwight Eisenhower to the presidency in 1952. Furthermore, Eisenhower's administration was full of Dewey men: Hagerty (White House press secretary), Dulles (secretary of state), and Brownell (attorney general). Dewey also became the mentor of Eisenhower's young vice president, Richard Milhous Nixon. In 1964 he tried, unsuccessfully, to prevent Barry Goldwater's nomination to the presidency and in 1968 recommended to Nixon a young Texas congressman named George Bush for vice presidential running mate. Thomas E. Dewey never became president of the United States, but his influence upon the Republican Party was great.

The day after the 1944 election, Dewey addressed reporters in New York. To the press, he seemed relaxed and happy that the campaign was finally over. He told reporters that he missed his two sons, Thomas Jr. and John Martin, and hoped to take the family on vacation soon. "It's a terrible thing," he said, "to get so far away from the kids, as many of you fellows know." He then articulated what he viewed to be the main achievements of the campaign: party unity, a close national popular vote, and the return of a Republican legislature to Albany. Aides also indicated that the governor felt his campaign had "got rid of the worst elements in the Republican party," and there was now a "whole-hearted acceptance of his foreign policy views by Republican leaders in and out of Congress." Accompanied by his wife and Paul Lockwood, Dewey then walked from the Roosevelt Hotel to the Grand Central Terminal and boarded a train for Albany. Before the train pulled away, however, the governor appeared on the rear platform of his private car, waved to reporters, and shouted "So long fellows!" A policeman, who was a part of Dewey's security detail in the city, shouted "Next time, governor!" Smiling, Dewey called back: "It's been a lot of fun this time."[12]

NOTES

INTRODUCTION

1. *Newsweek*, July 10, 1944, 40.

2. FDR did, however, qualify the statement, adding that he would "feel free to report to the people the facts about matters of concern to them and especially to correct any misrepresentations." Samuel I. Rosenman, *Working with Roosevelt* (New York: Harper and Brothers, 1952), 202.

3. *Newsweek*, October 9, 1944, 41.

4. "A Bad Campaign," *New Republic*, October 30, 1944, 549.

5. "Moving into High Gear," *U.S. News*, October 6, 1944, 27.

6. John A. Wells, ed., *Thomas E. Dewey on the Two-Party System* (Garden City, NY: Doubleday, 1966), 31.

7. *Official Report of the Proceedings of the Democratic National Convention, 1944.* Democratic National Committee, 1944, 32.

8. *Official Report of the Proceedings of the Twenty-Third Republican National Convention* (Washington DC: Judd and Detweiler, Inc., 1944), 170. "Roosevelt 'Lied Us into War,' Mrs. Luce Declares in Chicago," *New York Times*, October 14, 1944, 9.

9. Stanley Weintraub, *Final Victory: FDR's Extraordinary World War II Presidential Campaign* (Boston: Da Capo Press, 2012).

10. See V.O. Key, "A Theory of Critical Elections," *The Journal of Politics* 17, no. 1 (Feb. 1955): 3–18.

11. Allan J. Lichtman, *Prejudice and the Old Politics: The Presidential Election of 1928* (Chapel Hill: University of North Carolina Press, 1979), 201.

12. "War Election Proves to World America's Faith in Democracy," *Newsweek*, November 13, 1944.

13. Thomas M. Carsey, *Campaign Dynamics: The Race for Governor* (Ann Arbor: University of Michigan Press, 2001), 8.

14. Ibid., 9.

15. Ibid., 15.

16. "War Election Proves to World America's Faith in Democracy."

17. Hadley Cantril, "The Issues—As Seen by the American People," *The Public Opinion Quarterly* (Fall 1944): 334. George Gallup, "Roosevelt and Dewey Evenly Matched Recent Elections Show, Gallup Poll Finds," *New York Times*, May 21, 1944, 37.

18. George Gallup, quoted in David M. Jordan, *FDR, Dewey, and the Election of 1944* (Bloomington: Indiana University Press, 2011), 314.

19. George Gallup, "Roosevelt Given Slight Advantage over Dewey in Final Gallup Report," *The Washington Post*, November 6, 1944, 1.

20. Cantril, "The Issues—As Seen by the American People," 332.

21. Ibid., 342.

22. George H. Gallup, *The Gallup Poll: Public Opinion 1935–1971, Volume 1: 1935–1948* (New York: Random House, 1972), 453.

23. Cantril, "The Issues—As Seen by the American People," 332.

24. Ibid., 342.

25. *Time*, November 1, 1943, 15.

26. Harry S. Truman, quoted in Jean Edward Smith, *FDR* (New York: Random House, 2008), 626.

27. Robert H. Ferrell, *Choosing Truman: The Democratic Convention of 1944* (Columbia: University of Missouri Press, 1994), 1–2.

28. "Dewey's Career: 3rd Take," DNC Special Report on TED, July 8, 1944, 76. Records of the Democratic National Committee: Library Clipping File: Thomas E. Dewey File: Presidential Campaigns, 1944–1948, Box 63, Folder 1, Harry S. Truman Presidential Library, Independence, Missouri.

29. "The Pros at Work," *Time*, December 13, 1943.

30. Jack Redding Memorandum, Records of the Democratic National Committee: Library Clipping File: Thomas E. Dewey File: Presidential Campaigns, 1944–1948, Box 63, Folder 1, Harry S. Truman Presidential Library, Independence, Missouri.

31. George H. Mayer, "The Republican Party, 1932–1952," in Arthur M. Schlesinger Jr. and Fred Israel, eds., *History of U.S. Political Parties, Volume 3: 1910–1945—From Square Deal to New Deal* (New York: Chelsea House Publishers, 1973), 2264.

32. Henry O. Evjen, "The Willkie Campaign: An Unfortunate Chapter in Republican Leadership," *The Journal of Politics* (May 1952): 241.

33. Ibid., 241.

34. Ibid., 248, 241.

35. William S. White, *The Taft Story* (New York: Harper and Row, 1954), quoted in John A. Wells, ed., *Thomas E. Dewey on the Two-Party System* (Garden City, NY: Doubleday, 1966), viii.

36. Taft, quoted in James T. Patterson, *Mr. Republican: A Biography of Robert A. Taft* (Boston: Houghton Mifflin Company, 1972), 286, 269.

37. John A. Wells, ed., *Thomas E. Dewey and the Two-Party System*, 8.

38. Dewey, quoted in Richard Norton Smith, *Thomas E. Dewey and His Times* (New York: Simon and Schuster, 1982), 350.

39. Taft, quoted in Patterson, *Mr. Republican*, 269.

40. "Davenport Sees Defeat of Dewey," *New York Times*, November 7, 1944, 21.

41. Wells, *Thomas E. Dewey on the Two-Party System*, 50, 55.

42. Thomas E. Dewey, "The World We Want to Live In," May 1942, in Stanley Walker, *Dewey: An American of This Century* (New York: McGraw-Hill, 1944), 267.

43. *Public Papers of Thomas E. Dewey, Fifty-First Governor of the State of New York: 1944* (Albany, NY: Williams Press, 1946), 12.

44. Dewey, quoted in Barry K. Beyer, *Thomas E. Dewey, 1937–1947: A Study in Political Leadership* (New York: Garland Publishing, 1979), 103–4.

45. Wells, *Thomas E. Dewey on the Two-Party System*, 8–9.

46. Richard Norton Smith, "Thomas E. Dewey and the Evolution of Modern Republicanism." Unpublished Harvard senior honors thesis, 1975. Thomas E. Dewey Papers, Rhees Library, University of Rochester, New York.

47. Ford Bond, "Politics Made Easy or a Campaign and World Peace in One Easy Lesson." Unpublished. TED Papers, Rhees Library, University of Rochester.

48. Richard Norton Smith, "Thomas E. Dewey and the Evolution of Modern Republicanism."

1: THE TRIUMPH OF POLITICS AS USUAL

1. Haynes Johnson, quoted in John W. Jeffries, *Wartime America: The World War II Home Front* (Chicago: Ivan R. Dee, 1996), 4.

2. John W. Jeffries, *Wartime America: The World War II Home Front*, 18.

3. Richard Polenberg, ed., *America at War: The Home Front 1941–1945* (Englewood Cliffs, NJ: Prentice-Hall, Inc., 1968), 60.

4. Albert Guerard, "A National Government," *The New Republic*, February 1, 1943, 150, quoted in Richard Polenberg, ed., *America at War: The Home Front*, 71.

5. Ibid.

6. Edward J. Flynn, "Party Duty in Wartime," in *America at War*, ed. Richard Polenberg, 67.

7. Harold W. Dodds, "Political Parties in Wartime," *The Yale Review* 31 (June 1942): 703–12, quoted in Polenberg, *America at War*, 68.

8. Dwight Macdonald, "Why Politics?" *Politics* 1 (February 1944): 6–8, quoted in Polenberg, *America at War*, 74.

9. Gary Dean Best, *Herbert Hoover: The Post-Presidential Years, Volume 1: 1933–1945* (Stanford, CA: Hoover Institution Press, 1983), 205.

10. America First Dissolution Statement, quoted in Wayne S. Cole, *Roosevelt and the Isolationists, 1932–45* (Lincoln: University of Nebraska Press, 1983), 504.

11. Richard W. Steele, "Franklin D. Roosevelt and His Foreign Policy Critics," *Political Science Quarterly* (Spring 1979): 18.

12. George Britt, *The Fifth Column Is Here* (New York: Wilfred Funk, Inc., 1940).

13. Samuel I. Rosenman, *The Public Papers and Addresses of Franklin D. Roosevelt, 1940 Volume: War—And Aid to Democracies* (New York: Macmillan Company, 1941), 531–32.

14. FDR, quoted in Steele, "FDR and His Foreign Policy Critics."

15. FDR, quoted in ibid.

16. Biddle wanted to proceed cautiously and avoid the "extravagant abuse of prosecutions for sedition" that had characterized the American home front experience during World War I. Thus, the attorney general ordered the release of several individuals arrested for "seditious" statements early in the war, including a man who had told a small group that Roosevelt should be impeached for asking Congress for a declaration of war; another who had started a brawl by proclaiming that he was for Hitler and that Roosevelt was "no good"; and a Republican who had booed at Roosevelt's picture in a Chicago theater. Francis Biddle, *In Brief Authority* (Garden City, NY: Doubleday and Company, Inc., 1962), 237–38.

17. Flynn's remarks were evidently spurred by a statement made by the new publicity director of the Republican Party, Clarence Budington Kelland, in late January 1942. According to Kelland, "Politics is good in time of peace; in time of war politics is

indispensable. When political unity comes in at the door, human liberties go out of the window. It is political unity which has plunged this world into war." Donald Bruce Johnson, *Wendell Willkie and the Republican Party* (Urbana: University of Illinois Press, 1960), 202.

18. Polenberg, *America at War*, 66.

19. Johnson, *Wendell Willkie and the Republican Party*, 204.

20. Ibid., 204.

21. Robert A. Taft, quoted in Polenberg, *America at War*, 61–62.

22. Herbert Hoover, *Addresses upon the American Road: World War II, 1941–1945* (New York: D. Van Nostrand Co., Inc., 1946), 165.

23. Best, *Herbert Hoover: The Post-Presidential Years, Volume 1*, 210.

24. Roland Young, *Congressional Politics in the Second World War* (New York: Da Capo Press, 1972), 15. According to Young, Congress, which was concerned about its role in the war, had three choices: (1) it could organize a single committee that represented the whole of Congress and was made privy to administration secrets; (2) it could create several investigation committees that focused on various aspects of the war; or (3) it could continue business as usual with the existing party-based committee structure of exacting control. In the end, Congress chose a combination of the second and third options. "Multiplication, not contraction," Young noted, "was in order." Ibid., 18.

25. Ibid.

26. Vandenberg to Leo C. Lillie, January 7, 1942, quoted in Richard E. Darilek, *A Loyal Opposition in Time of War: The Republican Party and the Politics of Foreign Policy from Pearl Harbor to Yalta* (Westport, CT: Greenwood Press, 1976), 27.

27. Congress, Tobey insisted, had an obligation to "demand that those who may be called upon to make the supreme sacrifice shall not make that sacrifice because of inefficiency." Richard Darilek, *A Loyal Opposition in Time of War*, 24.

28. "Tobey's Criticism of Navy Raises Storm in Senate," *The Washington Post*, December 12, 1941, 7.

29. Ibid.

30. Ibid.

31. "Congress Asks for Details on Hawaiian Raid," *Chicago Daily Tribune*, December 10, 1941, 3.

32. Leo Egan, "War Is State Issue, Bennett Declares," *New York Times*, October 20, 1942, 17. Dewey was not, in fact, an opponent of Lend Lease.

33. Ibid.

34. Francis Brown, "National Unity—A Willkie Formula," *New York Times*, December 14, 1941, 11.

35. "Dewey's Speech Accepting Party Nomination for Governor," *New York Times*, August 25, 1942, 12.

36. Ibid.

37. Stanley Walker, *Dewey: An American of This Century*, 258.

38. "Mrs. Luce's Speech before Connecticut Republicans," *New York Times*, September 11, 1942, 17.

39. "Victory and Responsibility," *Time*, November 16, 1942. This article can be found at <http://www.time.com/time/magazine/articles/0,917,932828,00.html>. Overall, Republicans won 51.6 percent of the popular vote in 1942.

40. "Dewey Sees Vote as War Mandate," *New York Times*, November 4, 1942, 7.

2: THOMAS DEWEY AND THE DILEMMAS OF REPUBLICAN WARTIME OP-POSITION

1. Angus Campbell et al., *The American Voter* (Chicago: University of Chicago Press, 1976), 160.

2. Michael A. Davis, "Politics of the 1930s and the New Deal," in Aaron Purcell, ed., *The New Deal and the Great Depression* (Kent, OH: Kent State University Press), 2014.

3. Angus Campbell et al., *The American Voter*, 157; Davis, "Politics of the 1930s and the New Deal."

4. V.O. Key Jr., *The Responsible Electorate: Rationality in Presidential Voting, 1936–1960* (Cambridge, MA: Belknap Press of Harvard University Press, 1966), 31.

5. Ibid., 31, 34.

6. Kristi Anderson, *The Creation of a Democratic Majority, 1928–1936* (Chicago: University of Chicago Press, 1979), 9.

7. Samuel Lubell, *The Future of American Politics* (New York: Harper and Brothers, 1952), quoted in Anderson, ibid.

8. George H. Mayer, "The Republican Party, 1932–1952," in *History of U.S. Political Parties*, 3:2266, 2270–71.

9. Donald R. McCoy, *Landon of Kansas* (Lincoln: University of Nebraska Press, 1966), 327.

10. Ibid., 342.

11. William E. Luechtenburg, *The FDR Years: On Roosevelt and His Legacy* (New York: Columbia University Press, 1995), 13.

12. Malcolm Moos, *The Republicans: A History of Their Party* (New York: Random House, 1956), 399.

13. Ibid.

14. Lippmann, quoted in Clyde P. Weed, *The Nemesis of Reform: The Republican Party during the New Deal* (New York: Columbia University Press, 1994), 37.

15. Arthur Pound, quoted in Moos, *The Republicans*, 394.

16. Gary Best, *Herbert Hoover: The Post-Presidential Years, Volume 1: 1933–1945*, 173.

17. Willkie to Mark Sullivan, November 25, 1944, quoted in Steve Neal, *Dark Horse: A Biography of Wendell Willkie* (Lawrence: University Press of Kansas, 1989), 178–79.

18. Lewis L. Gould, *Grand Old Party: A History of the Republicans* (New York: Random House, 2003), 287.

19. Moos, *The Republicans*, 395.

20. Richard E. Darilek, *A Loyal Opposition in Time of War*, 8.

21. "Herbert Hoover to John W. Bricker, October 16, 1944." Herbert Hoover Post-Presidential Correspondence, Box 23, HHPL.

22. "Flagrant Misrepresentations at the Democratic Convention of 1944," Republican National Committee booklet, p. 5. Post-Presidential Subject File, Box 101, Printed Materials Folder, HHPL.

23. "'Appeasers' in U.S. Warned by Dewey," *New York Times*, February 13, 1942, 15. Dewey's remarks (and perhaps those of FDR) were strongly influenced by *New York World Telegram* editorial writer George Britt's *The Fifth Column Is Here*. Britt's explosive work, published in late 1940, claimed that over a million fifth columnists—"foreign shadow soldiers"—were on American soil, inciting treason, and spying on "our industries,

our defenses, [and] our homes. . . ." Britt also detailed the activities of "little Hitlers" such as Congressman Jacob Thorkelson, an obscure Montana Republican, who in the summer of 1939 read into the *Congressional Record* a German interview with Adolf Hitler in which Hitler insisted upon his innocent intentions. George Britt, *The Fifth Column Is Here*, 112.

24. Arthur H. Vandenberg Jr., ed., *The Private Papers of Senator Vandenberg* (Boston: Houghton Mifflin Company, 1952), 1.

25. James H. Madison, ed., *Wendell Willkie: Hoosier Internationalist* (Indianapolis: Indiana University Press, 1992), 103.

26. *The Private Papers of Senator Vandenberg*, 56.

27. Smith, *Thomas E. Dewey and His Times*, 265.

28. Thomas E. Dewey, "Looking Forward," in *Dewey: An American of This Century*, by Stanley Walker, 221.

29. Thomas E. Dewey, *Twenty against the Underworld* (Garden City, NY: Doubleday, 1974).

30. Roger Butterfield, "Thomas E. Dewey," *Look*, 1944, 104.

31. Ibid.

32. TED to Annie Dewey, July 21, 1944. Thomas E. Dewey Papers. Correspondence, 1939–1954. Rhees Library, University of Rochester.

33. Roger Butterfield, "Thomas E. Dewey," 110.

34. Ibid., 106.

35. Ibid., 100.

36. Ibid., 112.

37. Hickman Powell, *Ninety Times Guilty* (New York: Harcourt, Brace, and Company, 1939), 46.

38. "Dewey's Career, 3rd Take," July 8, 1944. DNC Papers, FDR Presidential Library, 76.

39. Bogart's name in the film was not "Tom Dewey," but "David Graham." The Luciano-like gangster, played by Eduardo Ciannelli, was named "Johnny Vanning."

40. Hoover to Roger Straus, October 5, 1939. Thomas E. Dewey Papers, Series 10, Box 20, Rhees Library, University of Rochester.

41. Hoover to TED, July 17, 1940. Thomas E. Dewey Papers, Series 10, Box 20, Rhees Library, University of Rochester.

42. Butterfield, "Thomas E. Dewey," 117.

43. "The Views of Mr. Dewey: What the Record Shows," *The United States News*, April 21, 1944, 15.

44. Ibid.

45. Thomas E. Dewey, "Our Home Front," *Vital Speeches of the Day* (February 15, 1942), 267–69.

46. Leo F. McCue, "Thomas E. Dewey and the Politics of Accommodation," PhD diss., Boston University, 1979, 67.

47. Wendell Willkie, "Isolation Policies and the League of Nations," *Vital Speeches of the Day* (June 1, 1942), 486.

48. Thomas E. Dewey, *The Case Against the New Deal* (New York: Harper, 1940), 114.

49. For example, in early 1942, Willkie announced the names of 12 men who, he believed, qualified to serve as New York's governor. Dewey's name was not on the list.

50. Dewey, quoted in Smith, *Thomas E. Dewey and His Times*, 344.

51. Hoover, *Addresses upon the American Road: World War II, 1941–1945*, 166–67.

52. Best, *Herbert Hoover: The Post-Presidential Years, Volume 1*, 211.

53. TED to Hoover, May 22, 1942. TED Papers, Series 10, Box 20.

54. Justus D. Doenecke, *Storm on the Horizon: The Challenge to American Intervention, 1939–1941* (Lanham, MD: Rowman and Littlefield Publishers, Inc., 2003), 158.

55. Dewey was not the only politician, Republican or Democrat, to make pre–Pearl Harbor statements that in hindsight looked weak and naïve. For example, after German forces poured into the Soviet Union in June 1941, Democratic senator Harry Truman of Missouri insisted that the United States should support whichever side seemed to be losing. "If we see Germany is winning we ought to help Russia, and if we see Russia is winning, we ought to help Germany, and in that way, let them kill as many as possible, although I wouldn't want to see Hitler win under any circumstances. Neither of them think anything of their pledged word." Truman, quoted in Gary Dean Best, *Herbert Hoover: The Post-Presidential Years, Volume 1: 1933–1944*, 187.

56. Stanley Walker, *Dewey: An American of This Century*, 260–61.

57. "Oil Dearth 'Phony' Fish Charges Here," *New York Times*, September 4, 1941, 15.

58. Smith, *Thomas E. Dewey and His Times*, 343; "Fish Is Called 'Dupe of Hitlerism,' Defends His War Stand in Debate," *New York Times*, September 20, 1941, 9.

59. "Former FDR Adversary Dies at Home at Age 102," *The Eugene* [Oregon] *Register-Guard*, January 20, 1991, 16A.

60. Dewey, quoted in Smith, *Thomas E. Dewey and His Times*, 345.

61. Ibid., 345.

62. "Willkie Approves of Dewey's Stand," *New York Times*, May 24, 1942, 37.

63. Smith, *Thomas E. Dewey and His Times*, 345.

64. "Willkie Approves of Dewey's Stand," *New York Times*, May 24, 1942, 37.

65. Since Dewey's remarks were extemporaneous, there was no prepared text to reference later. There was also no stenographer on hand during the speech.

66. James C. Hagerty, "Willkie Demands Clear Party Stand," *New York Times*, June 14, 1942, 27.

67. "? Thomas E. Dewey?" Advertisement, *New York Times*, June 15, 1942, 13.

68. "Dewey Is 'All Out' in Opposing Fish," *New York Times*, June 16, 1942, 15.

69. TED Papers, Series 4, Box 200, Folder 3.

70. Dewey, quoted in Smith, 346.

71. "Dewey Sees Vote as War Mandate," 7.

72. "Tom Dewey Gets There," *Time*, November 16, 1942, 22.

73. James Hagerty, "Dewey Now in Position for Presidential Coup," *New York Times*, November 9, 1942, E12.

74. Forrest Davis, "The Great Albany Enigma," *The Saturday Evening Post*, January 22, 1944, 52.

3: FRANKLIN ROOSEVELT AND THE CHALLENGES OF THE DEMOCRATIC MAJORITY

1. *The Gallup Poll: Public Opinion 1935–1971, Volume 1*, 363.

2. New Deal stalwarts such as Josh Lee of Oklahoma and William Smathers

of New Jersey, along with sympathizers such as George Norris of Nebraska (whom FDR had openly supported), went down to defeat. "Victory and Responsibility," *Time*, November 16, 1942. This article can be found at <http://www.time.com/time/magazine/articles/0,917,932828,00.html>.

3. Tom Reynolds to Steve Early, September 24, 1944, Thomas E. Dewey Papers, Rhees Library, University of Rochester.

4. "U.S. at War: The New Deal Falls Sick," *Time*, November 30, 1942. This article can be found at <http://www.time.com/time/magazine/articles/0,917,932828,00.html>.

5. Herbert Hoover to Joseph W. Martin, November 6, 1942. Herbert Hoover Post-Presidential Correspondence, Box 143, HHPL.

6. An excellent book to detail this move away from the Republican Party by black Americans is Nancy J. Weiss, *Farewell to the Party of Lincoln: Black Politics in the Age of FDR* (Princeton, NJ: Princeton University Press, 1983).

7. He announced the promotion of Colonel Benjamin O. Davis, the only African American of that rank in the regular Army, to brigadier general. In addition, the president appointed the NAACP's William Hastie as civilian aide to the secretary of war, and he created a special post of Negro advisor to the director of Selective Service, to be filled by Campbell Johnson.

8. In 1936, Roosevelt received almost 27,800,000 votes (or 61 percent of the popular vote) to his Republican Alf Landon's 16,700,000 votes (or 36.5 percent of the popular vote). In 1940, the president still garnered slightly over 27,000,000 votes, but Republican Wendell Willkie increased the Republican vote to almost 22,300,000 (or 44.7 percent of the popular vote).

9. Sam H. Jones, "Will Dixie Bolt the New Deal?" *The Saturday Evening Post*, March 6, 1943, 45.

10. Kari Frederickson, *The Dixiecrat Revolt and the End of the Solid South, 1932–1968* (Chapel Hill: University of North Carolina Press, 2001), 39.

11. Dixon, quoted in ibid.

12. Rankin, quoted in ibid.

13. Alf Landon to TED, June 2, 1944. Thomas E. Dewey Papers, Series 10, Box 24, Folder 10. Rhees Library, University of Rochester.

14. TED to Landon, June 6, 1944. Ibid.

15. George H.W. Bush, *All the Best, George Bush: My Life in Letters and Other Writings* (New York: Scribner, 1999), 48.

16. George H. Nash, *The Conservative Intellectual Movement in America since 1945* (Wilmington, DE: Intercollegiate Studies Institute, 1998), 1.

17. Godfrey Hodgson, *The World Turned Right Side Up: A History of the Conservative Ascendancy in America* (Boston: Houghton Mifflin, 1996), 34.

18. Friedrich A. Hayek, quoted in George H. Nash, *The Conservative Intellectual Movement in America*, 3–4.

19. Ludwig von Mises, *Omnipotent Government: The Rise of the Total State and Total War* (New Haven, CT: Yale University Press, 1944), 3.

20. Les K. Adler and Thomas G. Paterson, "Red Fascism: The Merger of Nazi Germany and Soviet Russia in the American Image of Totalitarianism, 1930s-1950s," *The American Historical Review* 75, no. 4 (April 1970): 1047.

21. Ibid., 1049.

22. *Wall Street Journal*, June 25, 1941, quoted in ibid., 1051.

23. Ibid.

24. Davies, quoted in John Lewis Gaddis, *The United States and the Origins of the Cold War, 1941–1947* (New York: Columbia University Press, 1972), 36.

25. Willkie, quoted in ibid., 40.

26. Ibid., 42.

27. Ibid., 56.

28. Ibid., 58.

29. Harry F. Byrd, "Economy in Government," *Vital Speeches of the Day* (May 1, 1944), 424–30.

30. Ibid., 426.

31 Ibid.

32. Hoover to Bricker, October 1, 1943. Herbert Hoover Post-Presidential Correspondence, Box 23, HHPL.

33. Letter, Constitutional Democrats of North Carolina. Herbert Hoover Presidential Library, Post-Presidential Period Subject File, Box 101. Folder: Printed Material and Clippings.

34. *Fourth Term Indefensible: An Editorial*. Pamphlet. Herbert Hoover Presidential Library, Post-Presidential Period Subject File, Box 101. Folder: Printed Materials and Clippings.

35. Norman D. Markowitz, *The Rise and Fall of the People's Century: Henry A. Wallace and American Liberalism, 1941–1948* (New York: The Free Press, 1973), 83.

36. FDR, quoted in Conrad Black, *Franklin Delano Roosevelt: Champion of Freedom* (New York: Public Affairs, 2003), 132.

37. Radio Address to *New York Herald Tribune* Forum, Washington DC, November 12, 1942. in John Grafton, ed., *Franklin Delano Roosevelt: Great Speeches* (Mineola, NY: Dover Publications, Inc., 1999), 135.

38. This paragraph was grounded in John Jeffries's excellent study, "The 'New' New Deal: FDR and American Liberalism, 1937–1945," *Political Science Quarterly* (Autumn 1990): 397–99.

39. Roosevelt signed the Servicemen's Readjustment Act (or the GI Bill), which embraced all of his points in the Fireside Chat of the previous summer, on 22 June 1944.

40. Eleanor Roosevelt, quoted in Lawrence and Cornelia Levine, eds., *The People and the President: America's Conversation with FDR* (Boston: Beacon Press, 2002), 495.

41. Fireside Chat, Washington DC, July 28, 1943. in Jeffries, "The 'New' New Deal," 144–45.

42. Levine and Levine, *The People and the President*, 503–9.

43. B.D. Zevin, *Nothing to Fear: The Selected Addresses of Franklin Delano Roosevelt, 1932–1945* (New York: Houghton Mifflin, 1946), 387–97.

4: MACKINAC AND THE MAKING OF A REPUBLICAN FOREIGN POLICY

1. George H. Gallup, *The Gallup Poll: Public Opinion, 1935–1971*, 340.

2. Polenberg, *America at War*, 153.

3. Robert Divine, *Second Chance: The Triumph of Internationalism in America during World War II* (New York: Atheneum, 1971), 119.

4. Ibid.

5. Ibid., 81.

6. Dewey, quoted in ibid.

7. Herbert Hoover, *Addresses upon the American Road: World War II, 1941–1945*, 8.

8. Ibid., 9.

9. Ibid., 10.

10. William Bradford Huie, "Stassen Challenges the Republican Party," *The American Mercury*, March 1943, 271.

11. Walter Lippmann, *U.S. War Aims* (Boston: Little, Brown and Company, 1944), 164.

12. Ibid.

13. Ibid., 167.

14. Richard H. Immerman, *John Foster Dulles: Piety, Pragmatism, and Power in U.S. Foreign Policy* (Wilmington, DE: Scholarly Resources, Inc., 1999), 22.

15. Ibid., 4–5.

16. Smith, *Thomas E. Dewey and His Times*, 303; "Men around Dewey," *Time*, May 29, 1944.

17. Immerman, *John Foster Dulles*, 21.

18. Ibid., 22.

19. John Foster Dulles, "Six Pillars of Peace," *Vital Speeches of the Day* (1943), 407.

20. Immerman, *John Foster Dulles*, 22.

21. Ibid., 23.

22. Smith, *Thomas E. Dewey and His Times*, 385.

23. *The Private Papers of Senator Vandenberg*, 45.

24. McCue, "Thomas E. Dewey and the Politics of Accommodation," 84.

25. Ibid.

26. Turner Catledge, "Dewey Proposes We Keep Alliance with the British," *New York Times*, September 6, 1943, 1.

27. "Paper Says Dewey 'Goes Anti-American,'" *New York Times*, September 7, 1943, 14.

28. Alf Landon to Herbert Hoover, September 15, 1943. Herbert Hoover Post-Presidential Correspondence, Box 118. Herbert Hoover Presidential Library, West Branch, Iowa.

29. Hoover to Landon, September 20, 1943. Herbert Hoover Post-Presidential Correspondence, Box 118. Herbert Hoover Presidential Library, West Branch, Iowa.

30. Landon and Hoover were not the only Republicans displeased with Dewey's performance at Mackinac. In a letter to a friend later that month, Senator Robert Taft of Ohio recalled that Dewey arrived at the conference "in a special car, with a bodyguard, and then was so arrogant and disagreeable that he turned most of the Republicans there against him." Robert Taft to David S. Ingalls, September 16, 1943. Clarence E. Wunderlin Jr., ed., *The Papers of Robert A. Taft, Volume 2: 1939–1944* (Kent, OH: Kent State University Press, 2001), 487.

31. TED to Anne T. Dewey. TED Papers, Correspondence, 1939–1954.

32. *The Private Papers of Senator Vandenberg*, 55.

33. McCue, "Thomas E. Dewey and the Politics of Accommodation," 82.

34. Ibid., 84.

35. *The Private Papers of Senator Vandenberg*, 59.

36. Hoover to Bricker, October 1, 1943.

37. Ellsworth Bernard, *Wendell Willkie: Fighter for Freedom* (Marquette: Northern Michigan University Press, 1966), 420.

38. Divine, *Second Chance*, 132.

5: DEMOCRATS AND THE POSTWAR WORLD

1. Franklin D. Roosevelt, "Our Foreign Policy: A Democratic View." *Foreign Affairs* (July 1928): 578.

2. Franklin D. Roosevelt, "Acceptance Speech for Vice-Presidential Nomination," in John Grafton, ed., *Franklin Delano Roosevelt: Great Speeches*, 3–4.

3. Ibid., 3.

4. Roosevelt, "Our Foreign Policy," 578.

5. Ibid., 56.

6. Saul Padover, ed., *Wilson's Ideals* (Washington DC: American Council on Public Affairs, 1942), 4.

7. Ibid., 5.

8. Divine, *Second Chance*, 168.

9. Edgar G. Sisson, "A Bigger Wilson Than We Knew," *The Saturday Review*, July 15, 1944, 8.

10. Gerald W. Johnson, *Woodrow Wilson: The Unforgettable Figure Who Has Returned to Haunt Us* (New York: Harper and Brothers, 1944).

11. Divine, *Second Chance*, 168.

12. Ibid., 169.

13. Karl Schriftgiesser, *The Gentleman from Massachusetts: Henry Cabot Lodge* (Boston: Little, Brown and Company, 1944), 351.

14. Darryl F. Zanuck, *Wilson*. Film. Twentieth Century Fox, 1944.

15. William D. Hassett, *Off the Record with F.D.R., 1942–1945* (New Brunswick, NJ: Rutgers University Press, 1958), 270.

16. Markowitz, *The Rise and Fall of the People's Century*, 47.

17. Henry A. Wallace, *The Century of the Common Man* (New York: Reynal and Hitchcock, 1943), 7.

18. Ibid., 11.

19. Ibid., 51.

20. Harry Byrd, "Economy in Government," *Vital Speeches of the Day* (May 1, 1944), 428.

21. Sumner Welles, "World Leadership to Protect Peace," *Vital Speeches of the Day* (New York: City News Publishing, June 15, 1942, Vol. 8, No. 17), 515.

22. Samuel I. Rosenman, ed., *The Public Papers and Addresses of Franklin D. Roosevelt, 1943: The Tide Turns* (New York: Harper and Brothers, 1950), 375–76.

23. *Herbert Hoover: The Post-Presidential Years, Volume 1*, 239.

24. *New York Times*, March 15 and 16, 1943, quoted in H. Bradford Westerfield, *Foreign Policy and Party Politics: Pearl Harbor to Korea* (New Haven, CT: Yale University Press, 1955), 147.

25. Westerfield, *Foreign Policy and Party Politics*, 149.

26. Ibid., 159.

27. Woods, *A Changing of the Guard*, 254.

28. Willard Range, "FDR—A Reflection of American Idealism," in Warren F. Kimball, ed., *Franklin D. Roosevelt and the World Crisis, 1937-1945* (Lexington, MA: D.C. Heath and Company, 1973), 249.

29. Michael Beschloss, *The Conquerors: Roosevelt, Truman, and the Destruction of Hitler's Germany, 1941-1945* (New York: Simon and Schuster, 2002), 49.

30. Ibid., 19, 103.

31. Ibid., 116.

32. "Would Save Oppressed: Dewey Asks U.S. to Act at once for Jews in Europe," *New York Times*, September 10, 1943, 25.

33. Beschloss, *The Conquerors*, 116.

6: JOHN W. BRICKER AND THE CONSERVATIVE REPUBLICANS

1. Robert A. Taft, "A 1944 Program for the Republicans," *The Saturday Evening Post*, December 11, 1943, 17.

2. Taft to John W. Bricker, June 10, 1943. in Wunderlin, ed., *The Papers of Robert A. Taft, Volume 2: 1939-1944*, 454.

3. Taft, quoted in James T. Patterson, *Mr. Republican*, 270.

4. Taft to David S. Ingalls, September 16, 1943. in Wunderlin, ed., *The Papers of Robert A. Taft, Volume 2*, 487.

5. Patterson, *Mr. Republican*, 270.

6. Taft was correct. He did in fact face a difficult bid for reelection in 1944, winning by a margin of only 17,740 votes. Patterson, *Mr. Republican*, 268.

7. Taft to Bricker, July 5, 1944. Wunderlin, ed., *The Papers of Robert A. Taft, Volume 2*, 566.

8. Taft to Bricker, June 10, 1943. Ibid., 454. Bricker humbly replied to Taft: "Bob, you don't have to explain anything to me at any time. I do want to say to you if at any time it becomes apparent that you are the man to be candidate for President, you have my support as you have had in the past." Ibid.

9. "Bricker Rests All on the Presidency," *New York Times*, November 16, 1943, 18.

10. Alf Landon to Bricker, November 16, 1943. John W. Bricker Papers, Correspondence, 1942-44, Box 23, Ohio Historical Society.

11. Hoover to Bricker, February 12, 1944. John W. Bricker Papers, Correspondence, 1942-44, Box 23.

12. William Bradford Huie, "The Man Who May Be President," *The American Mercury*, May 1943, 528.

13. Ibid., 530.

14. Michael J. Anderson, "The Presidential Election of 1944" (PhD diss., University of Cincinnati, 1990), 113.

15. Huie, "The Man Who May Be President," 532.

16. Richard O. Davies, *Defender of the Old Guard: John Bricker and American Politics* (Columbus: Ohio State University Press), 83.

17. Ibid.

18. Text of radio address, "Declaration of American Faith," Blue Network, 1 January 1944, Box 133, John W. Bricker Papers, Ohio Historical Society. Quoted in Davies, *Defender of the Old Guard*, 88.

19. John Hollister to Assistant Campaign Chairman, Everet Addison, 17 January

1944. Hollister Papers. Box 16. Folder 7, Cincinnati Historical Society, Quoted in Anderson, "The Presidential Election of 1944," 117.

20. Taft to Lester Bradshaw, May 30, 1944. Wunderlin, ed., *The Papers of Robert A. Taft, Volume 2,* 550.

21. John Whiteclay Chambers II, ed., *The Oxford Companion to American Military History* (Oxford: Oxford University Press, 1999), 405.

22. Philip J. Briggs, "General MacArthur and the Presidential Election of 1944," *Presidential Studies Quarterly* 22 (Winter 1992): 34.

23. *The Private Papers of Senator Vandenberg,* 77.

24. Ibid., 78.

25. Ibid., 82.

26. Incidentally, MacArthur's victory in Illinois was smaller than Dewey's 86 percent victory in that same primary four years earlier.

27. John McCarten, "General MacArthur: Fact and Legend," *The American Mercury,* January 1944.

28. *The Private Papers of Senator Vandenberg,* 84.

29. Ibid., 86.

30. Briggs, "General MacArthur and the Presidential Election of 1944," 39.

31. Ibid.

7: THE FALL OF WENDELL WILLKIE

1. Eugene Lyons, "Notes on Wendell Willkie," The *American Mercury,* May 1944, 520.

2. The first unsuccessful Republican presidential nominee to win the nomination a second time was Thomas Dewey in 1948. Twenty years later, Richard Nixon, who had lost the general election to John Kennedy in 1960, repeated this feat. Democrats, meanwhile, have been more forgiving to their losing nominees. For example, in 1892, former president Grover Cleveland, who had been defeated in his bid for a second term in 1888, was nominated for a third time. In 1900, Democrats embraced the unsuccessful William Jennings Bryan a second time, and in 1908, a third. Finally, in 1956, Adlai Stevenson, the unsuccessful nominee from 1952, once again secured his party's nomination.

3. Wendell Willkie, *One World* (New York: Simon and Schuster, 1943), 2.

4. Ibid., 179.

5. Ibid., 180.

6. Eugene Lyons, "Notes on Wendell Willkie," 524–25.

7. Taft to David S. Ingalls, May 14, 1943. Wunderlin, ed., *The Papers of Robert A. Taft, Volume 2,* 439.

8. D.B. Johnson, *Wendell Willkie and the Republican Party,* 261.

9. George Gallup, "Republican Voters Give Views on Leading Candidates for 1944," *The Washington Post,* March 7, 1943, B2.

10. "Republicans," *Time,* November 1, 1943, 15.

11. Best, *Herbert Hoover: The Post-Presidential Years, Volume 1,* 219.

12. Hoover, quoted in ibid.

13. Gallup, "Republican Voters Give Views on Leading Candidates for 1944," B2.

14. James A. Hagerty, "Willkie Declares Candidacy for '44; R.H. Cake Manager," *New York Times,* February 15, 1944, 1.

15. Willkie's gaffes and Dewey quote from Smith, *Thomas Dewey and His Times,* 388.

16. *The Gallup Poll: Public Opinion 1935–1971, Volume 1*, 414.

17. In the first week of his campaign in Wisconsin, Willkie delivered 30 speeches.

18. James Hagerty, "Willkie Speeches in Wisconsin Held as Aimed at Dewey," *New York Times*, March 21, 1944, 1.

19. James Hagerty, "Willkie Condemns Isolationist Views," *New York Times*, March 22, 1944, 1, 36.

20. James Hagerty, "Willkie Says Vote May Hinge on War," *New York Times*, March 25, 1944, 11.

21. Wendell Willkie, "Our Sovereignty: Shall We Use It?" *Foreign Affairs* (April 1944): 353–54.

22. James Hagerty, "Willkie Says Vote May Hinge on War," 11.

23. James Hagerty, "Willkie 'Proud' for His Enemies," *New York Times*, March 27, 1944, 19.

24. Walter Johnson, *The Battle against Isolation*, 238–39.

25. Letter from Clyde D. Eastus to Assistant Attorney General Tom C. Clark, Democratic National Committee Papers, FDR Presidential Library, Hyde Park, New York.

26. D.B. Johnson, *Wendell Willkie and the Republican Party*, 280.

27. "Newspapers Discuss Willkie's Withdrawal from Race," *New York Times*, April 6, 1944, 17.

28. D.B. Johnson, *Wendell Willkie and the Republican Party*, 273.

29. Lyons, "Notes on Wendell Willkie," 521.

30. Thomas E. Dewey Papers, Rhees Library, University of Rochester.

31. D.B. Johnson, *Wendell Willkie and the Republican Party*, 264.

32. Ibid., 264–65.

33. Lyons, "Notes on Wendell Willkie," 521.

8: THOMAS DEWEY AND THE STRUGGLE FOR REPUBLICAN CONSENSUS

1. Ibid.

2. Alf Landon to Roger Straus, November 5, 1943. TED Papers, Series 10: Box 24.

3. Barton to TED, May 7, 1943. TED Papers, Series 10: Box 3: Folder 4.

4. TED to Herbert Hoover, October 16, 1943. Thomas E. Dewey Papers, Series 10, Box 20, Rhees Library, University of Rochester.

5. Herbert Hoover to Harrison Spangler, November 16, 1943. Thomas E. Dewey Papers. Series 10, Box 20, Rhees Library, University of Rochester.

6. TED to Herbert Hoover, November 19, 1943. Thomas E. Dewey Papers. Series 10, Box 20, Rhees Library, University of Rochester.

7. Forrest Davis, "Dewey's April Choice," *The Saturday Evening Post*, August 12, 1944, 48.

8. Ibid.

9. *The New Masses*, quoted in Stanley High, "Why the Left Wing Fears Dewey," *The Saturday Evening Post*, October 14, 1944, 17.

10. Martin Van Buren, Horatio Seymour, Samuel Tilden, Grover Cleveland, Theodore Roosevelt, Charles Evans Hughes, Alfred E. Smith, and Franklin D. Roosevelt had all served as New York governors before becoming presidential nominees. Van Buren, Cleveland, and the two Roosevelts were the ones who actually won.

11. *Time*, November 1, 1943.

12. John N. Wheeler to Bruce Barton, Thomas E. Dewey Papers. Series 10, Box 3, Folder 4. Rhees Library, University of Rochester.

13. Butterfield, "Thomas E. Dewey," 116.

14. Dewey, quoted in Simon Topping, "'Never Argue with the Gallup Poll': Thomas Dewey, Civil Rights and the Election of 1948," *Journal of American Studies* 38 (2004): 181.

15. "Francis Rivers Named Aide to Dewey in NY," *The Afro American*, January 8, 1938, 12.

16. Herbert Brownell, *Advising Ike: The Memoirs of Attorney General Herbert Brownell* (Lawrence: University Press of Kansas, 1993).

17. "Edwin Jaeckle, 97, Lawyer and Backer of Thomas Dewey," *New York Times*, May 16, 1992.

18. Drew Pearson, "The Washington Merry-Go-Round," *The Washington Post*, June 27, 1944, 7.

19. Smith, *Thomas E. Dewey and His Times*, 389.

20. Anderson, "The Presidential Election of 1944," 154, 156.

21. Telegram, Thomas E. Dewey to Carl Rix, February 22, 1944. TED Papers, Series 2, Box 15, Folder 2. RRL-UR. Quoted in Anderson, "The Presidential Campaign of 1944," 155. Incidentally, one day after Dewey sent the telegram to Wisconsin delegates disavowing a presidential run, Leo Egan, a Dewey supporter, qualified the governor's statement, announcing: "Governor Dewey regards himself as *pledged not to seek* the Republican Presidential nomination, but considers himself free to accept it if the national convention should name him as its candidate [italics added]." Quoted in Johnson, *Wendell Willkie and the Republican Party*, 270.

22. Beyer, *Thomas E. Dewey, 1937–1947: A Study in Leadership*, 102.

23. Anderson, "The Presidential Election of 1944," 153.

24. Memorandum of Dinner with TED, March 29, 1944. Herbert Hoover Papers, PPI Box 315, Thomas E. Dewey Folder. Herbert Hoover Presidential Library. Quoted from Anderson, 157.

25. Anderson, "The Presidential Election of 1944," 163.

26. The Dewey supporter was Missouri Republican Barak Mattingly, who was a member of the Arrangements Committee for the Republican National Convention in 1944. Dewey's reply to Mattingly was "the answer to your wire is no." Quoted from Michael Anderson, "The Presidential Campaign of 1944," 152.

27. "The Cautious Young Man on a Campaign Trapeze," in Max Lerner, *Public Journal: Marginal Notes on Wartime America* (New York: The Viking Press, 1945), 198.

28. "GOP Senators Back Dewey in '44 Poll," *New York Times*, February 8, 1944, 34.

29. *Public Papers of Thomas E. Dewey, Fifty-First Governor of the State of New York: 1944*, 709.

30. Hoover to TED, May 1, 1944. TED Papers, Series 10, Box 20.

31. Taft to Frances Edwards, March 8, 1944. Wunderlin, ed., *The Papers of Robert A. Taft, Volume 2*, 531.

32. Adams, quoted in McCue, "Thomas E. Dewey and the Politics of Accommodation," 91.

9: THE REPUBLICAN NATIONAL CONVENTION

1. Meyer Bergers, "Convention Gives Dewey an Ovation," *New York Times*, June 29, 1944, 1.

2. Joseph Martin, *My First Fifty Years in Politics* (New York: McGraw-Hill, Inc., 1960), 161.

3. "Dewey Snaps GOP from Coma, But Enormous Task Lies Ahead," *Newsweek*, July 10, 1944, 35.

4. Ibid., 47.

5. "Dewey Bricker," *New York Times*, July 2, 1944, E1. Charles Hurd, "Nominations Made with Great Speed," *New York Times*, June 27, 1944, 13.

6. Nancy Weiss, *Farewell to the Party of Lincoln*, 211.

7. "'Never Argue with the Gallup Poll,'" 179.

8. Simon Topping, *Lincoln's Lost Legacy: The Republican Party and the African American Vote, 1928–1952* (Gainesville: University Press of Florida, 2008), 90.

9. "Two Strikes on Dewey," *Crisis*, April 1944, 104.

10. Mark Sullivan, "War Is Only Element That Tends to Increase F.D. Vote," *The Washington Post*, March 12, 1944, B5.

11. "Two Strikes on Dewey," 104.

12. *Public Papers of Thomas E. Dewey: 1944*, 594.

13. "Two Strikes on Dewey," 104.

14. "Quitting Bias Unit, 8 Criticize Dewey," *New York Times*, March 27, 1944, 19.

15. *Public Papers of Thomas E. Dewey: 1944*, 123.

16. Smith, *Thomas E. Dewey and His Times*, 444.

17. Ibid.

18. *Public Papers of Thomas E. Dewey: 1944*, 123.

19. "NAACP Charges Dewey Made the 'Wrong Choice' on FEPC Act," *The New York Age*, April 1, 1944, 2.

20. "Two Strikes on Dewey," 104.

21. Warren Moscow, "Dewey Builds Up Party Platform on 2 Major Points," *New York Times*, June 30, 1944, 11.

22. Wendell Willkie, *An American Program* (New York: Simon and Schuster, 1944), 7.

23. *Official Report of the Proceedings of the Twenty-Third Republican National Convention, 1944*, 133–34.

24. Charles Hurd, "Nominations Made with Great Speed," *New York Times*, June 27, 1944, 13.

25. *Official Report of the Proceedings of the Twenty-Third Republican National Convention*, 139, 140, 138.

26. Ibid., 166.

27. Ibid., 173–74.

28. Smith, *Thomas E. Dewey and His Times*, 396.

29. James A. Hagerty, "29 Leaders Join Dewey Movement," *New York Times*, June 23, 1944, 12.

30. James A. Hagerty, "Dewey Majority Appears Certain by Convention Eve," *New York Times*, June 24, 1944, 1.

31. Ibid.

32. Charles Hurd, "Bricker Fights On, with Help of Taft," *New York Times*, June 26, 1944, 9.

33. The memo, "Suggested Case for Presidential Campaign," was written by Harold Seymour, who knew Dewey in connection with USO activities. The Seymour memo was prepared after consultation with Lindsay Bradford and Prescott Bush. It was sent to Paul Lockwood, who then gave it to Brownell, who promised to forward it to Dewey. It was for-

warded, but there is no record of Dewey's views on it. Paul Lockwood to Herbert Brownell, May 16, 1944. Series 10, Box 6, Folder 1, TED Paper, University of Rochester.

34. Charles Hurd, "Bricker Fights On, with Help of Taft," *New York Times*, June 26, 1944, 9.

35. Davies, *Defender of the Old Guard*, 93.

36. *Official Report of the Twenty-Third Republican National Convention, 1944*, 193–97.

37. Ibid.

38. Ibid., 197.

39. Charles Eagan, "Bricker Nominated for Second Place," *New York Times*, June 29, 1944. Raymond Moley, quoted in Davies, *Defender of the Old Guard*, 94.

40. Taft to Bricker, July 5, 1944. Wunderlin, ed., *The Papers of Robert A. Taft, Volume 2: 1939–1944*, 566.

41. In many ways, then, Bricker was a better pick than Dewey's first choice (and ultimately his running mate in 1948), Earl Warren. In fact, a case could be made that, in the 1948 upset, the Dewey campaign would have greatly benefited from a running mate like Bricker.

42. John W. Bricker to Thomas E. Dewey, October 5, 1944. Thomas E. Dewey Papers, Rhees Library, University of Rochester.

43. Raymond Moley, *27 Masters of Politics: In a Personal Perspective* (New York: Funk and Wagnalls Co., 1949), 58.

10: DEWEY—"AN AMERICAN OF THIS CENTURY"

1. Ibid., 192.

2. *Official Report of the Twenty-Third Republican National Convention, 1944*, 233–34.

3. Ibid., 234.

4. Ibid.

5. Ibid.

6. Ibid., 240.

7. *Newsweek*, July 10, 1944, 40.

8. Ibid.

9. Ibid.

10. Ibid., 35.

11. S. Burton Heath, *Yankee Reporter* (New York: Wilfred Funk, Inc., 1940), 233–34.

12. Ibid., 215.

13. I.F. Stone, "Thomas E. Dewey," *The Nation*, May 20, 1944, 586–87.

14. Wolcott Gibbs, *St. George and the Dragnet: An Intimate Profile of a Presidential Candidate* (1940). Pamphlet. Herbert Hoover Post-Presidential Subject File, Box 100, HHPL.

15. "Dewey: The Man and His Record," *The New Republic*, September 25, 1944, 388.

16. Ibid., 407.

17. Ibid., 388.

18. One of the most substantive pro-Dewey works of 1944 was an article in *Life* by Roger Butterfield, simply entitled "Thomas E. Dewey." Another positive and informative account of Dewey was Forrest Davis's "The Great Albany Enigma," published in two parts in *The Saturday Evening Post* in January 1944.

19. "Rupert Hughes Tells Why Dewey Is Needed in the White House," *New York Jr. American*, October 16, 1944.

20. Stone, "Thomas E. Dewey," 586.

21. "Dewey's Career: 3rd Take," DNC Special Report on TED, July 8, 1944, 93. Records of the Democratic National Committee: Library Clipping File: Thomas E. Dewey File: Presidential Campaigns, 1944–1948, Box 63, Folder 1, Harry S. Truman Presidential Library, Independence, Missouri.

22. Stanley Walker, *Dewey: An American of This Century*, 32–33.

23. RNC Memo, September 30, 1944. TED Papers, Series 10, Box 6, Folder 2.

24. John Gunther, *Inside U.S.A.* (New York: Harper and Brothers, 1946), 529.

25. Ibid., 533.

26. John Gunther, *Inside U.S.A.*, 533.

27. Ibid.

28. Ibid.

29. Taft to Lester Bradshaw, May 30, 1944. Wunderlin, ed., *The Papers of Robert A. Taft, Volume 2*, 550.

30. Richard M. Nixon, *In the Arena: A Memoir of Victory, Defeat and Renewal* (New York: Simon and Schuster, 1990), 267.

31. Kenneth W. Thompson, ed., *Lessons from Defeated Presidential Candidates*, 112–13, 109–10.

32. TED to Henry Turnbell, October 4, 1944. Dewey Series 4, Box 187, Folder 18, Rhees Library, University of Rochester.

33. Carl Byoir to Herbert Brownell, August 17, 1944. Dewey Series 2, Box 15, Folder 8, Rhees Library.

34. Moley, *27 Masters of Politics*, 56.

35. Ibid., 57.

11: FRANKLIN ROOSEVELT AND THE PURSUIT OF DEMOCRATIC PARTY UNITY

1. Samuel I. Rosenman, ed., *The Public Papers and Addresses of Franklin D. Roosevelt, Volume 1: The Genesis of the New Deal, 1928–1932* (New York: Random House, 1938), 860.

2. *The Gallup Poll: Public Opinion 1935–1971, Volume 1*, 409.

3. "Says Party Is 'Sunk' without Roosevelt," *New York Times*, September 1, 1943, 21.

4. Quoted in Robert Dallek, *Franklin D. Roosevelt and American Foreign Policy, 1932–1945* (New York: Oxford University Press, 1979), 442.

5. Lawrence W. Levine and Cornelia R. Levine, eds., *The People and the President*, 547.

6. *The Gallup Poll: Public Opinion 1935–1971, Volume 1*, 371.

7. Ibid., 388.

8. "You're Right, Dewey Has a Good Chance!" *The Saturday Evening Post*, July 29, 1944, 92.

9. "The Pros at Work," *Time*, December 13, 1943.

10. Ibid.

11. *The Gallup Poll: Public Opinion 1935–1971, Volume 1*, 419.

12. Ibid.

13. Robert A. Garson, *The Democratic Party and the Politics of Sectionalism, 1941–1948* (Baton Rouge: Louisiana State University Press, 1974), 96, 100–102.

14. Allan Nevins, "A Portrait of FDR (Review)," *Saturday Review*, August 12, 1944, 9.

15. Ibid.

16. Frank Kingdon, *"That Man" in the White House: You and Your President* (New York: Arco Publishing Company, 1944), 58.

17. Ibid., 63.

18. Ibid.

19. Ibid., 64.

20. Robert Moses, "Why I Oppose the Fourth Term," *The Saturday Evening Post*, October 7, 1944, 17, 109–10.

21. Ferrell, *Choosing Truman*, 15.

22. J.R. Fuchs Oral History Interview with Edwin F. Pauley, March 1971. Harry S. Truman Presidential Library.

23. Ibid.; Thomas F. Eagleton and Diane L. Duffin, "Bob Hannegan and Harry Truman's Vice Presidential Nomination," *Missouri Historical Review* (April 1996): 268.

24. Eagleton and Duffin, "Bob Hannegan and Harry Truman's Vice Presidential Nomination," 268.

25. Robert L. Messer, *The End of an Alliance: James F. Byrnes, Roosevelt, Truman, and the Origins of the Cold War* (Chapel Hill: University of North Carolina Press, 1982), 18.

26. Pauley, quoted in Jonathan Daniels, *The Man of Independence* (Philadelphia: J.B. Lippincott Company, 1950), 238; Eagleton and Duffin, "Bob Hannegan and Harry Truman's Vice Presidential Nomination," 269.

27. Samuel I. Rosenman, ed., *The Public Papers and Addresses of Franklin D. Roosevelt, 1944–1945: Victory and the Threshold of Peace* (New York: Harper and Brothers, 1950), 80.

28. "Bob Hannegan and Harry Truman's Vice Presidential Nomination," 270.

29. Pauley memorandum for Daniels, quoted in Ferrell, *Choosing Truman*, 13.

30. McCullough, *Truman* (New York: Simon and Schuster, 1992), 341.

31. Roosevelt, quoted in ibid.

32. Ferrell, *Choosing Truman*, 14.

33. Eleanor Roosevelt, quoted in ibid., 15.

34. Ibid., 22–23.

35. John Morton Blum, ed., *The Price of Vision: The Diary of Henry A. Wallace, 1942–1946* (Boston: Houghton Mifflin, 1973), 366–67. Quoted in Ferrell, *Choosing Truman*, 24–25.

36. Ferrell, *Choosing Truman*, 20.

37. Ibid., 21.

38. Ibid.

39. James F. Byrnes, *All in One Lifetime* (New York: Harper and Brothers, 1958), 221.

40. Ibid., 222.

41. Truman, quoted in Ferrell, *Choosing Truman*, 33; ibid., 32.

42. Byrnes, *All in One Lifetime*, 224.

43. Ibid.

44. Ferrell, *Choosing Truman*, 32.

45. Byrnes, quoted in ibid., 33.

46. *What Is the P.A.C.?* Pamphlet, TED Papers.

47. Joseph Gaer, *The First Round: The Story of the CIO Political Action Committee* (New York: Duell, Sloan and Pearce, 1944).

12: THE DEMOCRATIC NATIONAL CONVENTION

1. Edward T. Folliard, "Kerr Attacks Dewey's Youth, Inexperience," *The Washington Post*, July 20, 1944, 1.

2. *Official Report of the Proceedings of the Democratic National Convention 1944* (Democratic National Committee: 1944), 37.

3. Ibid., 38.

4. Ibid., 32.

5. "Political Four-Flushing," Voice of the People, *Chicago Daily Tribune*, August 21, 1944, 10. Republicans, meanwhile, responded with a small pamphlet entitled *Flagrant Misrepresentations at the Democratic Convention of 1944*.

6. *Official Report of the Proceedings of the Democratic National Convention 1944*, 54.

7. Dewey Series 2, Box 15, Thomas E. Dewey Papers, Rhees Library, University of Rochester.

8. Dewey Series 2, Box 15, Thomas E. Dewey Papers, Rhees Library, University of Rochester.

9. Arthur Szyk: Artist for Freedom Exhibition, Library of Congress. <http://www.loc.gov/rr/print/swann/szyk/szyk-ex.html>.

10. *Hell-Bent for Election*, United Productions of America, 1944. <https://archive.org/details/Hell-bentForElection>.

11. Walter Brown to Harry Hopkins, 27 October 1944, Hopkins Campaigns, Misc. File, Franklin D. Roosevelt Library, Hyde Park, New York.

12. Franklin D. Roosevelt to Samuel D. Jackson, 14 July 1944, quoted in Thomas F. Eagleton and Diane L. Duffin, "Bob Hannegan and Harry Truman's Vice Presidential Nomination," *Missouri Historical Review* (April 1996): 274.

13. Arthur Krock, "The Inflammatory Use of a National Chairman," *New York Times*, July 25, 1944, 18.

14. Robert Ferrell, ed., *Dear Bess: The Letters from Harry to Bess Truman, 1910–1959* (New York: W.W. Norton and Company, 1983), 505.

15. Truman, quoted in McCullough, *Truman*, 308.

16. Ibid.

17. Ibid.

18. *Official Report of the Proceedings of the Democratic National Convention 1944*, 73.

19. Ibid., 79.

20. Ibid., 78.

21. Former Roosevelt intimate James Farley received one vote from New York.

22. *Official Report of the Proceedings of the Democratic National Convention 1944*, 189.

23. Samuel I. Rosenman, *Working with Roosevelt*, 202.

24. Halford R. Ryan, *Franklin D. Roosevelt's Rhetorical Presidency* (New York: Greenwood Press, 1988), 63.

25. *Official Report of the Proceedings of the DNC 1944*, 192–93.

26. "The President's Week," *Time*, August 28, 1944, 18.

NOTES TO 132–39 **221**

27. Rosenman, *Working with Roosevelt*, 462.

28. Truman, quoted in Ferrell, *Choosing Truman*, 89.

29. Drew Pearson, "Dewey Sees GOP Aided by Truman," *The Washington Post*, August 20, 1944, B5.

13: THOMAS DEWEY AND THE MAKING OF A WARTIME CAMPAIGN

1. "You're Right, Dewey Has a Good Chance!" *The Saturday Evening Post*, July 29, 1944, 92.

2. Cantril, "The Issues," 338–42.

3. Warren Moscow, "Dewey Heads East; Brownell at Helm," *New York Times*, July 1, 1944, 1.

4. TED Memo to Stanley High, September 5, 1944. Confidential and Personal Files. TED Papers.

5. *Public Papers of Thomas E. Dewey: 1944*, 725.

6. Warren Moscow, "Government Lags on Plans for Jobs, Dewey Declares," *New York Times*, August 1, 1944, 1.

7. Warren Moscow, "Dewey, at Pawling, Sets Ideal in War," *New York Times*, July 8, 1944, 7.

8. TED Memo to Stanley High, September 5, 1944. Confidential and Personal Files. TED Papers.

9. Republican National Committee, *What to Talk About* (September 1944), 6. TED Papers.

10. TED Memo to Stanley High, September 5, 1944.

11. Republican National Committee, *What to Talk About* (September 1944), 6. TED Papers.

12. TED Memo to Stanley High, September 5, 1944.

13. Edward T. Folliard, "Brownell Hits 'Bossism and Radicalism' of Democrats," *The Washington Post*, July 25, 1944, 1.

14. Arthur Krock, "The Inflammatory Use of a National Chairman," *New York Times*, July 25, 1944, 18.

15. Rosenman, *Working with Roosevelt*, 502.

16. "Clear with Sidney," RNC Flyer, TED Papers.

17. Irwin Silber, ed., *Songs America Voted By* (Harrisburg, PA: Stackpole Books, 1971), 277.

18. Confidential and Personal Files. Memo to Stanley High, September 5, 1944. Thomas E. Dewey Papers, Rhees Library, University of Rochester.

19. Warren Moscow, "Dewey at Owosso Hails 'Main Street,'" *New York Times*, September 10, 1944, 1.

20. "Dewey Declares Roosevelt Seeks to Sow Disunity," *New York Times*, September 27, 1944, 17.

21. Republican National Committee, *What to Talk About* (1944), 6.

22. Silber, *Songs America Voted By*, 277–78.

23. The Democratic nominee for president in 1900, William Jennings Bryan, who had pioneered the rear-platform campaign in 1896, delivered only 546 speeches.

24. Bricker, quoted in Davies, *Defender of the Old Guard*, 100.

25. Bricker, quoted in ibid., 100–101.

26. Warren Moscow, "Dewey Denounces 'Hitler-Like' Smith For Bricker 'Smear,'" *New York Times* (August 2, 1944), 1.

27. Hoover to Bricker, November 8, 1944. Herbert Hoover Post-Presidential Correspondence, Box 23, HHPL.

28. John W. Bricker, "Free Representative Government," *Vital Speeches of the Day* (September 1944), 708–11.

29. Brownell Interview, TED Papers.

30. Ford Bond, *Republican Radio Handbook 1944,* TED Papers.

31. "Statement of Policy Adopted by Republican Governors," *New York Times,* August 4, 1944, 9.

32. *Public Papers of Thomas E. Dewey: 1944,* 598–99.

33. Cordell Hull, *The Memoirs of Cordell Hull, Volume 2* (New York: Macmillan Company, 1948), 1689.

34. *Public Papers of Thomas E. Dewey: 1944,* 600.

35. Hull, *Memoirs,* 1690.

36. *Public Papers of Thomas E. Dewey: 1944,* 604.

37. Dewey interview with Challener, 15–16. Dulles Project. Rhees Library, University of Rochester.

38. Hull, *Memoirs,* 1693.

39. Ibid., 1690.

40. Ibid., 1693.

41. Ibid.

42. Ibid.

43. Hugh Gibson to Herbert Hoover, August 24, 1944. Herbert Hoover Post-Presidential Correspondence, Box 68. Herbert Hoover Presidential Library, West Branch, Iowa.

44. *The Private Papers of Senator Vandenberg,* 117.

45. Herbert Brownell to Hoover, August 17, 1944. Herbert Hoover Correspondence (Post-Presidential), Box 25, Herbert Hoover Presidential Library.

46. Michael Beschloss, *The Conquerors,* 119.

14: FDR: COMMANDER-IN-CHIEF

1. Richard Polenberg, *War and Society: The United States, 1941–1945* (New York: J.B. Lippincott, 1972), 189.

2. Ibid.

3. Ibid.

4. Polenberg, *War and Society,* 189.

5. *Official Proceedings of the Democratic National Convention 1944,* 20.

6. "Remember Me?" poster. Post-Presidential Period Subject File, Box 100, Herbert Hoover Presidential Library.

7. Mark Ethridge, *For What the Hell Should We Apologize.* Pamphlet, Democratic National Committee, 1944. TED Papers.

8. Harry S. Truman, *Memoirs, Volume One: Year of Decisions* (Garden City, NY: Doubleday and Company, Inc., 1955), 5.

9. Harry S. Truman, "Tried and Experienced Leadership," *Vital Speeches of the Day,*

Vol. X., No. 23, September 15, 1944.

10. Hamby, *Man of the People*, 285.

11. Ibid.

12. Harry Truman Oral History, 11. Harry S. Truman Presidential Library.

13. "Truth about Truman" Leaflet, TED Papers.

14. McCullough, *Truman*, 331.

15. Ibid.

16. John Gunther, *Inside U.S.A.*, 533.

17. *Cock-a-doodle Dewey*. Pamphlet, 1944. Subject File, Box 100, Folder 2, Herbert Hoover Presidential Library.

18. Arthur Krock, "Dewey Striving to Set Ruling Campaign Issues," *New York Times*, September 10, 1944. Thomas E. Dewey Scrapbooks, Vols. 73–74, September 9, 1944 to October 5, 1944, Roll 28, Rhees Library, University of Rochester.

19. Ibid.

20. Ibid.

21. William D. Hassett, *Off the Record with F.D.R.*, 265.

22. Franklin D. Roosevelt, "Radio Broadcast on the War in the Pacific," in *Nothing to Fear: The Selected Addresses of Franklin Delano Roosevelt*, 408.

23. "President on Air," *New York Times*, August 13, 1944, 1.

24. "The President's Week," *Time*, August 28, 1944, 19.

25. "FDR's Return," *New York Times*, August 20, 1944, E2.

26. B.D. Zevin, *Nothing to Fear*, 405.

27. Samuel I. Rosenman, *Working with Roosevelt*, 462.

28. Ibid.

29. Ibid.

30. "Roosevelt Gains in *Fortune*'s Poll," *New York Times*, August 17, 1944, 18.

31. Eleanor Roosevelt, *This I Remember* (New York: Harper and Brothers, 1949), 329.

32. Hugh E. Evans, *The Hidden Campaign: FDR's Health and the 1944 Election* (Armonk, NY: M.E. Sharpe, 2002), 46. Bruenn published his diagnosis of Roosevelt in the early 1970s. See Howard G. Bruenn, "Clinical Notes on the Illness and Death of President Franklin D. Roosevelt," *Annals of Internal Medicine* 72, no. 4 (1970): 579–91.

33. McIntire, quoted in Evans, *The Hidden Campaign*, 46.

34. According to the Society of Actuaries, the average blood pressure levels for males Roosevelt's age were 132/80. Ibid., 66.

35. Ross T. McIntire, *White House Physician* (New York: G.P. Putnam's Sons, 1946), 194. Quoted in Evans, *The Hidden Campaign*, 64.

36. Evans, *The Hidden Campaign*, 61.

37. *New York Times*, March 29, 1944, 1, col. 6. Quoted in ibid., 55.

38. "Roosevelt Is Well, His Physician Says," *New York Times*, October 13, 1944, 20.

39. "Whispering Drive Seen by Hannegan," *New York Times*, October 14, 1944, 8.

40. Harry Vaughn, Oral History, Harry S. Truman Presidential Library. Quoted in David McCullough, *Truman*, 327.

41. Ibid.

42. Henry Stimson and McGeorge Bundy, *On Active Service in Peace and War* (New York: Harper and Brothers, 1947), 575.

43. Brownell, *Advising Ike*, 59.

15: "THE LISTENING CAMPAIGN"

1. Harold J. Seymour, "Suggested Case for Presidential Campaign," May 3, 1944. Paul Lockwood to Herbert Brownell, May 16, 1944. TED Papers, Series 10, Box 6.

2. Warren Moscow, "Dewey's Campaign Tour Breaks with Tradition," *New York Times*, September 17, 1944, E10.

3. Ibid.; Arthur Krock, "Dewey Striving to Set Ruling Campaign Issues," *New York Times*, September 10, 1944, Thomas E. Dewey Scrapbooks, Vols. 73–74, Roll 28, University of Rochester.

4. "The Listening Campaign," *Time*, September 25, 1944, 13.

5. "The Great Silence," *Newsweek*, September 25, 1944, 38.

6. "The Listening Campaign," *Time*, September 24, 1944, 13.

7. Ibid.

8. Ibid.

9. Kenneth W. Thompson, ed., *Lessons from Defeated Presidential Candidates*, 100.

10. *Public Papers of Thomas E. Dewey: 1944*, 727.

11. "Hershey Sees a Million or Two out of Armed Forces after Reich Falls," *New York Times*, August 22, 1944, 8.

12. Samuel Rosenman, *Working with Roosevelt*, 472.

13. Ibid.

14. *Public Papers of Thomas E. Dewey: 1944*, 727, 728.

15. Tom Reynolds to Steve Early, September 24, 1944, FDRL.

16. "Hard-Hitting Candidate," *Elmira Star Gazette* (September 9, 1944), Thomas E. Dewey Scrapbooks, Vols. 73–74, Roll 28, Rhees Library, University of Rochester.

17. Landon to TED, September 7, 1944. Series 10, Box 24, TED Papers.

18. "Dewey on World Peace," *Jamaica Press*, September 9, 1944, Thomas E. Dewey Scrapbooks, Vols. 73–74, Roll 28, University of Rochester; *Public Papers of Thomas E. Dewey: 1944*, 730.

19. *Public Papers of Thomas E. Dewey: 1944*, 730.

20. Ibid., 733, 732.

21. "Dewey Steps Lightly," *New York Post*, September 9, 1944, Thomas E. Dewey Scrapbooks, Vols. 73–74, Roll 28, University of Rochester.

22. "Owosso Welcome," *Newsweek*, September 18, 1944, 40.

23. Warren Moscow, "Dewey at Owosso 'Hails Main Street,'" *New York Times*, September 10, 1944, 1.

24. Ibid.

25. Robert Divine, *Foreign Policy and U.S. Presidential Elections, 1940–1948* (New York: New Viewpoints, 1974), 132.

26. Warren Moscow, "Dewey Asks a Rise in M'Arthur Role in the Pacific War," *New York Times*, September 14, 1944, 1.

27. Major George Fielding Eliot, "Dewey Statement on MacArthur Is Called Disservice to Country," *New York Tribune*, September 19, 1944, Thomas E. Dewey Scrapbooks, Vols. 73–74, Roll 28, University of Rochester.

28. Warren Moscow, "Dewey Shows Fight in Far West Talks," *New York Times*, September 15, 1944, 12.

29. Robert J. Manning, "Dewey's Speech Shows What He Does Not Know—Ickes," *Auburn Citizen Advertiser*, September 16, 1944, Thomas E. Dewey Scrapbooks, Vols. 73–74, Roll 28, University of Rochester.

30. "Ickes Credits GOP for Jackson Hole," *New York Times*, September 16, 1944, 8.

31. Warren Moscow, "Dewey Cabinet Job Pledged Far West," *New York Times*, September 17, 1944, 40.

32. "The Listening Campaign," *Time*, September 25, 1944, 13.

33. Ibid.; *Public Papers of Thomas E. Dewey: 1944*, 736.

34. Tom Reynolds to Steve Early, September 24, 1944, FDRL.

35. Ibid.

36. *Public Papers of Thomas E. Dewey: 1944*, 739.

37. Ibid., 740.

38. Ibid., 740, 742.

39. Tom Reynolds to Steve Early, September 24, 1944, FDRL.

40. Howard Brubaker, quoted in John Gunther, *Inside U.S.A.*, 533.

41. Tom Reynolds to Steve Early, September 24, 1944, FDRL.

42. *Public Papers of Thomas E. Dewey: 1944*, 743–44.

43. Ibid., 745–46.

44. Samuel Rosenmen, *Working with Roosevelt*, 471.

45. Ibid., 472.

46. "Swing to Dewey," *Newsweek*, September 18, 1944, 42.

47. Rosenman, *Working with Roosevelt*, 473.

48. James MacGregor Burns, *Roosevelt: The Soldier of Freedom* (New York: Harcourt Brace Jovanovich, 1970), 522–25.

49. Smith, *Thomas E. Dewey and His Times*, 421.

50. Rosenmen, *Working with Roosevelt*, 478.

51. Eleanor Roosevelt, *This I Remember*, 336.

52. Burns, quoted in Gil Troy, Arthur M. Schlesinger Jr., and Fred Anderson, eds., *History of American Presidential Elections, 1789–2008, Volume 3: 1944–2008* (New York: Facts on File, 2012), 1149.

53. Dewey, quoted in John Chamberlain, "Pearl Harbor," *Life*, September 24, 1945, 111.

54. Ibid.

55. Warren Moscow, "Dewey's Campaign Plan Is to Keep Up Attack," *New York Times*, October 22, 1944, E12.

56. Ibid.; Smith, *Thomas E. Dewey and His Times*, 420.

57. Tom Reynolds to Steve Early, September 24, 1944, FDRL.

58. Ibid.

59. Samuel Rosenman, *Working with Roosevelt*, 478.

60. Ibid., 478–79.

61. *Public Papers of Thomas E. Dewey: 1944*, 747.

62. Ibid.

63. Ibid., 748.

64. Ibid.

65. John Burton to TED, September 26, 1944. TED Papers, Series 10: Box 3: Folder 4.

66. "Moving into High Gear," *U.S. News*, October 6, 1944, 27.

67. Gil Troy, "'Such Insulting Trash and Triviality': Franklin D. Roosevelt's Fala Speech Reconsidered," *Canadian Review of American Studies* (Winter 1995): 48.

68. TED to Robert McCormick, September 29, 1944. Series 10, Box 27, Rhees Library, University of Rochester.

69. Harold J. Seymour, "Suggested Case for Presidential Campaign," May 3, 1944. Paul Lockwood to Herbert Brownell, May 16, 1944. TED Papers, Series 10, Box 6.

70. Dewey, quoted in Smith, *Thomas E. Dewey and His Times*, 425.

16: "SUCH A SLIMY CAMPAIGN"

1. In fact, a 1944 survey conducted by the National Opinion Research Center (as well as one by Gallup) indicated as much.

2. Burns, *Roosevelt: Soldier of Freedom*, 528.

3. William Hassett, *Off the Record with F.D.R., 1942–1945*, 293.

4. Hughes, quoted in Smith, *Thomas E. Dewey and His Times*, 430.

5. McCormick to TED, October 9, 1944. TED Papers, Series 10, Box 27, Folder 5.

6. Dewey to McCormick, October 12, 1944.

7. John Chamberlain, "Pearl Harbor," *Life*, September 24, 1945, 110.

8. Army Board Report, quoted in John Chamberlain, "Pearl Harbor," *Life*, September 24, 1945, 110–20. TED Papers.

9. *Congressional Record,* September 7, 1944, 7581. Quoted in Robert A. Divine, *Foreign Policy and U.S. Presidential Elections, 1940–1948*, 145.

10. Ibid.

11. "Pearl Harbor Inquiry by Congress Is Urged," *New York Times*, September 19, 1944, 12.

12. Booth, quoted in Divine, *Foreign Policy and U.S. Presidential Elections, 1940–1948*, 146.

13. Walter Ruch, "Attacks Secrecy on Pearl Harbor," *New York Times*, September 21, 1944, 15.

14. Hugh Scott, quoted in Robert Divine, *Foreign Policy and U.S. Presidential Elections, 1940–1948*, 145; "TED, General Marshall and Pearl Harbor in the 1944 Campaign" Timeline. TED Papers.

15. Christopher Andrew, *For the President's Eyes Only: Secret Intelligence and the American Presidency from Washington to Bush* (New York: HarperCollins, 1995), 144.

16. Ibid.

17. "TED, General Marshall and Pearl Harbor in the 1944 Campaign" Timeline. TED Papers.

18. "Advisors Declare Dewey Had Pearl Harbor Secret," *The Milwaukee Journal*, September 21, 1945, 1; Smith, *Thomas E. Dewey and His Times*, 429.

19. Ibid.

20. "Advisors Declare Dewey Had Pearl Harbor Secret," *The Milwaukee Journal*, September 21, 1945, 1.

21. Robert A. Divine, *Foreign Policy and U.S. Presidential Elections, 1940–1948*, 147.

22. James M. Barnes to FDR, October 4, 1944, FDRL.

23. Zevin, *Nothing to Fear*, 415–17.

24. *Public Papers of Thomas E. Dewey: 1944*, 752–53.

25. Ibid., 753.

26. Ibid.

27. Ibid., 756.

28. "Willkie Congratulates Dewey, But Is Silent on Campaign Help," *New York Times*, June 29, 1944, 1.

29. Arthur Krock, "Mr. Willkie's Course of Watchful Waiting," *New York Times*, August 25, 1944, 12.

30. Warren Moscow, "Willkie to Confer with Dulles Here at Dewey Request," *New York Times*, August 21, 1944, 1.

31. Ibid.

32. Leo Egan, "Willkie Discusses Views with Dulles," *New York Times*, August 22, 1944, 1, 32.

33. Russell W. Davenport, "Why I Cannot Vote for Dewey," *The American Mercury*, October 1944, 392, 396.

34. Brownell, *Advising Ike*, 57, 63.

35. Dewey Papers, 13:8:13, the Harlan Philips Interviews, January 14, 1959, Rhees Library, University of Rochester.

36. Divine, *Foreign Policy and U.S. Presidential Elections, 1940–1948*, 146.

37. Ibid., 149.

38. Charles E. Martin, "Review," *The American Political Science Review* 38, no. 2 (April 1944): 391.

39. Samuel Rosenman, *Working with Roosevelt*, 481.

40. *Public Papers of Thomas E. Dewey: 1944*, 759.

41. Ibid.

42. Ibid., 760.

43. Ibid., 761.

44. Ibid., 762.

45. "Mr. Dewey on Foreign Policy," *New York Times*, October 20, 1944, 18.

46. Samuel Rosenman, *Working with Roosevelt*, 482.

47. C.P. Trussell, "President Defies Rain, Wind to Let New York See Him," *New York Times*, October 22, 1944, 1.

48. "Vast Throngs See Roosevelt on Tour," *New York Times*, October 22, 1944, 35.

49. Samuel Rosenman, ed., *The Public Papers and Addresses of Franklin D. Roosevelt, 1944–1945* (New York: Harper and Brothers, 1950), 341.

50. C.P. Trussell, "President Defies Rain, Wind," 1.

51. William Hassett, *Off the Record with F.D.R., 1942–1945*, 279.

52. Eleanor Roosevelt, *This I Remember*, 337.

53. C.P. Trussell, "President Defies Rain, Wind."

54. Samuel Rosenman, *Working with Roosevelt*, 483.

55. Eleanor Roosevelt, *This I Remember*, 338.

56. Burns, *Roosevelt: Soldier of Freedom*, 526.

57. William Hassett, *Off the Record with F.D.R., 1942–1945*, 281.

58. Burns, *Roosevelt: Soldier of Freedom*, 526.

59. Alexander Feinberg, "Dewey to Answer Roosevelt Tonight on Foreign Policy," *New York Times*, October 24, 1944, 1.

60. *Public Papers of Thomas E. Dewey: 1944*, 762.

61. Ball, quoted in Divine, *Foreign Policy and U.S. Presidential Elections, 1940–1948*, 151.

62. Lippmann, quoted in ibid., 153.

63. Challener interview with TED, Dulles Project, Rhees Library, University of Rochester.

17: ROOSEVELT AND VICTORY

1. Hoover to Landon, October 23, 1944. Hoover Correspondence, Box 118, Herbert Hoover Presidential Library.

2. Harold J. Seymour, "Suggested Case for Presidential Campaign," May 3, 1944. Paul Lockwood to Herbert Brownell, May 16, 1944. TED Papers, Series 10, Box 6.

3. Ibid.

4. "Dewey Declares Roosevelt Seeks to Sow Disunity," *New York Times*, September 27, 1944, 1.

5. "Pledges Crusade on Wars," *New York Times*, September 27, 1944, 17.

6. Samuel Rosenman, *Working with Roosevelt*, 472.

7. "Biddle Says Dewey Withholds Truths," *New York Times*, October 21, 1944, 30.

8. John Gunther, *Inside U.S.A.*, 532.

9. William D. Hassett, *Off the Record with F.D.R., 1942–1945*, 287.

10. "Hillman Attacks Dewey's Memory," *New York Times*, October 10, 1944, 16.

11. Bertram D. Hulen, "White House Hits Dewey's Charges," *New York Times*, October 15, 1944, 1.

12. Smith, *Thomas E. Dewey and His Times*, 434.

13. Harry S. Truman Papers: Senate and Vice Presidential Speech File. Draft File, June 2, 1944–April 3, 1945, Box 290, Harry S. Truman Presidential Library, Independence, Missouri.

14. "Truman Hits GOP on Defense," *P.M.*, October 17, 1994, Harry S. Truman Papers: Senate and Vice Presidential Speech File. Press Release File, Box 285, Harry S. Truman Presidential Library.

15. Samuel W. Bell, "Truman Asserts Dewey Resorts to 'Chicanery,'" *New York Herald-Tribune*, October 18, 1944, Harry S. Truman Papers: Senate and Vice Presidential Speech File. Press Release File, Box 285, Harry S. Truman Presidential Library.

16. "Asserts Dewey Helps Roosevelt," *New York Times*, October 31, 1944, 14.

17. C.P. Trussell, "Byrnes Says Shift Means Longer War," *New York Times*, October 31, 1944, 1.

18. Samuel Rosenman, ed., *The Public Papers and Addresses of Franklin D. Roosevelt, 1944–1945*, 354–55.

19. Ibid., 356–57; Rosenman, *Working with Roosevelt*, 487.

20. Ibid., 358.

21. Ibid., 358–59.

22. Rosenman, *Working with Roosevelt*, 495.

23. Ibid.

24. C.P. Trussell, "President Offers Post-War Program for Aiding Business," *New York Times*, October 29, 1944, 1.

25. Samuel Rosenman, *Working with Roosevelt*, 496.

26. Ibid., 496, 491.

27. Samuel Rosenman, ed., *The Public Papers and Addresses of Franklin D. Roosevelt, 1944–1945*, 373.

28. Ibid., 378.

29. *Public Papers of Thomas E. Dewey: 1944*, 771–74.

30. "Bricker Charges 'Sell-Out' to PAC," *New York Times*, September 16, 1944, 8.

31. Harlan Phillips Chronology of the 1944 Campaign, TED Papers; "Communists Run New Deal, Bricker Says," *The Washington Post*, October 31, 1944, 7.

32. "Commitments," October 19, 1944. Herbert Hoover Post-Presidential Subject File, Box 100, Herbert Hoover Presidential Library.

33. *Public Papers of Thomas E. Dewey: 1944*, 781–85.

34. Charles Breitel, quoted in Smith, *Thomas E. Dewey and His Times*, 433.

35. "Hillman Defense Made by Hanegan," *New York Times*, November 3, 1944, 14.

36. Ibid., 434.

37. William Hassett, *Off the Record with F.D.R., 1942–1945*, 289.

38. Samuel Rosenman, ed., *The Public Papers and Addresses of Franklin D. Roosevelt, 1944–1945*, 391.

39. Ibid., 404.

40. Ibid.

41. *Public Papers of Thomas E. Dewey: 1944*, 790.

42. J. Leonard Reinsch, Oral History, Harry S. Truman Library, Independence, Missouri.

43. *Public Papers of Thomas E. Dewey: 793–94.*

44. *National Election Study, 1944.* In late October 1944, the NORC performed a wave of preelection interviews with a sample of 2,564 people. Sixty percent of those surveyed were male, while 97 percent were white. Fifty-seven percent, meanwhile, were 40 years of age or older. A couple of weeks after the election, in late November, it conducted a second wave of interviews, in which 534 of the original respondents did not participate. Its report was one of the first of its kind and thus not as sophisticated as later ones, such as those by Columbia University and the University of Michigan. Still, it provided valuable information—and aside from Gallup and a few other polling organizations, the only non–Election Night statistical data available on the 1944 presidential election.

45. *Public Papers of Thomas E. Dewey:* 795.

46. William D. Hassett, *Off the Record with F.D.R., 1942–1945*, 294.

CONCLUSION: "NOT A WORD, NOT A COMMA"

1. Herbert Hoover notes on dinner with Arthur Krock, November 7, 1944. Hoover Post-Presidential Period Subject File, Book 100, Herbert Hoover Presidential Library.

2. Benjamin Stolberg to Herbert Hoover, November 29, 1944. Hoover Post-Presidential Correspondence, Box 223, Herbert Hoover Presidential Library.

3. "Dewey Declines to Guess on 1948; Hopes for Family Vacation Soon," *New York Times*, November 9, 1944, 21.

4. Hoover notes on dinner with Arthur Krock, November 7, 1944. Herbert Hoover Post-Presidential Period Subject File, Book 100, Herbert Hoover Presidential Library.

5. Samuel Rosenman, *Working with Roosevelt*, 478.

6. "Mr. Roosevelt Wins," *New York Times*, November 8, 1944, 16.

7. Willkie, *An American Program*, 7.

8. Henry Lee Moon, *Balance of Power: The Negro Vote* (Garden City, NY: Doubleday and Company, 1948), 33.

9. Ibid., 35.

10. Ibid.

11. Bond to TED, "Politics Made Easy," November 18, 1944, TED Papers.

12. "Dewey Declines to Guess on 1948; Hopes for Family Vacation Soon," *New York Times*, November 9, 1944, 21.

BIBLIOGRAPHY

Adler, Les K., and Thomas G. Paterson. "Red Fascism: The Merger of Nazi Germany and Soviet Russia in the American Image of Totalitarianism, 1930s–1950s." *The American Historical Review* 75, no. 4 (April 1970), 1046–64.

Adler, Mortimer. *How to Think about War and Peace*. New York: Simon and Schuster, 1944.

Anderson, Kristi. *The Creation of a Democratic Majority, 1928–1936*. Chicago: University of Chicago Press, 1979.

Anderson, Michael J. "McCarthyism before McCarthy: Anti-Communism in Cincinnati and the Nation during the Election of 1944." *Ohio History* 99 (Winter/Spring 1990): 5–28.

———. "The Presidential Election of 1944." PhD diss., University of Iowa, 1990.

Andrew, Christopher. *For the President's Eyes Only: Secret Intelligence and the American Presidency from Washington to Bush*. New York: HarperCollins, 1995.

Bailey, Thomas. *Woodrow Wilson and the Lost Peace*. New York: Macmillan Company, 1944.

Bateman, Herman E. "Observations on President Roosevelt's Health during World War II." *The Mississippi Valley Historical Review* 43 (June 1956): 82–102.

Beal, John Robinson. *John Foster Dulles: A Biography*. New York: Harper and Row, 1959.

Becker, Carl. *How New Will the Better World Be? A Discussion of Post-War Reconstruction*. New York: Knopf, 1944.

Bernard, Ellsworth. *Wendell Willkie: Fighter for Freedom*. Marquette: Northern Michigan University Press, 1966.

Beschloss, Michael. *The Conquerors: Roosevelt, Truman, and the Destruction of Hitler's Germany, 1941–1945*. New York: Simon and Schuster, 2002.

Best, Gary Dean. *Herbert Hoover: The Post-Presidential Years, 1933–1945*. Stanford, CA: Hoover Institution Press, 1983.

Beyer, Barry. *Thomas E. Dewey, 1937–1947: A Study in Political Leadership*. New York: Garland Publishing, Inc., 1979.

Biddle, Francis. *In Brief Authority*. Garden City, NY: Doubleday and Company, Inc., 1962.

Black, Conrad. *Franklin Delano Roosevelt: Champion of Freedom*. New York: Public Affairs, 2003.

Blum, John Morton, ed. *The Price of Vision: The Diary of Henry A. Wallace, 1942–1946*. Boston: Houghton Mifflin, 1973.

Bowen, Michael. *The Roots of Modern Conservatism: Dewey, Taft, and the Battle for the Soul of the Republican Party*. Chapel Hill: University of North Carolina Press, 2011.

Briggs, Philip J. "General MacArthur and the Presidential Election of 1944." *Presidential Studies Quarterly* 22 (Winter 1992): 31–46.

Brinkley, Alan. *The End of Reform: New Deal Liberalism in Recession and War*. New York: Vintage Books, 1996.

Britt, George. *The Fifth Column Is Here*. New York: Wilfred Funk, Inc., 1940.

Browder, Earl. *Teheran and America: Perspectives and Tasks*. New York: Workers Library, 1944.

Brownell, Herbert. *Advising Ike: The Memoirs of Attorney General Herbert Brownell*. Lawrence: University Press of Kansas, 1993.

Burns, James MacGregor. *Roosevelt: The Soldier of Freedom*. New York: Harcourt Brace Jovanovich, 1970.

Busch, Noel F. "Tom Dewey: New York's Young D.A. Has Become No. 1 Republican Hopeful." *Life*, April 22, 1940.

Bush, George H.W. *All the Best, George Bush: My Life in Letters and Other Writings*. New York: Scribner, 1999.

Butterfield, Roger. "Thomas E. Dewey." *Look*, October 9, 1944, 97–100, 102–4, 109–12, 115–17.

Byrnes, James F. *All in One Lifetime*. New York: Harper and Brothers, 1958.

Campbell, Angus, Philip E. Converse, Warren E. Miller, and Donald E. Stokes. *The American Voter*. Chicago: University of Chicago Press, 1976.

Campbell, James E. *The American Campaign: U.S. Presidential Campaigns and the National Vote*. College Station: Texas A&M University Press, 2000.

Cantril, Hadley. "The Issues—As Seen by the American People." *Public Opinion Quarterly* (Fall 1944): 331–47.

Carroll, Andrew, ed. *War Letters: Extraordinary Correspondence from American Wars*. New York: Scribner, 2001.

Carsey, Thomas M. *Campaign Dynamics: The Race for Governor*. Ann Arbor: University of Michigan Press, 2001.

Chamberlain, William Henry. "Information Please, about Russia." *Harper's Magazine*, April 1944, 405–12.

———. "The Russian Enigma: An Interpretation." *Harper's Magazine*, August 1942, 225–34.

Chambers, John Whiteclay II, ed. *The Oxford Companion to American Military History*. Oxford: Oxford University Press, 1999.

Cole, Wayne S. *Roosevelt and the Isolationists, 1932–45*. Lincoln: University of Nebraska Press, 1983.

Culver, John C., and John Hyde. *American Dreamer: A Life of Henry A. Wallace*. New York: W.W. Norton, 2000.

Dallek, Robert. *Franklin D. Roosevelt and American Foreign Policy, 1932–1945*. New York: Oxford University Press, 1979.

Daniels, Jonathan. *The Man of Independence*. Philadelphia: J.B. Lippincott Company, 1950.

Darilek, Richard E. *A Loyal Opposition in Time of War: The Republican Party and the Politics of Foreign Policy from Pearl Harbor to Yalta*. Westport, CT: Greenwood Press, 1976.

Davenport, Russell. "Why I Cannot Vote for Dewey." *American Mercury* 59, October 1944, 391–99.

Davies, Richard O. *Defender of the Old Guard: John Bricker and American Politics*. Columbus: Ohio State University Press, 1993.

Davis, Forrest. "The Cow Town That May Elect Dewey." *The Saturday Evening Post*, October 21, 1944, 19, 109–10.

———. "Dewey's April Choice." *The Saturday Evening Post*, August 12, 1944, 9–10, 46, 48.

———. "The Great Albany Enigma." *The Saturday Evening Post*, January 22, 1944. 9–11, 52.

———. "The Great Albany Enigma, Part II." *The Saturday Evening Post*, January 29, 1944, 26–27, 47, 50.

Dewey, Thomas E. "Can Religion Save the U.S.A.?" *Religious Digest*, July 1939, 7–10.

———. *The Case against the New Deal*. New York: Harper, 1940.

———. *Public Papers of Thomas E. Dewey, Fifty-First Governor of the State of New York: 1944*. Albany, NY: Williams Press, 1946.

———. *Thomas E. Dewey on the Two-Party System*. Edited by John A. Wells. Garden City, NY: Doubleday, 1966.

———. *Twenty against the Underworld*. Edited by Rodney Campbell. Garden City, NY: Doubleday, 1974.

Divine, Robert A. *Foreign Policy and U.S. Presidential Elections, 1940–1948*. New York: New Viewpoints, 1974.

———. *Second Chance: The Triumph of Internationalism in America during World War II*. New York: Atheneum, 1971.

Doenecke, Justus D. *Storm on the Horizon: The Challenge to American Intervention, 1939–1941*. Lanham, MD: Rowman and Littlefield, 2003.

Dos Passos, John. *The State of the Nation*. Boston: Houghton Mifflin Company, 1944.

Dulles, Foster Rhea. *The Road to Teheran: The Story of Russia and America, 1781–1943*. Princeton, NJ: Princeton University Press, 1944.

Dulles, John Foster. *War or Peace*. New York: Macmillan Company, 1950.

———. *War, Peace, and Change*. New York: Harper and Brothers, 1939.

Eagleton, Thomas F., and Diane L. Duffin. "Bob Hannegan and Harry Truman's Vice Presidential Nomination." *Missouri Historical Review* (April 1996): 265–83.

Evans, Hugh E. *The Hidden Campaign: FDR's Health and the 1944 Election*. Armonk, NY: M.E. Sharpe, 2002.

Evjen, Henry O. "The Willkie Campaign: An Unfortunate Chapter in Republican Leadership." *The Journal of Politics* (May 1952): 241–57.

Fay, Robert F. "An Evaluation of the Public Speaking of Franklin D. Roosevelt and Thomas E. Dewey in the Presidential Campaign of 1944." PhD diss., University of Iowa, 1947.

Ferrell, Robert. *Choosing Truman: The Democratic Convention of 1944*. Columbia: University of Missouri Press, 1994.

Ferrell, Robert, ed. *Dear Bess: The Letters from Harry to Bess Truman, 1910–1959*. New York: W.W. Norton and Company, 1983.

Foster, James Caldwell. *The Union Politic: The CIO Political Action Committee*. Columbia: University of Missouri Press, 1975.

Francis, J., John Foster Dulles, William Patton, Leo Pasvolsky, and S. McConnell. *A Basis for the Peace to Come: The Merrick McDowell Lectures for 1942*. New York: Abington Cokesbury Press, 1942.

Frederickson, Kari. *The Dixiecrat Revolt and the End of the Solid South, 1932–1968*. Chapel Hill: University of North Carolina Press, 2001.

Gaddis, John Lewis. *The United States and the Origins of the Cold War, 1941–1947*. New York: Columbia University, 1972.

Gaer, Joseph. *The First Round: The Story of the CIO Political Action Committee*. New York: Duell, Sloan, and Pearce, 1944.

Gallup, George H. *The Gallup Poll: Public Opinion 1935–1971, Volume 1: 1935–1948*. New York: Random House, 1972.

Garson, Robert A. *The Democratic Party and the Politics of Sectionalism, 1941–1948*. Baton Rouge: Louisiana State University Press, 1974.

Gosnell, Harold F. *Champion Campaigner: Franklin D. Roosevelt.* New York: Macmillan Company, 1952.

Gould, Lewis L. *Grand Old Party: A History of the Republicans.* New York: Random House, 2003.

Grafton, John, ed. *Franklin Delano Roosevelt: Great Speeches.* Mineola, NY: Dover Publications, Inc., 1999.

Gunther, John. *Inside U.S.A.* New York: Harper and Brothers, 1946.

Hamby, Alonzo. *Man of the People: A Life of Harry S. Truman.* New York: Oxford University Press, 1992.

Hart, Roderick P. *Campaign Talk: Why Elections Are Good for Us.* Princeton, NJ: Princeton University Press, 2000.

Hassett, William D. *Off the Record with F.D.R., 1942–1945.* New Brunswick, NJ: Rutgers University Press, 1958.

Hatch, Alden. *Franklin D. Roosevelt: An Informal Biography.* New York: Henry Holt and Company, 1947.

Heath, S. Burton. "Thomas Edmund Dewey: Political Resiliency." In *Public Men In and Out of Office,* edited by J.T. Salter. Chapel Hill: University of North Carolina Press, 1946: 56–65.

———. *Yankee Reporter.* New York: Wilfred Funk, Inc., 1940.

Hibbs, Ben. "Why the *Post* Is for Dewey." *The Saturday Evening Post,* September 23, 1944), 17.

High, Stanley. "The Case for Dewey." *Life,* March 17, 1948.

———. "Why the Left Wing Fears Dewey." *The Saturday Evening Post,* October 14, 1944, 17, 95.

———. *Yankee Reporter.* New York: Wilfred Funk, Inc., 1940.

Hinshaw, David. *The Home Front.* New York: G.P. Putnam's Sons, 1943.

Hodgson, Godfrey. *The World Turned Right Side Up: A History of the Conservative Ascendancy in America.* Boston: Houghton Mifflin Company, 1996.

Holbrook, Thomas M. *Do Campaigns Matter?* London: Sage Publications, 1996.

Hoover, Herbert. *Addresses upon the American Road: World War II, 1941–1945.* New York: D. Van Nostrand Company, Inc., 1946.

Hoover, Herbert, and Hugh Gibson. *The Problems of Lasting Peace.* Garden City, NY: Doubleday, Doran and Company, 1943.

Hughes, Rupert. *The Story of Thomas E. Dewey: Attorney for the People.* New York: Grosset & Dunlap Publishers, 1944.

Huie, William Bradford. "The Man Who May Be President." *The American Mercury,* May 1943, 528–31.

Hull, Cordell. *The Memoirs of Cordell Hull, Volume 2.* New York: Macmillan Company, 1948.

Immerman, Richard H. *John Foster Dulles: Piety, Pragmatism, and Power in U.S. Foreign Policy.* Wilmington, DE: Scholarly Resources, Inc., 1999.

Isserman, Maurice. *Which Side Were You On? The American Communist Party during the Second World War.* Middletown, CT: Wesleyan University Press, 1982.

Jeffries, John W. "The 'New' New Deal: FDR and American Liberalism, 1937–1945." *Political Science Quarterly* (Autumn 1990): 397–418.

———. *Wartime America: The World War II Home Front.* Chicago: Ivan R. Dee, 1996.

Johnson, Alvin. "The Issues of the Coming Election." *The Yale Review* (June 1944): 577–85.

Johnson, Charles S. "The Present Status Quo of Race Relations in the South." *Social Forces* (1944/1945): 27–32.

Johnson, Donald Bruce. *Wendell Willkie and the Republican Party.* Urbana: University of Illinois Press, 1960.

Johnson, Gerald W. *Woodrow Wilson: The Unforgettable Figure Who Has Returned to Haunt Us.* New York: Harper and Brothers, 1944.

Jones, Sam H. "Will Dixie Bolt the New Deal?" *The Saturday Evening Post*, March 6, 1943, 20–21, 42, 45.

Jordan, David M. *FDR, Dewey, and the Election of 1944.* Bloomington: Indiana University Press, 2011.

Kennedy, David M. *Freedom from Fear: The American People in Depression and War, 1929–1945.* New York: Oxford University Press, 1999.

Key, V.O. *The Responsible Electorate: Rationality in Presidential Voting, 1936–1960.* Cambridge, MA: Belknap Press of Harvard University Press, 1966.

———. "A Theory of Critical Elections." *The Journal of Politics* 17, no. 1 (Feb. 1955): 3–18.

Kimball, Warren F., ed. *Franklin D. Roosevelt and the World Crisis, 1937–1945.* Lexington, MA: D.C. Heath and Company, 1973.

Kingdon, Frank. *"That Man" in the White House: You and Your President.* New York: Arco Publishing Company, 1944.

Lazarsfeld, Paul. "The Election Is Over." *Public Opinion Quarterly* (Fall 1944): 317–30.

Lerner, Max. *Public Journal: Marginal Notes on Wartime America.* New York: Viking Press, 1945.

Levine, Lawrence W., and Cornelia R. Levine, eds. *The People and the President: America's Conversation with FDR.* Boston: Beacon Press, 2002.

Lichtenstein, Nelson. *Labor's War at Home: The CIO in World War II.* New York: Cambridge University Press, 1982.

Lichtman, Allan J. *Prejudice and the Old Politics: The Presidential Election of 1928.* Chapel Hill: University of North Carolina Press, 1979.

Lippmann, Walter. *U.S. War Aims.* Boston: Little, Brown and Company, 1944.

Logan, Rayford W., ed. *What the Negro Wants.* Chapel Hill: University of North Carolina Press, 1944.

Lubell, Samuel. *The Future of American Politics.* New York: Harper and Brothers, 1952.

Luechtenburg, William E. *The FDR Years: On Roosevelt and His Legacy.* New York: Columbia University Press, 1995.

Lyons, Eugene. "Notes on Wendell Willkie." *The American Mercury*, May 1944, 519–25.

Madison, James H., ed. *Wendell Willkie: Hoosier Internationalist.* Indianapolis: Indiana University Press, 1992.

Markowitz, Norman D. *The Rise and Fall of the People's Century: Henry A. Wallace and American Liberalism, 1941–1948.* New York: The Free Press, 1973.

Martin, Joseph. *My First Fifty Years in Politics.* New York: McGraw-Hill, Inc., 1960.

Mayer, George H. *The Republican Party, 1854–1966.* New York: Oxford University Press, 1967.

———. "The Republican Party, 1932–1952." In *History of U.S. Political Parties, Volume 3: 1910–1945—From Square Deal to New Deal,* edited by Arthur M. Schlesinger Jr. and Fred Israel, 2259–95. New York: Chelsea House Publishers, 1973.

McCoy, Donald R. *Landon of Kansas*. Lincoln: University of Nebraska Press, 1966.

McCue, Leo F. "Thomas E. Dewey and the Politics of Accommodation, 1940–1952." PhD diss., Boston University, 1979.

McCullough, David. *Truman*. New York: Simon and Schuster, 1992.

McIntire, Ross T. *White House Physician*. New York: G.P. Putnam's Sons, 1946.

McJimsey, George. *The Presidency of Franklin Delano Roosevelt*. Lawrence: University Press of Kansas, 2000.

Melosi, Martin V. "Political Tremors from a Military Disaster: Pearl Harbor and the Election of 1944." *Diplomatic History* 1 (Winter 1977): 79–95.

Messer, Robert L. *The End of an Alliance: James F. Byrnes, Roosevelt, Truman, and the Origins of the Cold War*. Chapel Hill: University of North Carolina Press, 1982.

Meyer, Agnes E. *Journey through Chaos*. New York: Harcourt, Brace and Company, 1943.

Moley, Raymond. *27 Masters of Politics: In a Personal Perspective*. New York: Funk and Wagnalls, 1949.

Moon, Henry Lee. *Balance of Power: The Negro Vote*. Garden City, NY: Doubleday and Company, 1948.

Moore, John Robert. "The Conservative Coalition in the United States Senate, 1942–1945." *Journal of Southern History* 33 (August 1967): 368–76.

Moos, Malcolm. *The Republicans: A History of Their Party*. New York: Random House, 1956.

Moses, Robert. "Why I Oppose the Fourth Term." *The Saturday Evening Post*, October 7, 1944, 17, 109–10.

Myrdal, Gunnar. *An American Dilemma: The Negro Problem and Modern Democracy*. New York: Harper and Brothers, 1944.

Nash, George H. *The Conservative Intellectual Movement in America, since 1945*. Wilmington, DE: Intercollegiate Studies Institute, 1998.

Neal, Steve. *Dark Horse: A Biography of Wendell Willkie*. Lawrence: University Press of Kansas, 1989.

Nixon, Richard M. *In the Arena: A Memoir of Victory, Defeat and Renewal*. New York: Simon and Schuster, 1990.

Official Report of the Proceedings of the Democratic National Convention, 1944. Democratic National Committee, 1944.

Official Report of the Proceedings of the Twenty-Third Republican National Convention, 1944. Washington: Judd and Detweiler, Inc., 1944.

Overacker, Louise. "Presidential Campaign Funds: 1944." *American Political Science Review* 39 (October 1945): 899–925.

Padover, Saul, ed. *Wilson's Ideals*. Washington DC: American Council on Public Affairs, 1942.

Patterson, James T. *Mr. Republican: A Biography of Robert A. Taft*. Boston: Houghton Mifflin Company, 1972.

Peters, Charles. *Five Days in Philadelphia: The Amazing "We Want Willkie!" Convention of 1940 and How It Freed FDR to Save the Western World*. New York: Public Affairs, 2005.

Polenberg, Richard. *War and Society: The United States, 1941–1945*. Philadelphia: J.B. Lippincott Company, 1972.

Polenberg, Richard, ed. *America at War: The Home Front, 1941–1945*. Englewood Cliffs, NJ: Prentice-Hall, Inc., 1968.

Powell, Hickman. "My Friend, Tom Dewey." *Colliers*, June 24, 1944, 12, 71.

———. *Ninety Times Guilty.* New York: Harcourt, Brace and Company, 1939.

Public Papers of Thomas E. Dewey, Fifty-First Governor of the State of New York. 1944. Albany: Williams Press, Inc., 1946.

Purcell, Aaron, ed. *The New Deal and the Great Depression.* Kent, OH: Kent State University Press. 2014.

Ratcliffe, S.K. "Dewey versus Roosevelt." *Contemporary Review* (July/December 1944): 137–41.

———. "President Roosevelt's Fourth Victory." *Contemporary Review* (July/December 1944): 325–30.

Robinson, Edgar Eugene. *They Voted for Roosevelt: The Presidential Vote, 1943–1944.* Stanford, CA: Stanford University Press, 1947.

Rodell, Fred. "Wendell Willkie: Man of Words." *Harper's Magazine*, March 1944, 305–12.

Roosevelt, Eleanor. *This I Remember.* New York: Harper and Brothers, 1949.

Roosevelt, Franklin D. "Our Foreign Policy: A Democratic View." *Foreign Affairs* (July 1928): 573–86.

Rosenman, Samuel I. *Working with Roosevelt.* New York: Harper and Brothers, 1952.

Rosenman, Samuel I., ed. *The Public Papers and Addresses of Franklin Delano Roosevelt, 1928–1932: The Genesis of the New Deal.* New York: Random House, 1938.

———, ed. *The Public Papers and Addresses of Franklin Delano Roosevelt, 1943: The Tide Turns.* New York: Harper and Brothers, 1950.

———, ed. *The Public Papers and Addresses of Franklin Delano Roosevelt, 1944–45: Victory and the Threshold of Peace.* New York: Harper and Brothers, 1950.

Ryan, Halford R. *Franklin D. Roosevelt's Rhetorical Presidency.* New York: Greenwood Press, 1988.

Salter, J.T., ed. *Public Men In and Out of Office.* Chapel Hill: University of North Carolina Press, 1946.

Schlesinger, Arthur M., Jr. *The Age of Roosevelt: The Politics of Upheaval.* Boston: Houghton Mifflin Company, 1960.

Schlesinger, Arthur M., Jr., and Fred L. Israel, eds. *History of American Presidential Elections, 1789–1968.* Vol. 4: *1940–1968.* New York: Chelsea House Publishers, 1971.

Schriftgiesser, Karl. *The Gentleman from Massachusetts: Henry Cabot Lodge.* Boston: Little, Brown and Company, 1944.

Sherwood, Robert E. *Roosevelt and Hopkins: An Intimate History.* New York: Harper and Brothers, 1948.

Silber, Irwin, ed. *Songs America Voted By.* Harrisburg, PA: Stackpole Books, 1971.

Smith, Jean Edward. *FDR.* New York: Random House, 2008.

Smith, Richard Norton. *Thomas E. Dewey and His Times.* New York: Simon and Schuster, 1982.

———. "Thomas E. Dewey and the Evolution of Modern Republicanism." Harvard senior honors thesis, 1975.

Spangler, Harrison E. "The GOP's New Stand." *The American Magazine*, February 1943, 24–25, 85–87.

Stassen, Harold E. "Wanted: A Forthright Republican Party." *The Saturday Evening Post*, May 15, 1944, 12–13, 53, 56.

Steele, Richard W. "Franklin D. Roosevelt and His Foreign Policy Critics." *Political Science Quarterly* (Spring 1979): 15–32.

Stimson, Henry. *On Active Service in Peace and War.* New York: Harper and Brothers, 1947.

Stolberg, Benjamin. "Thomas E. Dewey, Self-Made Myth." *American Mercury*, June 1940, 135–47.

Taft, Robert A. "A 1944 Program for the Republicans." *The Saturday Evening Post*, December 1943, 17, 50, 52, 57.

Takaki, Ronald. *Double Victory: A Multicultural History of America in World War II.* Boston: Little Brown, 2000.

Thomas, Norman. *What Is Our Destiny?* Garden City, NY: Doubleday, Doran and Company, Inc., 1944.

Thompson, Kenneth W., ed. *Lessons from Defeated Presidential Candidates.* Lanham, MD: University Press of America, Inc., 1994.

Topping, Simon. *Lincoln's Lost Legacy: The Republican Party and the African American Vote, 1928–1952.* Gainesville: University Press of Florida, 2008.

———. "'Never Argue with the Gallup Poll': Thomas Dewey, Civil Rights and the Election of 1948." *Journal of American Studies* 38 (August 2004): 179–98.

Troy, Gil. *See How They Ran: The Changing Role of the Presidential Candidate.* New York: The Free Press, 1991.

———. "'Such Insulting Trash and Triviality': Franklin D. Roosevelt's Fala Speech Reconsidered." *Canadian Review of American Studies* 25 (Winter 1995): 45–73.

Troy, Gil, Arthur M. Schlesinger Jr., and Fred Anderson, eds. *History of American Presidential Elections, 1789–2008.* New York: Facts on File, 2012.

Truman, Harry S. *Memoirs, Volume One: Year of Decisions.* Garden City, NY: Doubleday and Company, Inc., 1955.

Vandenberg, Arthur H., Jr., ed. *The Private Papers of Senator Vandenberg.* Boston: Houghton Mifflin Company, 1952.

Vital Speeches of the Day. See various volumes and editions listed in notes.

Von Mises, Ludwig. *Omnipotent Government: The Rise of the Total State and Total War.* New Haven, CT: Yale University Press, 1944.

Walker, Stanley. *Dewey: An American of This Century.* New York: McGraw-Hill Book Company, 1944.

Wallace, Henry A. *The Century of the Common Man.* New York: Reynal and Hitchcock, 1943.

Weed, Clyde P. *The Nemesis of Reform: The Republican Party during the New Deal.* New York: Columbia University Press, 1994.

Weintraub, Stanley. *Final Victory: FDR's Extraordinary World War II Presidential Campaign.* Boston: Da Capo Press, 2012.

Weiss, Nancy. *Farewell to the Party of Lincoln: Black Politics in the Age of FDR.* Princeton, NJ: Princeton University Press, 1983.

Westerfield, H. Bradford. *Foreign Policy and Party Politics: Pearl Harbor to Korea.* New Haven, CT: Yale University Press, 1955.

White, William S. *The Taft Story.* New York: Harper and Row, 1954.

Wilcox, Francis O. "Government Pamphlets on the War." *The American Political Science Review* 39 (February 1944): 58–71.

Willkie, Wendell L. *An American Program.* New York: Simon and Schuster, 1944.

———. "How the Republican Party Can Win in 1944." *Look*, October 5, 1943, 25–30.

———. "A Letter to the Editors." *Harper's Magazine*, April 1944.

———. *One World.* New York: Simon and Schuster, 1943.

———. "Our Sovereignty: Shall We Use It?" *Foreign Affairs* (April 1944): 347–61.

———. "Patriotism or Politics?" *American Magazine*, November 1942, 14–15, 114–15.

Winkler, Allan M. *Home Front U.S.A.: America during World War II*. Wheeling, IL: Harlan Davidson, Inc., 2000.

Woods, Randall. *A Changing of the Guard: Anglo-American Relations, 1941–1946*. Chapel Hill: University of North Carolina Press, 1990.

Wunderlin, Clarence E., Jr., ed. *The Papers of Robert A. Taft, Volume 2: 1939–1944*. Kent, OH: Kent State University Press, 2001.

Young, Roland. *Congressional Politics in the Second World War*. New York: Da Capo Press, 1972.

Zevin, B.D., ed. *Nothing to Fear: The Selected Addresses of Franklin Delano Roosevelt, 1932–1945*. New York: Houghton Mifflin Company, 1946.

INDEX